Web Marketing Applied

Joe Tracy

ADVANSTAR
MARKETING SERVICES
A Division of Advanstar Communications Inc.

Cleveland, Ohio

Printed in the United States of America

10 9 8 7 6 5 4 3 2

ISBN 0-929870-52-2

Library of Congress Catalog Card Number 99-66275

Published by Advanstar Communications Inc.

Advanstar Communications is a U.S. Business information company that publishes magazines, books and journals, produces expositions and conferences, and provides a wide range of marketing services.

For additional information on any magazines or a complete catalog of Advanstar Communications books, please write to Advanstar Communications Customer Service, 131 West 1st Street, Duluth MN 55802 USA. To purchase additional copies of Web Marketing Applied, please call 218-723-9180 or visit **www.advanstarbooks.com/ webmarketing/**

Product Manager: Danell Durica
Cover Design: Tom Jordan, Epic Software Group, The Woodlands, TX
Interior Design: Lachina Publishing Services, Inc., Cleveland, OH

About the Cover

The cover design for *Web Marketing Applied* was created by artists Tom Jordan and Kurt Larsen of the **epic software group, inc**. The primary software used for 3D modeling and rendering of the image was NewTek's LightWave 3D 5.6. Macromedia FreeHand 7 was used for typesetting. The epic software group is a ten-year-old multimedia production company located in The Woodlands, Texas. The fifteen artists, animators, programmers, and support staff who work at the company create interactive electronic catalogs, multimedia presentations, 3D graphics, and animated short features. Epic also provides basic and advanced training in LightWave and Inspire 3D. You can reach epic software group at 281-363-3742 (phone), 281-292-9700 (fax), epic@flex.net (email), or www.epicsoftware.com (Website).

About the Illustrator

Willie Lloyd has been illustrating technical books and magazines since 1984, bringing a sense of humor amid the complex data. Two previous Joe Tracy books have featured Willie's techno-cartoons. He has also worked for TV networks as a graphics artist, a 3D animator, and a digital video editor. Willie is currently living and laughing in Fort Myers, Florida, as a Microsoft Certified Systems Engineer. All of his cartoons are dedicated to his three boys: Dustin, Trevor, and Tanner. Willie can be contacted at willmation@aol.com.

About the Author

Joe Tracy is a Web marketing expert with the ability to drive over a million visitors a year to any Website, even when working within tight budget restraints, through the formation and execution of a strategic marketing plan. Joe has a degree in public relations from Pacific Union College and has been heavily involved in Web marketing for the past several years. In 1999 he began serving as the director of Internet marketing for American Computer Experience (ACE), the leading provider of summer computer camps for kids, driving tons of traffic to their Website at www.computercamp.com and www.ACEplanet.com. Joe is also the publisher of *Animation Artist Magazine* at www.animationartist.com and the editor of *Webmaster Techniques Magazine* at www.webmastertechniques .com. He offers Web marketing consulting services and has limited availability for speaking engagements. You can reach Joe Tracy at joetracy@earthlink.net.

Contents

Introduction

You never know where inspiration for a particular project will come from, as is the case with this book—*Web Marketing Applied.*

One day I was browsing through a large bookstore and decided to see what was available in the offering of Web marketing books. Being a savvy Web marketer, I was interested to see how well the subject of marketing online was being presented to Webmasters. Several books were available on the subject, but I found that each lacked three key elements:

1. Easy-to-follow instructions.
2. A dedicated and simple list of Web marketing ideas.
3. Detailed Web marketing information!

I was further shocked to discover that a number of the Web marketing books I thumbed through spent more time talking about how to build and design a Website than about how to market a Website that is already done!

It was clearly this moment that defined the next several months of my life—a dedication to putting my marketing experience in a published form to give Webmasters a clear path to Web marketing excellence.

To succeed on the World Wide Web, you must have a competitive edge. You are holding that competitive edge in your hands. You'll find that the three key missing elements in other books I mentioned above are all found in *Web Marketing Applied:*

1. Each chapter contains easy step-by-step instructions on how to apply the marketing ideas to any Website.
2. Chapter 2 alone gives you 101 Web marketing ideas—an idea per page!
3. You'll find the whole book dedicated to the subject of Web marketing.

Your adventure doesn't stop with this book. As a free bonus, I have designed a special marketing area on the Web for owners of this book. To access it, simply go to **www.webmastertechniques.com/webmarketing/**. Here you'll find a marketing forum and links to quickly get you to areas this book discusses.

Congratulations on your decision to take your Website to the next level by professionally marketing it. And please keep me posted on your success stories! You can reach me via email at **joetracy@earthlink.net** or on the World Wide Web at **www.webmastertechniques.com**. Here's to wishing you the best of success always!

Cheers,

Dedication

This book is dedicated to my wonderful wife, Vicki Tracy, with whom I have spent ten wonderful years. If truly there were ever an inspiration, she is it. Vicki was also of great assistance in editing this book and giving additional suggestions.

Acknowledgments

I would like to thank and acknowledge my book production manager, Danell Durica, who managed my last two books. She is always a pleasure to work with.

Dr. James Chase, communication chairman of Pacific Union College, gets my deepest gratitude for the leadership he provided me with throughout my college years and beyond. His guidance is what made me a savvy learner.

Kelly Haggard, my office companion at ACE, gets my appreciation for helping with the editing of this book. Life is never dull at the office.

I thank Michael Forcillo, my boss for the past three years, for his insight, his ability to keep me very busy, and his further ability to keep me always guessing.

Thank you Mark and Diane Stross (and family) for your friendship and advice.

I'm grateful for the regular encouragement I get from all my relatives, including my wonderful grandmother, mom, dad, and even my wife's family (it's great to get along with your in-laws).

Finally, I'd like to thank Lachina Publishing Services for the design and production of this book.

1 Web Marketing 101

Every day, thousands of new Web pages appear on the World Wide Web. As the Web gets more crowded, getting recognized becomes more difficult. Part of the problem is how most people approach the Web. They build a Website, use a free submission tool to get listed on search engines, and then wait for thousands of visitors to arrive. There's only one problem—*the visitors never show up.*

Marketing is 80 percent of the success of your product or service. This percentage does not change on the Web. With that in mind, let me be among the first to congratulate you, because by purchasing *Web Mar-*

keting Applied, you have proven that you are serious about having a competitive edge on the World Wide Web. Purchasing this book is only the first step, however. Your consistent implementation of the ideas within and your marketing strategy are what will bring you your ultimate success.

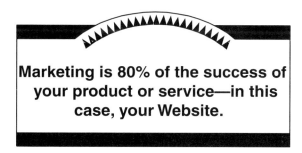

Marketing is 80% of the success of your product or service—in this case, your Website.

Throughout the rest of this chapter, you will find a step-by-step introduction into the world of successful Web marketing. I will also give you real-life examples on how I apply these ideas to Websites I market, such as Animation Artist (**www.animationartist.com**) and Webmaster Techniques (**www.webmaster techniques.com**). At the end of the chapter you will find a summary followed by a question-and-answer section that gives detailed responses to some popular marketing questions.

Step 1: Understand What Others Want

In order to market to the Web surfing community, you must first understand what Web surfers want from the World Wide Web. There are four key things that people look for on the Web:

1. **Information and content.** The Web is the world's biggest library, where people go to find a wealth of information on any topic. For example, if you were to go to a regular library and try to find information on how to prevent canker sores, you would be lucky to find three or four references in an entire day of searching. Yet on the Web you can find hundreds of pages of information on canker sore prevention in less than an hour. No matter what the topic, the Web has become the first choice to find the answer. If your Website doesn't have the information or

answers that someone is looking for, then that person will quickly go elsewhere and never think twice about visiting your site again.

There is a saying about Websites that "content is king." That saying has been true since day one of the Web and will most likely remain so for decades to come.

2. **Interactivity.** Besides being the world's biggest library, the Web is also the world's biggest entertainment empire. People can play games, post their opinions, chat with other people, participate in polls, and even send multimedia greeting cards to friends. Many Websites are incorporating interactivity through the use of high-end programs such as Flash. Interactivity is fun and can keep a person coming back again and again. Just look at how popular Slingo is on AOL. It's the only reason my wife purchased an AOL account a few months ago!

3. **Shopping.** The Mall of America is huge. It is the biggest shopping center in the United States, with more than 35 million visits a year. It's so big, in fact, that it contains a seven-acre indoor amusement park, an eighteen-hole miniature golf course, and over 500 stores. It even has a weekly newspaper! It would take 24,336 parked school buses to fill up the Mall of America! The mall has an economic impact on Minnesota in the amount of $1.5 billion a year. Those are pretty impressive facts. That is, until you compare it to the Web.

The Web has tens of thousands of shopping locations. Estimates by Jupiter Communications put online spending at $11.9 billion for 1999. It is expected to rise to $41 billion by 2002. Who would have ever thought in the early 1990s that companies called eToys and Amazon.com would bring fear to Toys "R" Us and Barnes & Noble? The Web once again dominates, this time as the world's largest shopping mall.

4. **Free Stuff.** The fourth main reason that people turn to the Web is for free stuff. This includes free software (*freeware*), free contests, free trials, free email, and free advice. You can even play lotteries for free on the Web (check out **www.freelotto.com**). If you win the million-dollar jackpot, I do accept tips.

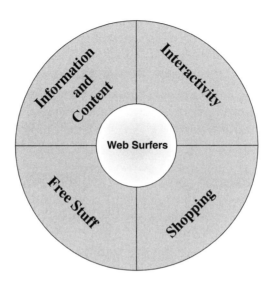

Now that you understand what people want from the Web, you need to be able to deliver these elements to your visitors. After all, the more of the four key elements you can deliver, the better position you will be in to drive traffic to your Website and to keep that traffic coming back.

REAL-LIFE EXAMPLE www.animationartist.com

Animation Artist is a great and fun Website to market because it targets the four key elements of what people are seeking. First, there are nearly a thousand pages of content and information aimed at the animation enthusiast. This includes interviews, reviews, feature stories, daily news, tutorials, animation behind-the-scenes information, and so on. Second, there is an entire interactive area called "Animation Artist Playland" with fun and entertaining interactive adventures. There are also voting polls and opinion areas for people to express their thoughts. Third, there is a huge mall area connected with affiliate programs, organized in a "directory" manner similar to what you see when you enter a shopping mall and go to the directory to find certain stores. Animators can easily find animation supplies here, too. Finally, there are many free things for visitors including contests (with prizes aimed at animators), free email, and free advice.

Step 2: Understand What You Want (Internal Goal Statement)

The second step to Web marketing is defining what you want out of your Website and out of those who visit your Website. Why does your site exist on the Web? Is it there as a hobby or as something for friends to look at? Perhaps you built it for shopping or for the purpose of improving it, then selling it? Maybe you want to drive lots of traffic there to make it attractive to advertisers?

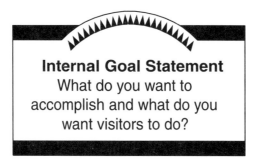

Internal Goal Statement
What do you want to accomplish and what do you want visitors to do?

Because you wisely purchased this book, my guess is that you want to make money with your Website by attracting more visitors to see (and hopefully purchase) your products and services or to increase the value of your ad space. Whatever the reason, you need to write it down as an *internal goal statement* so that you clearly understand why your site exists and what you want visitors to ultimately do. The more specific you can be with your internal goal statement, the better. Here's a real-life example:

REAL-LIFE EXAMPLE   www.webmastertechniques.com

"Webmaster Techniques exists to provide Webmasters with the information and tools they need to build better Websites. By increasing our visitor count to at least 4,000 unique visitors a day, we will be able to offer a strategic Web banner advertising program to increase both revenue and the value of the Website. The ideal visitor is a Webmaster who returns on a regular basis, purchases from our affiliate stores, purchases *Web Marketing Applied,* and participates in the interactive areas."

In the real-life example, I identified how much I wanted my visitor count to be (4,000 a day), what the results of that will be (the strategic Web banner advertising program to increase revenue and site value), and what I want visitors to do (shop through our affiliates and purchase this book). It is important to note that the internal goal statement is for your personal information only. You should frame it and place it just above your computer, reading it every day and aiming toward making the statement come true. *This is not a mission statement.* Please see Chapter 2 for more information on mission statements and Chapter 9 for the difference between an internal goal statement and a mission statement.

Once you have identified what you want, it is time to move to Step 3.

Successful Web Marketing
is the creative and consistent use of
strategies and tactics aimed at drawing
a long-term interest in your Website.

Step 3: Commit to What It Takes to Be a Successful Web Marketer

To understand what it takes to be a successful Web marketer, there must be a clear and easy definition of successful Web marketing. Here is my definition:

Successful Web marketing is the creative and consistent use of strategies and tactics aimed at drawing a long-term interest in your Website.

With that definition in mind, let's get down to the nitty-gritty and look at the attributes it takes to be a successful marketer. These are the things you *must have* in order for your marketing efforts to be successful.

1. **You must have discipline.** Large portions of today's society are pro-crastinators. Unfortunately, I fall into that category. We are the type that will go out and buy a book on eliminating procrastination, yet never get around to reading it. But even for procrastinators, there must be some amount of discipline in our lives. As long as you apply that discipline to the right aspects of your life, you can still accomplish important tasks in a timely fashion. One of those important tasks is Web marketing. Web marketing is not something that you do once and then wait for the results. You must do it several times a day, every day. You must get in the habit of doing it. For example, I'm in the habit of taking vitamins every morning. I disciplined myself to do it every day and after a few weeks it became a natural habit.

   With Web marketing, you must establish a list of daily activities that you strictly follow. If you find this hard to do, then use a discipline/reward process, in which you don't allow yourself to do something you like until a task is completed. Trust me, it cures the procrastination problem pretty quickly! For example, I love to sell and buy auction items on eBay (a great marketing technique, as I'll show you in Chapter 2). So when I'm faced with an important task that must be accomplished, I refuse to allow myself to check eBay until I've completed that task. It works!

Delegating certain duties can also be a big help in your marketing efforts. For example, I recruited my mom and dad to submit Animation Artist to Free For All Link (FFA) pages on a daily basis! They do it faithfully every day. I know because of the hundreds of autoresponses I get every day from the FFA sites (see Chapter 4 to learn how to avoid this). Delegate certain aspects of your marketing to people you can trust and be sure to reward them when you are successful.

2. **You must have patience.** In today's rush-rush society, it is easy to want everything to happen overnight. In the world of Web marketing, however, successful sites are built one day at a time. The Web marketing strategies you apply must be strategically woven so that they help achieve long-term goals and results as well as your short-term goals. You want your Web visitors to return, right? If so, then you must have your marketing strategy in place to get visitors to return *before* you market for people to initially visit your Website. After all, you never get a second chance to make a good first impression —and that first impression determines whether a person returns or not.

   Remember that Web marketing is a consistent effort applied on a daily basis. You will see the results begin to add up as time goes on. Sure, you may get only ten new people a day who begin visiting regularly, but over the course of a year that number has built to 3,650 loyal visitors a day! That's a pretty impressive number that will pay off big. With the first site I ever managed, it took me one year to build traffic up to 89,000 visitors a month. It was the number one Website in the company I worked for, which put out more than 50 sites. The success came through discipline and patience.

3. **You must have realistic goals.** Setting realistic goals goes hand in hand with patience. For example, "getting forty thousand new visitors in one

week" is not a realistic goal. And even if it were, do you have the marketing tools in place to keep the visitors coming back on a regular basis? When *Animation Artist Magazine* reached 1,000 visitors a day and had 400 people on its mailing list, my wife (the editor) and I sat down to establish what our new goals would be for the next two months. We figured that within two months we could realistically double both numbers. So we set out to achieve 2,000 daily visitors and 800 mailing list subscribers. We surpassed the 2,000 daily visitors (by a couple of hundred) and came in slightly under the 800-member mailing list goal. Our new goal, for the following two-month period, was 3,000 visitors and 1,100 mailing list members, with a stronger marketing focus being put on getting newsletter subscribers. Once you set a realistic goal, you must do everything in your power to meet and exceed that goal. Keep daily track of your progress, even if it means putting a hand-drawn goal chart on your wall to track your progress. If you can visualize your goals being accomplished, it will help motivate you to market your site even more.

4. **You must have a desire to succeed.** Everyone has a role model—someone that you have looked up to and have tried to shape aspects of your life after. My role model has always been Walt Disney. Here is a man who, when younger, was always told that it couldn't be done. He was told that no one would pay to see a full-length animated movie. He was told that Disneyland wouldn't succeed. Everywhere he went he heard "It can't be done," "That's impossible," "People won't be interested," and other negative comments.

   After the success of *Snow White and the Seven Dwarfs* and other full-length Disney animated features, Walt Disney looked back, saying, "You should have heard the howls of warning when we started making a full-length cartoon. It was prophesied that nobody would sit through such a thing."

   Walt Disney had a desire to succeed and a will to make his dreams come true. He knew that obstacles are what you see when you take your eyes off the goal. Walt Disney never saw any obstacles (because he didn't allow himself to)—only success.

When you set a goal, it is important to zero in on that goal and do everything in your power to make that goal become a reality. If, by some chance, you fail the first time, get right back on your feet and start after the goal again. You will succeed. Never give up the desire and always remember these quotes:

"The best way to predict the future is to create it."—*Peter Drucker*

"If you can imagine it, you can achieve it."—*Anthony Robbins*

"What would you do if you knew you could not fail?"—*Robert Schuller*

Now do it!

5. **You Must Have Ethics.** Unfortunately, the Web is plagued with marketers who use unethical methods to try to drive traffic to their sites or to the sites of their advertisers. Such unethical methods include forcing new windows to open when you try to leave a site, using search engine keywords that have nothing to do with their site, lying to visitors, and deceiving visitors. A few centuries ago, similar unethical methods would have meant the loss of one's honor—the ultimate punishment. If you want your marketing success to mean something, then you must avoid unethical behavior at all costs. Always be honest to your visitors and advertisers. Such honesty will only increase your loyalty.

A few years ago I watched as a gentleman with a good reputation decided to enter the world of magazine publishing. He did a huge marketing push, recruiting experts in his field to write and to give "pre-testimonials" (testimonials before the product was done) as to how the publication was the best in the field. He emphasized that his publication was number one and that what it offered blew away any competitors. He promised great things—a consistently delivered magazine with nearly 200 pages and great bonuses to those who signed up. At every turn you saw a lot of hype—and it was working, as hundreds of people started to subscribe. But then some interesting things started to happen. The first issue was very late, and when it finally came out, the bonuses weren't included. People started to complain. The second issue was much later than the first. Instead of facing subscribers and telling them that he had gotten in over his head, this individual began making up stories about fires and other disasters being responsible for the delays. Emails from readers weren't returned, refunds weren't being given, and the "best magazine in the field" had delivered only two issues in a one-year period.

Meanwhile, behind the scenes, the individual was trying to sell the publication to publishing companies who wouldn't touch it because of the amount of debt it had incurred (I worked for one of the publishing companies he approached). Finally, he announced that the parent company had screwed up everything and he wasn't associated with the parent company, so he was not part of the problem. Those who researched further found out that *he* was the parent company! Instead of being honest with readers and admitting his mistakes, this individual continued to build upon his lies. This resulted in threats of class-action lawsuits and hundreds of public posts condemning his behavior. There are now hundreds, if not thousands, of people who will never trust this person again because he was unethical in the treatment of his clients.

I cannot emphasize enough how important it is to always maintain your credibility and honor. Never lie to your visitors and never lie to your advertisers. Don't use deceptive methods to drive traffic to your site and don't lie about your statistics. Once you lose your honor, you can never regain it. Those you deceived will always be skeptical. When mob families were big in the early 1900s, dishonoring the family often meant a quick death. Even in medieval times, a person who betrayed one's own king to help another to the throne was sometimes put to death by the very king he helped. Why? Because the new king knew that the person who betrayed the former king could also betray him.

So how can you keep your honor from being lost?

a. Don't announce things you aren't ready to deliver. Besides, it will tip off your competitors, as we'll discuss in Chapter 4.

b. Don't overhype your product, service, or Website; it will only lead to disappointment.

c. Choose your words carefully; it is not easy to take them back.

d. Be willing to admit when you are wrong, and be willing to apologize.

e. Never be misleading.

A Strategic Marketing Plan
is the personalization of Web marketing strategies
and tactics into a plan aimed at increasing the
number of visitors to your Website, establishing
visitor loyalty, and reaching specific goals.

Step 4: Design a Strategic Marketing Plan

When you purchase a new product, such as a software program, you turn to the manual to learn how to operate the software. The manual becomes your guide; the better the manual is written, the quicker you learn the program. In marketing, your guide is your *strategic marketing plan,* which you will draft based on the advice and worksheets in Chapters 9 and 10. Your strategic marketing plan is *the personalization of Web marketing strategies and tactics into a plan aimed at increasing the number of visitors to your Website, establishing visitor loyalty, and reaching specific goals.*

Step 5: Execute Your Strategic Marketing Plan and Marketing Ideas

Executing your strategic marketing plan and marketing your ideas is the most important element to your marketing success. You've laid the foundation and now you're ready to execute your plan.

Chapter 2, "101 Web Marketing Ideas," will be your source for great methods for marketing your Website. The chapter has been organized to present you with 101 individual ideas, to let you know which ideas work best, and to inform you as to what purpose each idea serves (for example, attracting visitors or developing loyalty). The consistency with which you execute these ideas and the strategies you implement from your strategic marketing plan will be the key aspect in how many visitors you get and whether those visitors form a loyalty to your Website.

Before you start executing your strategic marketing plan and all of the ideas in Chapter 2, make sure that you have accomplished the following:

1. You have a plan in place to turn a first-time visitor into a repeat visitor.
2. You have a plan in place to encourage the visitor to sign up for your email newsletter.
3. Your site is optimized for branding (see Chapter 5, "Marketing Your Website's Image").
4. You have a way to track your Website statistics (most providers hosting your site will provide these for you).
5. You are prepared to immediately respond to any inquiries (see Chapter 8, "The Role of Public Relations in Web Marketing").

Once these five requirements are met, it's time to market, market, market! Now you may have questions such as, "How do I encourage visitors to sign up for my email newsletter?" "How do I make an email newsletter?" "How do I encourage repeat visits?" All of these questions are answered either in the question-and-answer section of this chapter or throughout the book.

Step 6: Always Have an Excuse to Market Something on Your Website

Every update you do to your site (preferably you do so daily) results in an opportunity to market your Website. For example, every time *Animation Artist Magazine* publishes an online interview, I go to forums, bulletin boards, and newsgroups that would be directly interested in such an interview and post information on it. The important thing is to include some content with your announcement so that your message is more interesting and informative (to the point where it might create an interesting discussion among members of the forum). Another approach is to include a teaser that gets people interested in visiting your new feature.

REAL-LIFE EXAMPLE   www.animationartist.com

When *Animation Artist Magazine* interviewed key crew members who brought to life the animated film *The Iron Giant,* I went to the Warner Bros. *Iron Giant* message boards to post details of the interview along with a link. Here's an actual message I used: "*Animation Artist Magazine*—**www.animationartist .com**—has published an interview with *The Iron Giant*'s head of animation, Tony Fucile. You can get to it from the Animation Artist Interviews pages at **www.animationartist.com/interviews/**. Most interesting is his revelation about a cut scene that gives some history on the Giant . . . " We received numerous visits from that forum. In addition, posted responses from other members about the excellent quality of the interviews helped draw more traffic to the Animation Artist Website. Here's one response that a member publicly posted regarding one of our other interviews we publicized on the forum: "Big cheers and more than a few thank you's to *Animation Artist Magazine,* for all the artist interviews with *The Iron Giant* staff, especially this latest one with Mark Whiting. Since I despair of ever seeing a well-done book (if any at all) on the making of the film, I've been saving and printing these pieces along with stories from the message boards."

As a savvy Web marketer, you will always find an excuse to launch a new marketing campaign that will drive traffic to your Website. You will also learn that the more you help readers find your great content (without spamming), the more they will appreciate you. I didn't limit my participation on the *Iron Giant* message board to just listing details of new information on the Animation Artist Website. I also added my opinion on certain subjects and sought out some hard-to-find articles online (one that had appeared in the *Los Angeles Times*) to share with everyone.

Step 7: Hold Regular Marketing Meetings and Evaluate Your Programs

Preferably once a week, hold a marketing meeting that goes over the strategies being used and how well those strategies are working. Now you may say, "But I'm the only one doing marketing." Even if you are a solo Webmaster, it is important to get another person involved, even if it is a relative or friend, to help keep you on track and to help brainstorm or execute ideas with you. You can even recruit marketing help online, by holding weekly meetings in a chat-based community such as Microsoft Chat Communities.

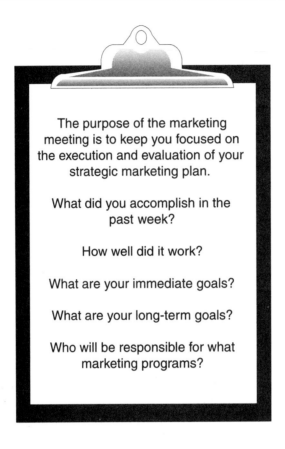

The purpose of the marketing meeting is to keep you focused on the execution and evaluation of your strategic marketing plan.

What did you accomplish in the past week?

How well did it work?

What are your immediate goals?

What are your long-term goals?

Who will be responsible for what marketing programs?

The purpose of the marketing meeting is to keep you focused on the execution and evaluation of your strategic marketing plan. What did you accomplish in the past week? How well did it work? What are your immediate goals? What are your long-term goals? Who will be responsible for what marketing programs? Prepare an agenda for each meeting, and take detailed notes during the meeting. Immediately after the conclusion of the meeting, write out minutes based on the notes you took. This will not only reemphasize the ideas in your mind, but will also be on paper in an organized fashion to make your action items easier to execute. *Action items?* Yes. At every meeting you should make a list of action items, which are items that must be accomplished prior to the next meeting. At the following meeting, you will go over the previous action items to make sure each was accomplished and to give a report on the results. The more organized you are in your marketing efforts, the better the results will be.

SUMMARY

There are seven main steps to launching a successful marketing campaign:

Step 1: Understand what others want.

Step 2: Understand what you want (internal goal statement).

Step 3: Commit to what it takes to be a successful Web marketer.

Step 4: Design a strategic marketing plan.

Step 5: Execute your strategic marketing plan and marketing ideas.

Step 6: Always have an excuse to market something on your Website.

Step 7: Hold regular marketing meetings and evaluate your progress.

By following this seven-step process, you will be able not only to drive traffic to your Website, but to also turn the majority of first-time visitors into regular visitors.

QUESTIONS AND ANSWERS

QUESTION: How, exactly, is success achieved in Web Marketing?

ANSWER: The key is to be very broad-minded in your approaches. *Successful marketing is the execution of many successful ideas in a strategic manner.*

Successful Marketing
is the execution of many successful
ideas in a strategic manner.

What's your favorite TV show? For many Americans, their favorite TV show throughout the 1990s was a top-rated show called *Home Improvement* that aired on ABC and starred Tim Allen. What would you say made that show successful? One might guess that the success of the show was the actors or the acting. While those definitely played a major role, the success actually came from a number of different areas brought together in a strategic fashion. Here are just three of many:

1. **The writers.** These people came up with the initial concept for the show and created the lines that made *Home Improvement* so funny and enjoyable to watch.

2. **The directors.** The director guides the production in the right direction and make sure the process is executed perfectly.

3. **The test audience.** This was a bold move to test jokes prior to filming, something that very few comedy shows have ever done.

In September 1998, my wife and I visited Universal Studios on a Wednesday. Our first stop was the TV show ticket booth to see whether any shows were playing that needed a live audience. We were the first ones to arrive at the booth and when we asked if there was anything interesting to see, the gentleman asked us, "How do you like the show *Home Improvement?*"

We responded that we liked the show and he told us that there was a test run being done that afternoon that would require 20 audience members.

"Test run?" we inquired.

"Yes, that's when there's a run-through of the entire show with a small audience so that the writers can see what parts work and what parts don't work, so that they can improve the show."

The concept was thrilling, so my wife and I signed up. At 3:30 that afternoon we were bussed to Disney Studios and taken to the set of *Home Improvement.* We were greeted by Jennifer, one of the writers on the episode we were about to see. She told us that in the actual filming, the audience is seated in bleachers, somewhat separated from the action, but that we would be seated right on the set, just a few feet away from the actors and actresses.

Sure enough, we were taken onto the set and seated in folding chairs right where the cameras would normally be. All the writers of the show sat directly behind us to evaluate our reactions to the script. The episode was titled "Chop Shop 'Til You Drop" and was about Tim and Jill buying a new car only to have it stolen. Tim and Al then go undercover to try and find the car. The whole gang was there—Tim Allen, Patricia Richardson, Earl Hindman (we got to see his face), Richard Karn, and the rest—and all were acting just a few feet in front of us.

After the show, the writers went into a back room where they rewrote parts of the script that the audience didn't laugh at (where the writers were hoping they would). On Thursday, the cast got a revised script and on Friday night it was filmed before a live audience for TV.

That evening was one of the most memorable times my wife and I had ever enjoyed (thanks for the *Home Improvement* hat, Jennifer). It is also an example of what I call "genius marketing"—doing something smart to improve your product or service that your competitors aren't doing. The producers of *Home Improvement* took the extra effort to add an extra step to their production, which made it a better show. Once the show was tested with a smaller audience, they enhanced the script and produced a better product because of it. No wonder *Home Improvement* was so popular!

I encourage you to always explore new ways of marketing that will make the experience for your visitors all the more pleasant, fun, and rewarding. Success in Web marketing is achieved when you take the time to better understand your audience, constantly improve your Website, and implement a series of excellent ideas with a strong consistency.

QUESTION: How do I establish visitor loyalty?

ANSWER: Establishing visitor loyalty is one of the most overlooked aspects in Web marketing. Most people think of Web marketing as "just getting visitors." What's more important than getting visitors is keeping the ones you have! Why be a pit stop on the information superhighway when you can be the racetrack?

Here are seven factors that will help increase visitor loyalty. Each one is discussed in much further detail throughout the book.

1. **Branding.** Chapter 5, "Marketing Your Website's Image," takes an in-depth look at branding and the importance of securing your image in the mind of your visitors through consistency in style, design, and impressions. Branding must always be consistent in order to be effective.

2. **Fresh content.** Fresh content on a regular basis (preferably daily) will help establish your Website as a leader in the field it covers. The result will be more return visits, a major step toward gaining visitor loyalty.

3. **Interactivity.** Getting visitors involved in your Website through interactive features helps establish loyalty through participation. Interactivity could be surveys, contests, questions of the day, polls, trivia, and so on. The more involved your visitors become, the more they will "feel at home."

4. **Informative email newsletters.** Every serious Website must have an informative newsletter that feeds subscribers great content via email on a regular basis. *Animation Artist Magazine* puts out a weekly newsletter every Monday that contains some tips and information that the Website doesn't. In addition, the newsletter gives an inside look at a completed, but not yet posted, project. For example, whenever we complete an interview with an artist, we prepare it for publishing on the Web, then "sit on it" just long enough to give a sneak peek to our email subscribers one to two days in advance. Since the interview is complete, we're not promising the subscribers something we can't deliver, and we're giving them great advance content. It gives more value to being a subscriber. Email newsletters also let you get a little more personal with your visitors. Always include a short introduction and welcome, written as if you were writing to a friend. Your visitors need to know that there is a human running your Website, not a machine.

5. **Quick response.** There is nothing more annoying than sending an email to a customer service department only to get an autoresponse email in return. What's worse is that some Websites are set up so that when you send an email, it looks for keywords to "guess" what you are writing about and then sends what it thinks is the correct autoresponse back to you. I once emailed an auction Website with a detailed complaint about one of their features not working correctly. In my conclusion I thanked the company for taking the time to view my complaint and then thanked them for their service. About fifteen minutes later, I received an autoresponse, disguised as an actual "signed" response by a customer service representative that stated, "On behalf of ____, you are very welcome. Thank you for affording us the opportunity to serve you! We hope that your experiences at ____ are pleasant and successful." My complaint was never addressed! Apparently the autoresponder picked up on the words *thank you* and thought my email was a thank-you letter, so it sent a "signed" generic autoresponse that didn't address my issues.

Autoresponders are not personal and do nothing to increase visitor loyalty. In fact, sometimes autoresponders can increase visitor frustration. But imagine if you sent an email to a company and had a response from a real person within five minutes. You'd be impressed, wouldn't you? So will your visitors. Work on responding to any email inquiries within one hour (within reason of course) and you'll be amazed at the results. We'll explore this more in Chapter 8, "The Role of Public Relations in Web Marketing."

6. **Personalize your Website.** The more personal your Website is, the more the reader can begin to relate to a "person" versus a computer screen. This means posting your own "signed" welcome messages, adding an image to your editorials, and so on. All the little things you do to personalize the experience of the visitor, without going overboard or looking like you're just promoting yourself, will go a long way to building a relationship with the person "on the other side of the computer."

7. **Beta test with current users.** Giving visitors the opportunity to test new areas of your Website before those areas open to the public not only increases participation in your site but also builds a sense of "ownership" with those who participate in the beta testing. In addition, you get some great feedback to improve your Website! Use your email newsletter to announce that you need beta testers to assist in some new projects you are preparing for your Website. Direct those who respond to a secret URL that hosts your new area; be sure to include a lot of questions that will help you gain valuable feedback for improving your Website. See the next question for more details.

QUESTION: How do I form a beta testing program?

ANSWER: Here is a step-by-step process:

Step 1: Have something to beta test. If you are posting something as simple as an interview, then there is no reason to ask for beta testers to look at it in advance. Beta testing is reserved for a new site redesign, a whole new area of your site, new interactive features, and so on. It is for areas that you can genuinely use some good advice about so that you can work on improvements.

Step 2: Make the request. An email newsletter is a great place to ask for beta testers. See the following real-life example for an example request. Be specific as to what you want the reader to do in order to be part of the program. We asked for the person's age in the real-life example because we wanted to know whether certain features of our new areas appealed differently to the various age groups.

REAL-LIFE EXAMPLE   www.animationartist.com

On Tuesday, August 17, 1999, *Animation Artist Magazine* put out a call for beta testers in its weekly email newsletter that read as follows:

BETA TESTERS NEEDED:

Animation Artist Magazine has been hard at work creating new features for **www.animationartist.com**. Some of these new features require beta testing before they are released. We are looking for 10–20 people willing to donate their time to lend a helping hand by beta testing a new area we are set to open at the end of next week. Beta testing won't begin until this weekend, but we are accepting sign-ups now. If you're interested, send an email to **vtracy@animationartist.com** with the words "BETA TEST REQUEST" in the subject line. In the body of the message tell us your name, age, and email address. We will then send a "beta test nondisclosure agreement" to you via email. Once you've agreed to it, you will be given more details about the program. Please note that we expect that the beta testing will take up 2–5 hours of your time, including some time in an online focus group where all those involved in the beta testing will discuss the concept.

Step 3: Email out a Beta Test Nondisclosure Agreement. When you email those who respond, be sure to thank them for being willing to assist you through your beta test program. Ask them to read your beta test nondisclosure agreement and, if in agreement, respond to the message (without changing or erasing anything) with the words "I agree." At the end of your message you'll add a couple of spaces and then include your beta test nondisclosure agreement, which is a short statement that gets you a promise from your beta testers that they will not disclose information on what they view to anyone prior to it going public. To see an example of a beta test nondisclosure agreement, go to **www.webmastertechniques.com/webmarketing/**. If you don't care about whether your beta testers discuss it with others (possibly even your competitors), then go ahead and skip this step altogether.

Step 4: Email details! Once your beta testers have responded, give them detailed instructions on what you are trying to accomplish. For example, one of the things we beta tested was a new logo design for Animation Artist. Because the site was becoming extremely popular (that's what marketing will do), we knew that if we were going to brand an identity we had to make any visual changes now (or never). So we came up with different logo designs and slapped them on a secret URL, labeling them Logo A, Logo B, Logo C, and so on. We then asked the beta testers to look at all the designs and to tell us what they thought of each one, which one was their first choice, and what they would change. From the responses we received, we were able to fine-tune the logo of choice (Logo F, in this case) before launching it publicly. We then used the same beta test team to look at some new interactive areas we were preparing to open. In your message, be sure to include the secret URL and any instructions or questions needed.

Step 5: Send personal thank-you notes. When your beta testers respond, be sure to send each one an individual thank-you note for his or her ideas and suggestions. Print all the suggestions, giving each one serious consideration in your redesign efforts. If you can afford it, reward your beta testers by sending them a free T-shirt or by mentioning their names online (with their permission). Keep in mind that beta testers are also an excellent source for quotes if you are constructing a press release about your new offerings.

QUESTION: Is Web marketing just a technique to drive traffic to a Website?

ANSWER: Web marketing is not a technique to simply drive people to your Website. Different marketing techniques serve different purposes. While the most popular marketing techniques are aimed at getting visitors, you must also know what type of marketing you will apply after you get the visit.

Here are the four key categories into which your marketing techniques will fall:

1. **Initial Contact.** Use marketing to try to drive traffic to your Website; FFA links and banner ads fit into this category.

2. **Revisits.** Encourage visitors to return to your Website; a regular email newsletter and easy methods for visitors to bookmark your page fit into this category.

3. **Participation.** Encourage visitors to participate in your site; focused contests and trivia fit into this category.

4. **Loyalty and Trust.** Work on developing a visitor's loyalty and trust; immediate email answers and privacy statements fit into this category.

In Chapter 2, "101 Web Marketing Ideas," every single one of the 101 ideas fits into one of these four key Web marketing categories, and every one is labeled as to whether it is used to generate initial contact, revisits, participation, or loyalty and trust. When you have a balance of all of these in consistent operation, you have truly achieved Web marketing excellence.

Speaking of Chapter 2, you're almost there! Chapter 2 is the core of *Web Marketing Applied* because it holds all the marketing ideas organized to give you the information you need to decide whether it fits into your strategic marketing plan.

2 *101 Web Marketing Ideas*

The bulk of your achievements in Web marketing will come from the successful implementation of strategic marketing ideas. This chapter is dedicated to giving you the ideas you need to succeed—**101 ideas**! You will find an idea per page in this chapter along with helpful information at the top of each page:

1. **The Web marketing idea name.**
2. **Does it cost money (to implement the idea)?** If a marketing idea costs money to implement, you'll see a "Yes" next to this question. If the marketing idea is free (meaning it doesn't cost money, just some of your time), you'll see a "No" next to this question.

3. **How well does it (the idea) work?** I've devised a five-star (★★★★★) rating system to identify how well each marketing idea works, based on my experience. I've also organized all the ideas based on their star rating. Ideas at the beginning of this chapter are five-star (★★★★★) ideas, which are the ones that will have the biggest overall impact (some short term, some long term). The ideas that don't have a big impact, but may still be worth an effort, are one-star (★) ideas. You'll find one-star ideas near the end of the chapter. Then, of course, the four-star, three-star, and two-star ideas appear in-between the five-star and one-star ideas.

4. **What does it develop?** As discussed at the end of Chapter 1, these Web marketing techniques fall into four key categories: **Initial Contact**, **Revisits**, **Participation**, and **Loyalty & Trust**. Please refer to the end of Chapter 1 for full descriptions of each. It is important that you understand each of these and the role they play in your marketing efforts. Ultimately, you are looking for a strong balance.

At the end of this chapter you will find more questions and answers pertaining to the ideas presented. Also, be sure to check out **www.webmaster techniques.com/webmarketing/** for quick links to every URL mentioned in this chapter.

WEB MARKETING IDEA   Seek Out Sites for Links

 DOES IT COST MONEY? No

 HOW WELL DOES IT WORK? ★★★★★

 ....WHAT DOES IT DEVELOP? Initial Contact

Asking another Webmaster to link to your Website is one of the best available methods of marketing your Website. In fact, the benefits are twofold:

1. The more Websites you are on, the easier it will be for people to find your Website.
2. The more Websites you are on, the better you'll rank on some search engines.

You may be curious as to how getting links on other people's Websites helps your ranking on some search engines. *Search engines* use a number of equations to determine how high or low you are placed. *Meta tags* and *descriptions* play an important role in these decisions. On some search engines, your Website's popularity is also figured into the equation. Your popularity is determined by how many Websites link to you. You want to be on as many Web pages as possible.

How do you think most people find your Website? Would your answer be search engines? If so, you may be interested in the survey results from a Georgia Institute of Technology study conducted in 1997. The study found that *most people find new Websites from other people's Websites.* Coming in a close second was search engines.

Here's what you need to do to apply this marketing idea:

1. Draft a nice letter politely introducing the recipient to your Website and asking him or her to please consider linking to your Website. Save the letter so that you can use it over and over.
2. Search the Internet for sites that relate to yours. For example, if your Website is about Pomeranian dogs, search for "Pomeranian," "Pomeranians," "toy dogs," and so on. Visit the sites you find one by one and see if the site has a link page. If so, find the Webmaster's email address and send him or her a copy of the letter. If the Webmaster puts his or her name on the site (for example, "this site made by Joe Tracy"), be sure to address your letter with that name to better personalize it. *Send out five emails a day—every day.*

See Web Marketing Idea #84, "Keep Track of Who Is Linking to You" for a related technique.

WEB MARKETING IDEA Place Strong Titles on Every Page

    DOES IT COST MONEY?   No
    HOW WELL DOES IT WORK?   ★★★★★
....WHAT DOES IT DEVELOP?   Initial Contact

The title of your Website plays an important role (as do meta tags, descriptions, and so on) in the entire process that determines where your pages show up on a search engine. The first three lines of your Web page HTML code usually look like this:

```
⟨HTML⟩
⟨HEAD⟩
⟨TITLE⟩Your Web Page Title Here⟨/TITLE⟩
```

Most Web page creation programs (such as NetObjects Fusion) have a space for you to enter the title without using HTML. Either way, you need to make sure that the title you give includes some important keywords for people to find you. See my examples of a bad title and a good title for an imaginary Website focusing on the movie *First Knight*:

Bad Title:

```
⟨TITLE⟩My Movie Page for fans of the movie First Knight to get
information⟨/TITLE⟩
```

Good Title:

```
⟨TITLE⟩First Knight Site! Sean Connery as King Arthur, Richard Gere
as Lancelot⟨/TITLE⟩
```

Titles should be short, as you will have a chance to fully describe the site in your meta tag description (see Web Marketing Idea #3). As a rule of thumb, search engines display your title in the results of each search. Since the title also helps determine ranking, you want to use as many keywords as possible. In the bad example, there are a lot of irrelevant words. In fact, the only relevant words are "*First Knight.*" Yet the good example was packed with relevant keywords, such as "*First Knight,*" "Sean Connery," "King Arthur," "Richard Gere," and "Lancelot." Make sure that your title uses relevant words.

WEB MARKETING IDEA   Use Meta Tags in Your HTML

DOES IT COST MONEY?   No

HOW WELL DOES IT WORK?   ★★★★★

....WHAT DOES IT DEVELOP?   Initial Contact

Meta tags give search engines details about your Website that help the search engines establish the ranking of your site. Use the following meta tags on every page of your documents:

```
<meta name="description" content="put your description here">
<meta name="keywords" content="list keywords here">
<meta name="author" content="put the Webmaster's name or page
   author's name here">
<meta name="revisit-after" content="the number of days before the next
   search engine visit—usually 30 days">
<meta name="robots" content="usually set to 'all'—determines which
   pages a search engine should and shouldn't index">
<meta name="rating" content="is your rating 'general'—all audiences—
   or 'adult'?">
<meta name="copyright" content="your copyright information goes here">
```

Using the *First Knight* example from Web Marketing Idea #2, here is how I would use meta tags:

```
<meta name="description" content="First Knight Site! Join Sean Connery,
   Richard Gere, and Julia Ormond in this medieval adventure where King
   Arthur and Lancelot both share the love of Lady Guinevere. Interviews,
   news, forums, and more—updated weekly!">
<meta name="keywords" content = "First Knight, Sean Connery movies,
   Richard Gere, Julia Ormond, medieval films, midevil, medeival, knights
   of the round table, sword battles, King Arthur, Sir Lancelot, Lady
   Guinevere">
<meta name="author" content="Joe Tracy">
<meta name="revisit-after" content="30 days">
<meta name="robots" content="all">
<meta name="rating" content="general">
<meta name="copyright" content="All content on the First Knight Website
   is © copyright 1999 Joe Tracy. All rights reserved.">
```

Notice how specific I was in the description and keywords. Also, I purposely misspelled *medieval*, knowing that it is a commonly misspelled word that could work to my advantage. For more detailed information on using meta tags, read Chapter 3, "Offensive Marketing Techniques."

WEB MARKETING IDEA Submit Your Website
                                              to Search Engines

DOES IT COST MONEY?   No

HOW WELL DOES IT WORK?   ★★★★★

WHAT DOES IT DEVELOP?   Initial Contact

You've spent a lot of time priming your Website for search engines and directories by adding carefully planned titles and meta tags to every single page. Now what? Now it's time to submit your Website to each search engine. There are three ways you can do this:

1. Hire someone to do it for you.
2. Use a "free submission service."
3. Do it yourself.

If you can find a reputable company, with a proven track record, to submit for you at a fee you find agreeable, then option 1 is appealing. Option 2 is dangerous . . . very dangerous. Most free submission services don't give you a list of sites they're submitting to, or a report on whether the submissions were successful. In fact, they may not have submitted your Website at all! My choice would be option 3. After all, you've spent a lot of time making sure everything was perfect with your wording, keywords, description, and so on, so why let your guard down now with the submission process?

Even with option 3 there are two ways you can proceed. The first is to go to **www.selfpromotion.com**, which uses scripts to assist you in your individual submissions. The second is to go to each search engine and directory yourself to submit. If the latter is your choice, go to **www.webmastertechniques.com/webmarketing/** for a full list of search engines and directories you should be submitting your Website to, along with a direct link to each one. In the meantime, here's what I consider the top five search engines and directories to get listed on:

1. **Yahoo.** Go to **http://docs.yahoo.com/info/suggest/** for directions on getting listed.
2. **AltaVista.** Go to **www.altavista.com/cgi-bin/query?pg=addurl** for submission information.
3. **Lycos.** Go to **www.lycos.com/addasite.html** for submission information. Also, note that this search engine requires that you submit each individual page (versus submitting one page, and a spider finds the rest by following links). So make sure you add *every single page* on your Website to this search engine.
4. **Infoseek.** Go to **www.go.com/AddUrl?&pg=SubmitUrl.html** for submission information.
5. **HotBot.** Go to **www.hotbot.com/addurl.asp** for submission information.

WEB MARKETING IDEA Use the Multisubmit Strategy

    DOES IT COST MONEY?   No
    HOW WELL DOES IT WORK?   ★★★★★
....WHAT DOES IT DEVELOP?   Initial Contact

The multisubmit strategy does not mean submitting your home page URL over and over to the same search engines and directories. Such actions could have you penalized by some search engines. Using the multisubmit strategy means that you treat portions of your Website as separate distinct sections and submit the main page of each section to search engines and directories. For example, *Animation Artist Magazine*—**www.animationartist.com**—has distinct sections such as Interviews, Tutorials, Columns, Opinions, New Products, and so on. We treat each of these sections as a separate Website; each section contains its own unique descriptions, keywords, and so on. I then submit these areas as if I were submitting separate Websites.

Interviews	Tutorials
Interviews with industry leading animators, artists, and directors.	Tutorials covering all the major graphics and animation programs.
Columns	**New Products**
Columns that give insight and opinions into the world of animation.	Information on the latest products available for animators and artists.

Each section of Animation Artist is distinct enough to stand on its own, even though it is all one Website, and therefore perfect for submitting as separate pages to search engines.

In September 1999, *Animation Artist Magazine* added numerous new sections to its Website: a Voices in Animation Message Board, a Screening Room, and Animation Artist Playland. As soon as the sections were uploaded (with proper titles, descriptions, and meta tags), I submitted the different sections to search engines and directories that otherwise would not have known they existed for a while, if at all.

Remember to submit only the main page of each section to the search engines and directories. The only exception to this is Websites such as Lycos that require you to submit every page you want indexed.

WEB MARKETING IDEA Develop a Strategic Marketing Plan

DOES IT COST MONEY?   No

HOW WELL DOES IT WORK? ★★★★★

WHAT DOES IT DEVELOP?   Initial Contact, Revisits, Participation, Loyalty & Trust

As discussed in Chapters 1, 9, and 10, the blueprint to your success in Web marketing will be your strategic marketing plan. It will be the key to obtaining initial contact, revisits, participation, and loyalty and trust.

Here are five reasons why you should have a detailed strategic marketing plan:

1. **It is your blueprint to success.** Let's say that you are looking at two contractors to build your house. You interview the first contractor, who walks you through the process, starting with the detailed blueprints that are drawn for your new home to make sure the process is smooth and perfect. The second contractor you go to doesn't have a process. "We just build it," he says. "Forget blueprints—those take too long to make." Which would you be more likely to select for your home?

2. **It keeps you on schedule.** By reviewing your strategic marketing plan every day, you stay on target to accomplish your goals in a timely fashion.

3. **It gives you direction.** With a strategic marketing plan, there's never a question of what you'll do next or where to go from here.

4. **It can make you more money.** Many excellent Websites are usually swallowed by larger companies who spend millions of dollars in purchasing those sites. Imagine that a millionaire is looking at two Websites with the intent of purchasing one. The are equal in quality, visitor traffic, and so on. However, you have something that the other doesn't—a detailed strategic marketing plan and a detailed business plan. Which will the millionaire purchase?

5. **It allows you to experience success.** With a strategic marketing plan, you gain the feeling of true accomplishment and success as you see your plan being perfectly executed. You know where the results are coming from.

Make your strategic marketing plan your top priority and review it on a daily basis so that you can evaluate your goals and your continued path to ultimate success.

WEB MARKETING IDEA   Develop a "Top 10" Program

DOES IT COST MONEY?   Yes and No

HOW WELL DOES IT WORK?   ★★★★★

WHAT DOES IT DEVELOP?   Initial Contact

When you start getting 600–1,000 visitors a day, you will want to implement what I consider one of the best techniques to aid the initial contact growth of your Website—a Top 10 program.

A Top 10 program is a CGI script that allows Webmasters to sign up and compete against other Webmasters to see who can drive the most traffic to your Website. The more traffic the Webmaster brings to your site (from his or her site), the higher his or her Website will rank on your Top 10 list. The list is displayed on your Website, showing the referrers ranked from number 1 through number 10. It also provides direct links to those listed in the Top 10. In a way it is like a link exchange, except that you get the best deal because of the competition factor of all the Webmasters trying to be number 1. It's a great program and can get you great placement on some high-traffic Websites as they compete to send you the most visitors. Most scripts are customizable to allow you to do Top 20, 30, 40, or 50 programs. Some allow you to customize the program for advertising and include great administrative functions.

So the big question now is, where do you find such a script? There are many free Top 10 scripts on the market. There are also scripts that cost up to $250. You can find all of these programs at **http://cgi.resourceindex.com/Programs_and_Scripts/ Perl/Website_Promotion/Top_Sites/**.

WEB MARKETING IDEA Organize a Task List and Update
Your Website Daily

DOES IT COST MONEY? No

HOW WELL DOES IT WORK? ★★★★★

WHAT DOES IT DEVELOP? Revisits

Without a task list (also known as a things-to-do list), it is easy to get yourself in a position where you don't know what to do next. Everything you have to do can appear so overwhelming that you don't feel like doing any of it. This is where the task list comes in handy. With a daily task list you know exactly where to begin and what your priorities are, and you can see progress being made. You know what to do next.

A task list will greatly increase your marketing efforts by giving you a timely focus. Here is a sample of one of my daily task lists (remember that it will change daily according to your strategic marketing plan and your short- and long-term goals):

____ 1. Send out five email link requests (see end of Web Marketing Idea #1).

____ 2. Review yesterday's log files and identify most popular sections and referrers.

____ 3. Write marketing article for next week's Webmaster Techniques newsletter.

____ 4. Update awards section with two new awards received.

____ 5. Submit Animation Artist and Webmaster Techniques to FFA program.

____ 6. Email minutes of yesterday's marketing meeting to those in attendance.

____ 7. Look into cheaper event chat opportunities for Animation Artist.

I have clearly identified the tasks that need to be done for the day. Now it is just a matter of focusing on one, completing it, and moving on to the next. It's a great feeling when you've completed them all and can relax or reward yourself (eBay!).

Use a word processing program to create a task list. Print it. Now place it in a prominent area and as you complete each task, put a checkmark to the left of it and then cross out the entire task (double the satisfaction of completing it).

WEB MARKETING IDEA   Offer a Major New Service,
                                                 Such as Email

    DOES IT COST MONEY?   Yes and No

    HOW WELL DOES IT WORK?   ★★★★★

....WHAT DOES IT DEVELOP?   Revisits, Participation, Loyalty & Trust

The most popular part of the Internet is not the World Wide Web. It is email. Email has emerged as the standard communication vehicle for business and personal matters. Web-based email has gained a lot of popularity in recent years because it allows a user to check his or her email anywhere at any time. You can easily check it at trade shows, while on vacation, or even at the office.

Webmasters now have the ability to take advantage of the email craze by offering email accounts from their Websites. For example, in September 1999, *Animation Artist Magazine* started giving away free email accounts that had the extension animation artist.net. So if you registered as Webb (the book's mascot—see illustrations), your email address would be **Webb@animationartist.net**! It's a great way to build a community around your domain name.

"Wait a minute," you may ask. "Why isn't your extension *animationartist.com*?"

Great question. When we registered **www.animationartist.com**, we immediately registered **www.animationartist.net** and **www.animationartist.org** so that no one else would take those names. Instead of letting those URLs rot away in the "I was just put here so no one else would take me" world, I decided to put the URLs to good use. So we turned **www.animationartist.net** into our email service, and we're getting ready to launch a whole new idea for **www.animationartist.org**.

So where can you sign up to offer free email accounts? Two places, **www.big mailbox.com** and **www.everyone.net**, offer this service to you for free! The catch is that **www.bigmailbox.com** takes 80 percent of your advertising (you get the other 20 percent), while **www.everyone.net** splits it with you 50/50. Look very closely at both before deciding, because functionality is a very important part of the experience. You may also want to look at **www.ghostmail.com**.

If you would like to have 100 percent control over the advertising on your email service, consider a monthly fee-based service such as **www.netflyer.net** or **www.alias-mail.com**.

For our Animation Artist email program, we use Coconut Software, located at **www.coconutsoftware.com**.

WEB MARKETING IDEA Develop a Strong Logo

DOES IT COST MONEY?   Yes

HOW WELL DOES IT WORK?   ★★★★★

WHAT DOES IT DEVELOP?   Revisits, Loyalty & Trust

In order for your branding efforts (Web Marketing Idea #12) to be successful, you need to start off with a strong logo and slogan (Web Marketing Idea #11). Your logo and slogan will be used to identify you for the lifespan of your company, so make it good the first time around.

Your logo is one of the first parts of your corporate identity that people see. It is also the part of your corporate identity that people will most identify you with in the years to come. Therefore you should give strong consideration and plenty of time to the development of your logo.

Developing a logo isn't easy. At ACEplanet.com, dozens of logo ideas were passed around before one was decided on (see image). Notice that the name is easy to read and the visual part of the logo (the planet) is simple and smooth. Go to **www.aceplanet .com** to see it in color.

There are many things to consider when building a logo. How good will it look with your Website? Do the artwork and colors present the image you want people to see on your Website? Will it look good on stationery, business cards, and T-shirts? Your logo must create a lasting impression in the minds of your visitors for maximum effectiveness. Does it do that? If you are a graphic artist, you have probably already given a strong logo a lot of thought and will create it yourself. If you're not a graphic artist, you may want to invest a couple of hundred dollars in having one create a logo for you. Look around on the Internet; you can find some great companies to create logos at reasonable prices.

WEB MARKETING IDEA   Develop a Strong Slogan

    DOES IT COST MONEY?   No
    HOW WELL DOES IT WORK?   ★★★★★
....WHAT DOES IT DEVELOP?   Revisits, Loyalty & Trust

What do you think of when I say the following phrases:

"Don't leave home without it."

"Got milk?"

"Just do it."

"The happiest place on earth."

These are four classic examples of successful slogans that were well branded. Chances are you correctly guessed each one (American Express, milk, Nike, Disneyland). If I were to mention "Think Different," what would you think of? You probably said "Apple." The "Think Different" slogan and campaign were so popular that a video called *The Making of Think Different* was produced and the campaign won many prestigious awards.

Did you know that some companies charge up to $40,000 to create a slogan for you? I can think of 100 other great marketing ways to spend $40,000 than on your slogan. Even so, you need one and it should convey a strong thought relating to your company. Here are a couple of great ones I came across while surfing the Net:

"Helping Your Site Succeed"—Everyone.net

"The Internet's Biggest Toy Store!"—eToys

"Your Gateway to the Internet"—CompuServe

"Your Personal Internet Guide"—Lycos

"Turning Technology into Good Business"—eCommerce Corporation

Your slogan should be short, with a unique and descriptive punch—something that is easy to remember and not hard to pronounce. Once you get it, stick with it. It's really sad to see some companies such as Visa use their slogan only temporarily and lose the effectiveness they gained by changing it, as discussed under Web Marketing Idea #12.

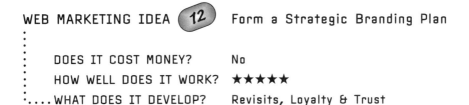

Chapter 5 is dedicated to the entire subject of marketing your website's image, otherwise known as *branding*. Branding is a long-term goal. It takes a long time to achieve, but is very effective once you've reached branding success.

The biggest mistake that companies make today is changing their logos and slogans. The companies that are most effective at branding have never changed their logo or slogan. So it should be with your Website.

Every time a visitor enters your Website, that visitor sees your logo and slogan. As both are emphasized on every page of your Website, the message is implanted deeper into the mind of your returning guest. To abruptly change either, especially after years of success, is downright foolish in achieving your branding goal and forces you to start from square one.

Intel's logo and slogan are one of the most recognized in the industry. The slogan is simply "Intel Inside" and is emphasized in every medium—from TV commercials to stickers on computers. Imagine if every year Intel changed its "Intel Inside" logo and slogan—it would quickly lose its branding effectiveness.

Your first step to effective branding is to create a branding plan that covers the following areas:

1. Research of your industry and logos in your industry.
2. Specific logo ideas (match your industry, but with a unique flair).
3. Specific slogan ideas.
4. Avenue of research to determine the effectiveness of your logo and slogan (online focus groups, hire a marketing firm, and so on).
5. The strategic methods you'll use to brand your logo and slogan.

Keep in mind that logos and slogans aren't the only thing that can be branded. People and characters can be effectively branded too. Just look at Mickey Mouse!

WEB MARKETING IDEA **13**   Brand Every Web Page

DOES IT COST MONEY?   No

HOW WELL DOES IT WORK?   ★★★★★

WHAT DOES IT DEVELOP?   Revisits, Participation, Loyalty & Trust

"The Spirit of Animation"

As mentioned in the last tip, branding every page of your Website with your logo and slogan is very important to achieving long-term branding.

The home page of *Animation Artist Magazine* contains a large version of our logo with the slogan built in, as you can see in the grayscale image on this page. Every single other page in the Website contains a smaller version of the exact same logo with the slogan built in. It is always in the same spot at the top of *every* page.

We chose to build our slogan into our image for the following two reasons:

1. It looked great as part of the logo.
2. It keeps the two items (logo and slogan) together, emphasizing both in all branding techniques, including merchandise (T-shirts, hats, bumper stickers, and so on).

For branding to succeed, your image must appear everywhere, without being annoying or intrusive. I recommend a large logo on your front page (with slogan under or built in), followed by a smaller logo on the top left-hand corner of all other pages, linked back to your home page. Your slogan should appear under or to the right of the smaller logo on every page.

WEB MARKETING IDEA Form a Directory Listing for
:   Banner Exchange Program
:   DOES IT COST MONEY?   No
:   HOW WELL DOES IT WORK?   ★★★★★
:....WHAT DOES IT DEVELOP?   Initial Contact, Participation

A few years ago I came up with a "Directory Listing for Banner Exchange Program" that proved to be a valuable success to my Website, to those who participated, and to my visitors. The concept behind this idea is to give a 50-word listing to any Website that puts your banner on their home page with a link back to your Website! As you get more participants, you start to form a valuable resource directory for your visitors (versus a simple links page). As the directory grows, you can split it into categories. You'll find that the more popular it becomes, the more people want to be in it. Here are some step-by-step instructions:

Step #1: Build six banners (some animated) that promote your Website and upload those to your directory listing page or a special "sign-up" page.

Step #2: Add listing information to your directory home page (or sign-up page) with information such as "Add a link to *Animation Artist Magazine* and have the favor returned! Select one of the six banners below to display on the home page of your Website, then link it to **http://www.animationartist.com**. In return we'll establish a link to your Website and publish a description of 50 words or less on what your Website is about!"

Step #3: Give reasons why a Webmaster should participate in the program. Here's an example: "As an established leader in the animation industry, Animation Artist is the perfect place to promote your Website."

Step #4: Give clear step-by-step instructions for the person to save your banner, display it, and notify you that it is up (include your email address). You may want to include an easy form on your Website for them to email their 50-word listing to you.

When you're notified that a participant has added your banner, go check to make sure it is properly displayed and working. If it is, then *immediately* add the listing to your directory.

WEB MARKETING IDEA Become Active in Discussion Groups

DOES IT COST MONEY?   No

HOW WELL DOES IT WORK?   ★★★★★

WHAT DOES IT DEVELOP?   Initial Contact, Revisits, Loyalty & Trust

One of the best techniques you can use to introduce people to your Website, gain revisits, and build loyalty and trust is to simply participate, on a regular basis, in discussion groups. This doesn't mean posting messages that just promote your Website. This means giving out valuable advice and answers to questions that establish you as an expert. The key to this idea is in your signature, which contains the link to your Website. For example, at the end of my messages you will always see my signature:

Best Wishes,

Joe Tracy, Publisher
Animation Artist Magazine—"The Spirit of Animation"
http://www.animationartist.com

Animation Artist Magazine is a free resource of animation news, features, and information that is updated every day, including holidays and weekends.

In this example I've given my credentials (Publisher), the Website name (Animation Artist Magazine), the slogan ("The Spirit of Animation"), and a URL. I've also added a simple one-sentence description of my Website. The whole promotion is very simple and nonintrusive. If the person enjoyed the insight given in my message, chances are that he or she will pay a visit to my Website.

Check out **www.deja.com** for a quick and easy way to access newsgroups that deal with the focus of your Website. Be helpful. Don't participate in flaming (putting others down), and always be courteous. Doing this with consistency will help bring you a lot of targeted traffic.

WEB MARKETING IDEA Turn "File Not Found" Errors into
Marketing Messages

DOES IT COST MONEY?   No

HOW WELL DOES IT WORK? ★★★★★

....WHAT DOES IT DEVELOP?   Initial Contact, Revisits

Have you ever tried to go to a Web page only to get a "File Not Found" error message? Chances are that it happens to you several times a day. Did you know that as a Webmaster you can customize that error message to redirect users to your home page versus losing them altogether?

 **File Not Found**

The file you are trying to access could not be found on this server. If you got here by clicking on a link from the Animation Artist Magazine Website, please let us know what link you clicked on so that we can immediately fix the problem. The email address is fixit@animationartist.com.

You may be able to find what you're looking for with a simple trip to one of our main areas. Click on one of the links below:

Animation Artist Magazine Home Page

Animation Artist Magazine Interviews

Animation Artist Magazine Tutorials

Animation Artist Magazine Voices in Animation

Animation Artist Magazine Upcoming Animated Movies

Nearly all Web hosting companies provide a way for you to upload your own Web page to replace the default "File Not Found" error page. Some have you create an HTML file named *missing.html* or *404.html* and upload it to your root directory to replace the default on the server. When doing this it's a good idea to put up your logo, a "File Not Found" title, and then a short message followed with links to different areas of your Website (see image). It's a great way to also have readers let you know when one of your links isn't properly working!

Check the online manual of your Web hosting company or email them for the exact details of changing your File Not Found error message. Then watch misguided traffic find its way to your home page!

WEB MARKETING IDEA   Post and Adhere to a Privacy
:   Statement
:   DOES IT COST MONEY?   No
:   HOW WELL DOES IT WORK?   ★★★★★
:....WHAT DOES IT DEVELOP?   Participation, Loyalty & Trust

Internet users are sick and tired of spam. It is annoying and unwanted and arrives unsolicited. The rise in spam has caused many people to become very defensive in giving out any information to Websites, particularly an email address.

If you value your visitors, you will post and strictly adhere to a privacy statement that assures your visitors that any personal information they give you will not be sold to any third parties. Here is an excerpt from *Animation Artist Magazine's* privacy statement:

> Animation Artist Magazine is committed to strict privacy standards and the protection of any information gathered from visitors on the Animation Artist Magazine Website. Animation Artist Magazine has created this privacy statement as a demonstration of our firm commitment to the privacy of visitors. The following contains information regarding privacy issues on the Animation Artist Website as they relate to information gathering, posting, or third party participation.
>
> **Interactive Areas Where Visitor Information May Be Gathered or Viewed:**
> The Voices in Animation *Message Board* on the Animation Artist Website is a very interactive public area that we offer to registered visitors. Please remember that any information that is disclosed in these message boards becomes public information. You should exercise caution when deciding to disclose any personal information . . .

To read the entire privacy statement, and thus gain a good understanding to help you write your own, go to **www.animationartist.com** and scroll down to the bottom of the screen. Click on "Privacy Statement."

Your privacy statement should be linkable from every page of your Website. Simply title the link "Privacy Statement" and link it to a page where your entire policy is available.

For great information on privacy issues and privacy statements, visit **www.truste .org**. You can even use their very detailed Privacy Wizard to help build your own privacy statement!

WEB MARKETING IDEA 〖18〗   Build Another Website to Help
                                                             Market Your Current One

    DOES IT COST MONEY?   Yes

    HOW WELL DOES IT WORK?   ★★★★★

....WHAT DOES IT DEVELOP?   Initial Contact, Revisits

If you are the Webmaster of an online store, you may find that getting people to purchase from your store isn't easy. For one, there is a lot of competition. Then there's the issue of trust. This Web Marketing Idea will be one of the best tips you can implement in order to drive more traffic to your store, where people will order from you with confidence. It is also a great traffic builder for content Websites.

The idea? *Build another Website.*

Let's say that I'm the Webmaster of an online store that sells accessories for dogs (T-shirts, leashes, name tags, and so on). That's not an easy project to market, especially if it's a startup. The whole process, however, becomes much easier when you build a *content Website* to help support and drive traffic to your online store. So in this case, what if I built an entire content Website around dogs—something like **www.dogsdaily.com** [this URL was unregistered as of September 15, 1999]. The Website would focus on all issues of concern to dog owners—advice, feature articles, training, and so on.

Wouldn't you agree that it would be much easier to market a free information content Website like Dogs Daily (**www.dogsdaily.com**) than a dog accessory store? Of course it is! Now you use **www.dogsdaily.com** to market the dog accessory store! As people visit Dogs Daily on a daily basis (because as a good Webmaster you would update it daily), they start to become loyal. Knowing that the accessory store is operated by the same people as Dogs Daily will pass that trust on to the store. Suddenly you are getting a lot of business, have a great Website, and may even receive advertising inquiries about your Website!

This tip is also for content providers. For example, early on Animation Artist realized that Disney's *Dinosaur* animated movie (scheduled for release on Memorial Day Weekend 2000) had the potential to be a big hit. So we reserved the URL **www.dinosaurmovie.com** and built a big site just on the movie. We give great information on the movie and strongly market *Animation Artist Magazine* from that site!

Building another Website will cost you money through additional hosting fees.

WEB MARKETING IDEA   Network Your Websites

DOES IT COST MONEY?   Yes

HOW WELL DOES IT WORK?   ★★★★★

WHAT DOES IT DEVELOP?   Initial Contact, Revisits, Participation

As you begin building multiple Websites on the Web, you'll want to begin strategically linking (networking) the Websites to achieve maximum marketing results. If a person is going to leave your Website for any reason, it should be to go to one of your other Websites!

Website networking is the art of building a strong connection between two Websites even though they may be about two different subjects. It is about giving the visitors of one of your Websites a reason for entering another of your Websites.

Here are five ideas to better network your Websites:

1. **Email.** Does one of your Websites (Website A) offer free email, but not the other (Website B)? Be sure to allow the visitors to Website B the opportunity to sign up for Website A's free email service.

2. **Banners.** Banner ads don't have to be reserved only for advertisers. Be sure to use your own banner ads on all your sites to promote your other Websites.

3. **Menus.** In your home page menu system, have a "Partners" or "Networked" heading with links to all your other Websites under it.

4. **A logo.** If you have a company logo that all your Websites reside under, you can place that same logo in the menu system of all your Websites. For example, Studio Visions (*www.studiovisions.com*) is my company. It owns about six Websites including Animation Artist, Webmaster Techniques, The Creativity Factory, and Playable Magazine. This presents a great opportunity to place a Studio Visions logo on all the sites with the words *part of the Studio Visions network* on the logo. It is, of course, clickable and will take the visitor to a page that promotes all the Websites (like a portal entry).

5. **Story links.** If one of the news or feature stories you have on Website A relates to Website B, be sure to find a way to mention Website B in the story with a link.

Networking your Websites is an excellent way to keep traffic flowing between your sites. Maybe one of your sites has interactive games for people to play, but your other one doesn't—there's a great opportunity to interlink this area for everyone to enjoy. Always think of ways to drive traffic to areas of your other Websites so that you keep the traffic flowing within your own little network of Websites.

WEB MARKETING IDEA   Form Strategic Partnerships

DOES IT COST MONEY?   No

HOW WELL DOES IT WORK? ★★★★★

WHAT DOES IT DEVELOP?   Initial Contact, Revisits

In Chapter 3, "Offensive Marketing Techniques," I mention that one of the greatest offensive strategies you can have is to ally with other Websites. By creating strategic partnerships with certain key Websites you can effectively "share the wealth" of visitors and grow at a much quicker rate. There are many different types of partnerships available on the Web, including the following six:

1. **Ad partnerships.** Two Websites exchange ad banners to run throughout each other's Websites.
2. **Co-branding partnerships.** These are very popular on the Web with larger companies. A Website offers you a valuable service for your visitors, but gets to share banners on the service. If you are using the service, the co-branding gives you an added benefit to your visitors while introducing them to the company that provided the benefit. An example is many of the free email services. You sign up to offer free email to your Website visitors and the email provider sticks a banner on the main email page along with a "Powered by [us]" button. If you have a great service few other Websites have, you may want to consider sharing it in exchange for a co-branding opportunity to introduce more people to your services and Website.
3. **Partners.** Each site places the name of the other Website under a "Partners" heading with a link to that Website.
4. **Hosting partnerships.** Where a large company agrees to host your Website for free in exchange for banner space and the ability to announce that you are part of their network.
5. **Event partnerships.** Two Websites join forces to offer a specific event (such as a live interview with a well-known person). The Websites split the costs and jointly market the event.
6. **Content partnerships.** Two Websites join forces to exchange content and information (the bios at the end of articles and so on link back to the Website providing the content).

The types of partnerships you can form are nearly endless. What matters is that you're on the same team helping each other out. Having an ally is always much preferable to having an enemy.

WEB MARKETING IDEA 21   Answer Your Emails
in a Timely Manner

DOES IT COST MONEY?   No

HOW WELL DOES IT WORK? ★★★★★

WHAT DOES IT DEVELOP?   Revisits, Participation, Loyalty & Trust

Have you ever gone into a restaurant without getting service? One day my wife and I invited a couple of friends to go out to breakfast with us. We went to a nice local bagel place that I had visited before without any problems. The four of us sat down at a table and waited . . . waited . . . waited . . . After we had been ignored about 20 minutes, a woman yelled to us, "If you want to order, you have to come up to the counter." This was odd because we had always been brought menus and served from our tables in the past. So we went to the counter—and again we were ignored! We couldn't believe it and started to wonder if we were invisible to the staff of six people serving others and ignoring us. We left in disgust. I will never go back there and will never recommend it to family or friends.

Your Website is a place of business. When people email you, they expect to get a response. When their emails go ignored, it implants a negative image in the mind of the visitor. It gives them the feeling that they're not important. You must avoid this image at all costs!

Organize your email system for maximum results in being able to respond to visitor inquiries. Create folders such as Respond Immediately, Research Further, and Finished. When you get a message in your inbox, deal with it immediately. If it is something you can give a quick response to, then do so. If it will require some research, then respond letting the person know that you will research an answer for him or her and reply as soon as possible.

Your inbox should always be empty because you'll sort messages into your Respond Immediately, Research Further, and Finished folders. And never go to bed at night until your Respond Immediately folder is completely empty! Set aside an hour a day to go through your Research Further folders to come up with answers. Keep in constant and immediate contact with those who email you, and their participation, visits, and loyalty to your Website will vastly improve.

I always leave my email program running so that I can look at a message the second it comes in. One day I received a message that one of the pages of my Website had some information that was incorrect. I immediately went to that page and fixed the problem and responded to the individual that it had been corrected and I was very thankful to him for bringing it to our attention. From the time he sent his email to the time I emailed him (that the problem had been corrected) was *three minutes*! His response was simply, "Wow, you are quick! I'm impressed!"

WEB MARKETING IDEA Offer Targeted Contests

    DOES IT COST MONEY?   Yes
    HOW WELL DOES IT WORK?   ★★★★★
....WHAT DOES IT DEVELOP?   Initial Contact, Revisits, Participation

How many contests do you see to "Win a Million Dollars" or "Win a New Car"? Now how many of those contests have you entered and won? Probably none. It seems that we have a better chance of getting struck by lightning than winning any million-dollar contest (perhaps it's true).

Let's create a hypothetical scenario and say that two contests are running, but you can only enter one of the contests. The first is a chance to win a million dollars. There is only one prize available. The second is a chance to win $100. There are 10,000 of those prizes available. Which do you feel you have the better chance of winning? Both add up to a million dollars, but one becomes more appealing because your chance of winning the $100 is dramatically better than the near impossibility of winning the million dollars.

The preceding analysis presents you with a great opportunity to incorporate contests into your Website where your visitors have better chances of winning prizes *that are targeted at their interest*. On the *Animation Artist Magazine* Website, we have dozens of contests running simultaneously. Only a few prizes are worth a lot of money, but the majority are small things, such as sealed packages of animation trading cards. The cards cost us less than a dollar per pack (when bought in bulk), but are a perfect gift for animation enthusiasts—especially when you import cards from other countries that are hard to find for our many U.S. readers. Since a sealed packet of cards can fit into an envelope, it is very cost-effective to send (the cost of a first-class stamp). It also allows us to have several fun little contests going at once, thus increasing the participation and revisits of our members.

Think of interesting items that would appeal to your visitors that you can purchase in mass quantities to offer through a series of contests on your Website. Because offering more prizes increases a person's chance of winning, you should see participation skyrocket. And don't forget the occasional "expensive" prize too. Also, remember that when you send a prize to a winner, it is the perfect opportunity to plug your site again in a congratulatory letter to the winner. Never just send a prize. Make sure there's the personal touch too.

WEB MARKETING IDEA   Produce an E-Newsletter

DOES IT COST MONEY?   No

HOW WELL DOES IT WORK? ★★★★★

WHAT DOES IT DEVELOP?   Revisits, Participation, Loyalty & Trust

An e-newsletter is a newsletter that you send out via email to those who sign up to receive it. It is one of the best marketing ideas to increase revisits, participation, and loyalty and trust. It is a great way to deliver extra news, extra content, and a behind-the-scenes look at your Website. When you start to get thousands of subscribers, it will also become an important ad medium (discussed in my next book, *Web Profits Applied*).

If you've never done an e-newsletter, it is rather simple. First, you sign up for a service that will deliver your email newsletters to your users. Three such services are ListBot (**www.listbot.com**), ONElist (**www.onelist.com**), and Topica (**www.topica .com**). Be sure your list is set to "announce only" so that you are the only one allowed to send messages to the list. Once you sign up, you will be provided with HTML to place on your Website to allow users to easily subscribe to your newsletter.

Creating the newsletter is a matter of having good material to place in it. It's good to usually start your newsletter with a personalized message from you. Then launch into the various announcements. In addition to news, announcements of upcoming events, and so on, you can add features to your newsletter such as "Most Visited Page of the Week," which provides a link to the page that got the most hits on your Website (outside of your home page).

Whenever we interview someone for *Animation Artist Magazine,* we always hold on to the interview a few extra days to give our email newsletter subscribers a sneak peek at some of the comments made by the interviewee. We also post some of our "upcoming animated movie tips" to the email newsletter before putting it online.

Most important, make sure that you put the newsletter out on a regular basis, provide a link to the newsletter archives (get this from the free service you sign up for), and market it strongly on your Website to increase the number of signups.

For a related tip, see Web Marketing Idea #29 on registering and publicizing your newsletter.

WEB MARKETING IDEA   Create a Daily Email Update Service

DOES IT COST MONEY?   No

HOW WELL DOES IT WORK? ★★★★★

WHAT DOES IT DEVELOP?   Revisits, Participation, Loyalty & Trust

If your site offers daily updates (news, features, and so on), you may want to consider creating a daily email update service. This service allows users to sign up to receive an update every day that contains links to everything that has been updated on your Website for that day! It's a great way to put that daily reminder before those on the list to "visit today because there's something new!"

Here's a sample of how a daily email update message would look:

Per your request, here's a list of areas that have been updated on the Animation Artist Website today:

Interview with Mark Whiting, Production Designer for The Iron Giant
http://www.animationartist.com/interviews/Artists/Mark_Whiting/mark_whiting.html

Pixels:3D 3.1 Released for Macintosh
http://www.animationartist.com/products/Pixels3D/pixels3d.html

New Tip for Disney's Toy Story II
http://www.animationartist.com/upcoming/ToyStory2/toystory2.html

Weekend Box Office Results for Warner Bros.' The Iron Giant
http://www.animationartist.com/upcoming/IronGiant/irongiant.html

That's it for today's update. Thank you for your continued interest in Animation Artist Magazine. I'll have more updates for you first thing tomorrow morning.

[Signature]

The daily updates are short and to the point. But this tip is useful only if you update on a daily basis and have at least three or four items to place in each update. Users love the service because it allows them to click on the link to go directly to the update, versus searching for it through your Website. Like the e-newsletter (Web Marketing Idea #23), it could eventually turn into a great advertising opportunity when enough people sign up.

WEB MARKETING IDEA Offer a Rewards Program

    DOES IT COST MONEY?   No
    HOW WELL DOES IT WORK?   ★★★★★
....WHAT DOES IT DEVELOP?   Revisits, Participation, Loyalty & Trust

You've seen reward programs with airlines, credit cards, ATMs, and about anything that involves money. Now apply that model to a program to reward your regular and loyal visitors. Build an incentive program that rewards your visitors for their participation in your site.

An incentive program is no easy thing to build. You must decide on what types of prizes you can award, how the point program (if it is a point program) works, how many points are needed for what prizes, how points are tallied on a regular basis, how visitors can access their statistics to know how many points they have to spend, how distribution of the rewards will take place, and so on.

Even though it isn't easy to operate, there are a lot of rewards that come with a successful rewards program. Higher revisits, participation, and loyalty are the three main ones. Furthermore, it is a branding effort if you give away the right prizes. Branding? You bet. Make most of your prizes useful items with your logo on them, such as T-shirts, carry bags, and so on, and when your visitors use those items, they will be advertising your Website!

Be very careful in your planning before deciding to offer a rewards program. It is something you want to be able to continue without going broke. That means planning for growth. Don't make items too easy to get, but not too hard that it discourages people from participating. The way Animation Artist structures its rewards program is through participation. If a person's quote in our forum is used on the front page as the Quote of the Day, then they get points. If they find certain things in the Website (a mini–scavenger hunt), they win points. If they win contests, they additionally win points, and so on. There's a "Rewards" page that lists all the items available and what the point costs are for the items. Be sure to have posted rules (points cannot be combined with those of other members, and so on).

To keep the whole program interesting, add more things people can get points for and refresh your prizes often (adding new ones, removing old ones, and so on). Get some companies to sponsor items! If you have limited availability on some products, say so. There's a ton of great opportunities in a well-planned awards program.

WEB MARKETING IDEA Study Your Log Files

    DOES IT COST MONEY?   No
    HOW WELL DOES IT WORK?   ★★★★★
....WHAT DOES IT DEVELOP?   Revisits, Participation

The best marketing research you can do to help improve initial contact, revisits, and participation on your Website is to study your daily log files that contain the statistics of your Website. Log files present the opportunity for you to find out the following:

1. How many people visited your Website.
2. Which pages were most popular.
3. Where your traffic was referred from.
4. Which pages most people left your site from.
5. How many errors visitors experienced on your Website.
6. Tons of more statistics (browser types, top visitors, and so on).

Studying your log file presents you with opportunities to see what's hot, what's not, and how you can improve the flow of traffic throughout your Website. It allows you to create a plan to improve navigation and to strengthen your promotion in pages from which most people are exiting your site.

The problem with statistics tracking is that most new Webmasters don't know how. The good news is that your Web hosting company should have a statistics program for you. Some even email all your stats to you on a regular basis. Your support department can also direct you to the location of your log files should you decide to download them and use another program (such as Webtrends) to keep track of your statistics.

Another option is to grab a hit counter from a place such as **www.hitbox.com**. One of the newest programs, HitBOX Site Analysis, will give you a detailed real-time analysis of your entire site. You do have to insert HTML code and it does install a small ad on your site, but for free you can't beat it. To get rid of the ad, you can purchase an Enterprise edition for $20 a month (for sites that have up to 10,000 page views a month). Use your statistics to plan your strategies!

WEB MARKETING IDEA Submit a Press Release

   DOES IT COST MONEY?   Yes
   HOW WELL DOES IT WORK?   ★★★★★
....WHAT DOES IT DEVELOP?   Initial Contact, Revisits, Participation,
                                         Loyalty & Trust

A press release is one of the key ways to reach media with the potential of getting some coverage of your Website. Writing a good press release isn't easy, and you have to create some unique angles in order to get the press interested in covering your story—especially since there are hundreds of new Website press releases being issued every week!

If your press release is channeled through the right distributors, you may get additional coverage from other Websites that will republish your press release.

Chapter 8, "The Role of Public Relations in Web Marketing," covers in detail what you need to make an effective press release and how to increase your chances of being recognized. Be forewarned, however, that mass distribution of your press release can cost *a lot* of money. For maximum effectiveness, we're talking about $500–$600. For minimum effectiveness, distribution will cost around $150.

In general, a press release should cover something truly newsworthy and unique. The more unusual it is (especially if it is a "first" on the Web), the better chance you have of your phone ringing (yes, you must put a phone number on your press release) and of mass publicity coming your way.

Be prepared before sending out a press release. Make sure there are no "Under Construction" areas on your Website. Also, be sure that your site can handle the increased traffic that could come as a result of your press release. Make sure you also have a press page (Web Marketing Idea #36) on your Website and a way for reporters to access your press kit (Web Marketing Idea #28) online. The more information you can get to press, the better.

Read Chapter 8 for details on writing an effective press release and to learn what media are available for distribution.

WEB MARKETING IDEA Create a Press Kit

DOES IT COST MONEY?   Yes

HOW WELL DOES IT WORK? ★★★★★

....WHAT DOES IT DEVELOP?   Initial Contact, Revisits, Participation,
                             Loyalty & Trust

A press kit contains vital information about your Website, the company behind it, and any recent press releases you have put out. Generally speaking, a press kit contains the following five items:

1. A nice folder with your logo on the cover and inserts on the inside to hold all your material (plus a slot for your business card).
2. Copies of any articles that have been written about your Website or company.
3. A detailed background of your Website or company.
4. A "Quick Reference" fact sheet on your Website or company.
5. Any recent press releases about your Website or company.

In addition, here are some optional items that you can include:

1. A black-and-white photo of the front page of the Website.
2. A color photo of the front page of the Website.
3. A list of awards your Website has won (if the list is impressive).
4. Copies of any physical award certificates your Website has won.

Make sure that everything in your press kit is relevant to your purpose for distributing it. Keep a strong focus on your Website. In Chapter 8, "The Role of Public Relations in Web Marketing," you will learn where to get media names and addresses to send your press kits to.

In addition, you may want to consider putting your media kit online! If you don't want everyone to see it, then password-protect it. That way you can distribute the URL and password via your printed press kit and email the URL and password to any new contacts you make. If you don't care about who sees your press kit (including competitors), then you may want to link directly to it from your front page.

A press kit is different from a media kit. A media kit (which the upcoming *Web Profits Applied* book thoroughly discusses) is meant to *attract advertisers*. A press kit is meant to *attract publicity*. So your media kit will contain detailed information on prices for advertising on your Website, whereas your press kit won't.

Read Chapter 8 for more details on creating and distributing a press kit.

WEB MARKETING IDEA   Register and Publicize Your
:   Email Newsletter
:
:   DOES IT COST MONEY?   No
:   HOW WELL DOES IT WORK?   ★★★★
:....WHAT DOES IT DEVELOP?   Initial Contact

Once you have an email newsletter (Web Marketing Idea #23) and have started marketing it to your Website visitors, you will want to register it and publicize it to places
outside of your Website. Registering your email newsletter (also known as an e-zine)
with e-zine directories has the same effect for your newsletter that registering your
Website with search engines has on your Website.

Right now there are only a handful of e-zine directories on the Web compared to
the vast number of search engines and Website directories.

Here is a list of places where you should register your email newsletter:

1. www.meer.net/~johnl/e-zine-list/submit.html

2. www.arl.org/scomm/edir/template.html

3. www.published.com/add/

4. http://gort.ucsd.edu/newjour/submit.html

5. www.newsletteraccess.com/database/reg.html

6. www.lifestylespub.com/cgi-bin/publishers.cgi?$id

7. http://scout.cs.wisc.edu/caservices/new-list/input.html (geared
   more toward mailing lists than e-zines)

8. www.coalliance.org/ejournal/forms/ej.suggest.shtml

Pay close attention to the instructions within each registry. Remember that you can
access these links directly via www.webmastertechniques.com/webmarketing/.

You'll also want to apply many of the tips you learn in this chapter to the promotion of your email newsletter. Make sure you have a page on your Website dedicated
strictly to the promotion and sign-up of your newsletter so that you can send traffic
that way. Considering offering contest drawings, strictly for mailing list members, on
a monthly basis.

WEB MARKETING IDEA Become a Seller on Auction Sites Such as eBay

DOES IT COST MONEY? Yes (but you also <u>make</u> money)

HOW WELL DOES IT WORK? ★★★★

....WHAT DOES IT DEVELOP? Initial Contact

If I were to rank these marketing ideas on a fun scale, this one would definitely rank #1 (for me, at least). The eBay site alone is a fun place to hang out, which also makes it a fun place to apply marketing strategies.

Every day, *Animation Artist Magazine* receives 40 to 60 unique visitors from eBay. Why? Because I market Animation Artist on everything I sell on eBay. Furthermore, I take advantage of the "About Me" eBay utility to further market *Animation Artist Magazine*.

Notice the opening paragraph on my "About Me" eBay page (see image). I promote *Animation Artist Magazine* by stressing the fact that most things I buy on eBay are given away for free on Animation Artist. This attention grabber (which is true, by the way) helps draw an added interest to my site. After all, someone I outbid in an auction may end up getting that item for free by winning a contest on Animation Artist! To see how the rest of the "About Me" page looks, visit `http://members.ebay.com/aboutme/joetracy/`.

Welcome to Joe Tracy's Ebay Page!

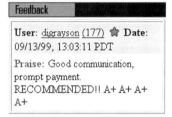

A Welcome to You

Welcome to my eBay page. I'm glad you took the time to stop by. As I've recently discovered, eBay can be pretty addicting. Luckily it doesn't interfere with the work I do for Animation Artist Magazine - www.animationartist.com. In fact, the purpose of most of my eBay purchases is to **give away the items I bid on for free at the Animation Artist Magazine Website!**

Feedback

User: digrayson (177) ★ Date: 09/13/99, 13:03:11 PDT

Praise: Good communication, prompt payment. RECOMMENDED!! A+ A+ A+ A+

By using the "About Me" feature and by adding a simple "Visit My Website at `www.animationartist.com`" to every page of items I'm selling, I gain hundreds of weekly visitors to *Animation Artist Magazine.*

While eBay is by far the most popular of the auction sites, you can equally apply this to other auction sites, such as the ones at `Amazon.com` and `Yahoo.com`.

WEB MARKETING IDEA   Create a "Best of the Web"
:   Award Program
:   DOES IT COST MONEY?   No
:   HOW WELL DOES IT WORK?   ★★★★
:....WHAT DOES IT DEVELOP?   Initial Contact

Once your Website becomes established as a strong leader in its field, you may want to give serious consideration to offering your own "Best of the Web" award program to honor outstanding Websites. Be forewarned, however, that this can be very time-consuming, as it will require going to potentially hundreds of Websites a week. It is difficult to maintain, but can be rewarding in new traffic and in further establishing links to you from around the Web.

There are three key elements you need to offer when establishing an awards program:

1. A well-designed award graphic.

2. Very detailed rules, instructions, and qualifications.

3. A way for people to submit their Websites for consideration.

The most time-consuming part of offering an awards program is managing the whole thing. Luckily, a free software program called FastAward will save you count-less hours in this process; it can be downloaded from **http://www.amusive.com/ scripts/**. It is a CGI script, so you will need to be familiar with the installation of such scripts. If you have any problems or questions, just drop by the Web Marketing Applied Reader Forum at **www.webmastertechniques.com/webmarketing/** and you should be able to find some quick assistance.

When you send out the congratulatory letter to winners, either attach the award GIF or direct the winner to a URL where they can save it. Try to be specific as to why the site won your award, as many Websites publish such comments with the award. If desired, include link instructions so the recipient can link the award to your Website! Be sure to register your award program with the various award sites (for example, **http://www.focusa.com/awardsites/introduction.htm**).

WEB MARKETING IDEA Keep Visitor Comfort in Mind

DOES IT COST MONEY?   No

HOW WELL DOES IT WORK? ★★★★

....WHAT DOES IT DEVELOP?   Revisits, Participation

If you want visitors to return and participate in your Website, you need to do everything in your power not to annoy them. The following are some things that could become very annoying to your visitors to the point of driving them away. Avoid these at all costs!

Top Annoyances That Drive Visitors Away:

1. Pop-up banners and ad boxes.

2. Forcing a new window open on a person's browser that opens a new Web page when he or she exits your site.

3. Graphics that take forever to load (use an optimizer program such as the free online one at **www.jpegwizard.com** to avoid this).

4. Clicking on a button or link on a Website only to get a "File Not Found" error message (be sure to help combat this with Web Marketing Idea #16).

5. Not being able to find information. If a Website has bad navigation and a lack of direction or focus, the result could be the visitor not being able to find what he or she is looking for.

6. A cluttered site. Some Web pages could win the "Cluttered Site of the Year" award for trying to pack an entire book onto one page. Analyze the layout of a nice magazine before designing your Website and avoid the cluttered look!

7. Using a noisy background pattern behind text (especially one that hasn't been ghosted) that makes text unreadable and therefore useless.

When a visitor comes to your Website, you want to make the experience as pleasant as possible. Produce a nice clean site that is easy to navigate around. Don't clutter your site with too many ads or too much information in one place. Make it easy for visitors to contact you and to make recommendations. Make the experience as enjoyable as possible for everyone. The result will be more visits and stronger participation in your Website.

WEB MARKETING IDEA   Make Linking to an Article Easy

DOES IT COST MONEY?   No
HOW WELL DOES IT WORK?   ★★★★
WHAT DOES IT DEVELOP?   Initial Contact, Participation

Chances are that many Webmasters of other Websites will visit your site. Some of them will have sites dealing with the same subject as yours. Many of these Webmasters are looking for great stuff to link to and additional content for their Websites. Whenever you publish an interview, tutorial, feature, or anything of interest, include a little statement for Webmasters at the bottom of the page (see first image). Your goal is to make linking to one of your pages *as easy as possible*.

Webmasters - feel free to link directly to this article. The URL is:
http://www.animationartist.com/interviews/Animators/Richard_Bazley/richard_bazley.html

You should also provide a very direct request to Webmasters from your home page. See the second image for an example.

Attention Webmasters
Your support is greatly appreciated! Please take a second to provide a link from your site to ours using the following URL: http://www.animationartist.com
Feel free to also grab a banner by clicking here. Thank you for your support!

Notice that in the second image I've also given Webmasters a quick way to find an Animation Artist banner. Make everything easy and convenient to find, and the result will be more links to your Website. You're also encouraging participation of Webmasters who will always know that good information can be found on your Website with simple link instructions.

Couple this idea with Web Marketing Idea #44 for maximum effectiveness.

WEB MARKETING IDEA 34   Help Make Your Website
                                 Their Home Page

DOES IT COST MONEY?   No

HOW WELL DOES IT WORK?   ★★★★

WHAT DOES IT DEVELOP?   Revisits, Participation

Microsoft's Internet Explorer has passed Netscape as the #1 browser online. The most-used version of Internet Explorer (as of this writing) is Internet Explorer 5.0. The great thing about visitors coming to your site with Internet Explorer 5.0 is that you can incorporate some cool scripts for your marketing efforts.

One script is the "Click here to automatically make this page your home page" script. With this script, all that users of Internet Explorer 5.0 have to do is click the link (first image), confirm the request (second image), and it's done! Your page is now their home page! Visitors who don't use Internet Explorer 5.0 won't see the option (third image); it will appear as a blank space. The script will not interfere with the browsing experience of those not using Internet Explorer 5.0.

Monday
September 13, 1999

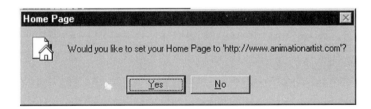

Monday
September 13, 1999

If you are using Internet Explorer 5.0 or above, go to **www.animationartist.com**; you'll notice that the option to make Animation Artist your home page appears at the top and at the bottom of the page. You'll find that the highest compliment you can get as a Webmaster is a visitor making your Website his or her home page.

To get the code for the script, go to **http://wsabstract.com/script/script2/ homepage.shtml**.

WEB MARKETING IDEA **35**   Use Your Email Signature

> DOES IT COST MONEY?   No
> HOW WELL DOES IT WORK? ★★★★
> ....WHAT DOES IT DEVELOP?   Initial Contact, Revisits

Nearly every email program on the market has an easy way for you to set an *email signature* (see images—both from Microsoft Outlook). An email signature automatically places text on every outgoing email message.

A signature is convenient because it is automatically placed in every email message you send out. This gives you a great opportunity to create a tagline to attract more visitors and increase your branding. Your email signature doesn't have to be fancy. As you can see in the second image, I simply stated the name of the Website (Animation Artist Magazine), the URL, our slogan ("The Spirit of Animation") and the fact that it is updated daily. An email signature is easy and free, so make sure you set yours up immediately.

WEB MARKETING IDEA Add a Press Page to Your Website

DOES IT COST MONEY? No

HOW WELL DOES IT WORK? ★★★★

WHAT DOES IT DEVELOP? Initial Contact, Participation, Loyalty & Trust

A press page on your Website serves three purposes:

1. It informs visitors of any press releases you have put out.
2. It helps direct press inquiries to the right person.
3. It adds credibility to your Website.

The first purpose is to inform visitors of any press releases you have put out. From your home page, you need a link to your press page. Your press page needs to contain links to press releases that you have put out. Usually, on the front page, you will have the title of the press release, the URL, the date it was released, and a short description. Visitors can then click on the link for further information. In addition to your company press releases, you'll want to have a separate area that contains links to any press stories about the company that appear on other Websites.

The second purpose for a press page is to help direct press inquiries to the right person. Right on the front page you should have a "Press Contact" with a name, email address, and phone number (optional). Each of your press releases should also contain contact information, as discussed in Chapter 8.

Finally, your press page adds credibility to your Website. It helps you look more prestigious and professional. It also enhances your communications with the press and your visitors and it shows that you have a clear direction.

WEB MARKETING IDEA   Introduce a Forum on Your Website

    DOES IT COST MONEY?   Yes and No
    HOW WELL DOES IT WORK?   ★★★★
....WHAT DOES IT DEVELOP?   Participation

A forum on your Website can be a great way for your members to participate. There are, however, a number of things to consider before starting one:

1. **How many visitors do you currently get?** You should probably wait until you're getting at least 750 visitors a day before starting a forum. Dead forums are like graveyards.

2. **You must promote your forum.** Without promotion, your forum will never get off the ground. You must have a plan. How will you direct visitors there? How will you encourage visitors to use your forum?

3. **Rules.** What are your forum rules? Will your forum be "family-safe"? If so, you need a forum that allows you to censor bad language in advance. Will you require your visitors to register in order to participate in the forum? This is generally a good idea in case you start to have problems. How will your forum be moderated?

4. **Design.** What will be the look and feel of your forum? Do you have design elements that you can create to personalize the look and feel?

Once you've examined these considerations, it's time to make your decision on what forum program to use.

There are two main leaders in the forum arena. One costs just over $150 (Ultimate Bulletin Board) and the other one is free (UltraBoard). For *Animation Artist Magazine,* I use the Ultimate Bulletin Board; you'll see that many prestigious companies such as Warner Bros. also use this package. Of course, you'll need to decide for yourself which one is best for your needs. Here are the URLs to both programs:

1. Ultimate Bulletin Board—www.ultimatebb.com

2. UltraBoard—www.ultrascripts.com

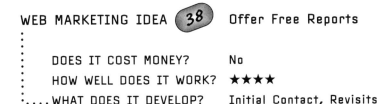

WEB MARKETING IDEA **38**   Offer Free Reports

DOES IT COST MONEY?   No

HOW WELL DOES IT WORK?   ★★★★

WHAT DOES IT DEVELOP?   Initial Contact, Revisits

Free reports are a great way to attract new interest in your Website. These are specialized reports that you write up and then publish on your Website. You then focus your marketing efforts on letting people know about your free reports. From the free reports, you publicize the home page of your Website to drive more internal traffic.

Let's assume that your Website deals with lawn care. You can create a series of short "free reports" that deal with the subject—for example:

"16 Ways to Help Your Lawn Grow Greener"

"How to Get Rid of Gophers Overnight"

"Five Ways to Landscape Your Lawn"

You get the picture. Near the end of each of these reports you include a *major* plug for your Website. Let's take the first example. You have a well-crafted abbreviated report and you save your last paragraph for your plug: "These tips I've shared with you are just a small part of the huge lawn care resource you'll find at my Website, Ideal Lawn— **www.ideallawn.com** [this URL was unregistered as of September 15, 1999]. Visit our home page to get dozens of more tips on creating a greener lawn."

Since your free reports are marketed to a deeper part of your Website (for example, **www.ideallawn.com/freereports**), you want to make sure to channel the reader to your front page. Furthermore, since your free reports are on your site, you can include your navigation bar and teasers to lead the reader from your free report to other areas of your Website.

Your free report can also now double as content you provide to other Webmasters, as discussed in Web Marketing Idea #48.

WEB MARKETING IDEA   Keep a Percentage of Your Website
                                           Income for Marketing

   DOES IT COST MONEY?   No

   HOW WELL DOES IT WORK?   ★★★★

....WHAT DOES IT DEVELOP?   Initial Contact, Revisits, Participation,
                             Loyalty & Trust

If you want to take full advantage of your marketing efforts, you will have to spend some money on a consistent basis. The biggest complaint I hear from Webmasters in this area is "I don't have any money to spend." Your job is to "create" money to spend. Here's what to do:

1. Start making money on your Website (read my upcoming book *Web Profits Applied* for some great ideas). This could be affiliate programs, advertising, member fees, and so on. Whatever it is, begin generating some type of monthly or quarterly revenue.

2. Create a bank account (or subaccount from your bank account) called "Marketing." This is where your marketing budget will reside.

3. Set aside 20 percent of all incoming revenue to go directly into your marketing account. This money cannot be touched for any purpose except for marketing your Website.

Let's say that you're an Amazon.com affiliate and you bring in $1,000 a quarter (not unrealistic if done right). As soon as you receive that check, you would place $200 into your Marketing bank account and use the rest for Website expenses, your pay, prizes, and so on. Now when you run across any marketing ideas in this chapter that cost money, you will have the money to start executing some of these ideas.

The more successful your Website becomes, the more money you will make. Stick strictly to the scenario, placing 20 percent away for marketing. Soon you'll have a hefty budget to do great things—just make sure that those great things are consistent!

WEB MARKETING IDEA Create a "Scoop" for a
                                        High-Traffic Website

    DOES IT COST MONEY?   No

    HOW WELL DOES IT WORK?   ★★★★

....WHAT DOES IT DEVELOP?   Initial Contact

Many Websites enjoy trying to discover "scoops" in order to be the first to report it to the world. In the entertainment industry, sites such as Ain't It Cool News (AICN) and Cinescape gain a lot of traffic by providing daily scoops. So what happens when you come across one? The second you get a strong scoop, you should do a little write-up on it and submit it to sites much bigger than yours asking them to credit you. The result is that they will still "get the scoop" (which you can also publish on your Website) and you will get the credit, resulting in more traffic to your Website. Animation Artist has gained tons of immediate traffic using this method, as we've had information appear on both AICN and Cinescape.

For this to work, you need to start analyzing who the leading Websites are in your subject matter. These should be sites that get a lot of traffic, have daily news, and specialize in "inside stories." Find an email address to submit tips to and consider an introductory email, letting them know that you exist and would like to submit tips or scoops from time to time.

Ultimately, you want to be the Website that is getting all the scoops, inside information, and traffic. Until then, take advantage of the traffic you can get from other Websites that are already highly successful.

WEB MARKETING IDEA   Offer Monthly Prizes to Sites
                                                 Displaying Your Banner
    DOES IT COST MONEY?   Yes
    HOW WELL DOES IT WORK?   ★★★★
....WHAT DOES IT DEVELOP?   Initial Contact

Contests don't have to be just for your visitors. Contests can also be used to encourage Webmasters to participate in your programs. For example, why not offer a monthly drawing for Webmasters who place one of your banner ads on their Website?

Here's how the program works:

1. Make a series of banners and place them on a Web page that you will promote from the front page of your Website.
2. Clearly explain how the program works—Webmasters place a banner on their Website and email you that it has been done, and every month you hold a drawing. Once the winner's name is drawn and you confirm that he or she has the banner up, you mail the winner a prize.
3. List the prizes that are available for that month.
4. Every month list the winner, contact the Webmaster for an address, and ship out the stated prize. Be sure to check the Website of the winner first to make sure your banner is still there!

This brings up the subject of prizes. You should set aside a portion of your Website's income (usually 5 to 10 percent) just for prize money. You can find great items for prizes on eBay, at bookstores, or at software stores. Furthermore, if you have connections in your industry, you may be able to have prizes donated (for all your contests). The key is to have a reward system in place, as it gives people more of an incentive to participate. The amount of additional traffic it will bring you far outweighs the cost of the prizes.

WEB MARKETING IDEA   Survey Your Website Visitors

DOES IT COST MONEY?   No

HOW WELL DOES IT WORK? ★★★★

WHAT DOES IT DEVELOP?   Participation, Loyalty & Trust

Want to improve your Website while increasing participation? Find out what visitors like best and focus on presenting more of the great while improving the areas visitors find least appealing. This is accomplished through simple Website surveys.

Conducting Website (and even email) surveys is an important step in your marketing research. Many large corporations are so in tune with the value of Website and email surveys that they pay up to $60,000 just for advanced software to conduct and analyze survey results.

Luckily, setting up your own survey won't cost you $60,000 but it will require some research along with thoughtful questions and possible answers. I find that the survey results that help me the most are answers to open-ended questions, in which visitors are not given a list of possible responses, but rather answer the question in their own words. Here are some examples of open-ended questions:

1. What is the main reason you visit *Animation Artist Magazine*?

2. What can *Animation Artist Magazine* do to better serve your needs?

3. What section on the Animation Artist Website would you like to see updated more often?

Use open-ended questions and a reward mechanism (for example, offer a prize drawing with a cool prize for those that respond). Most of all, pay close attention to the results. Your visitors have spoken. Listen to them!

WEB MARKETING IDEA Compile Your Competitors'
                                       Strengths into Your Site

   DOES IT COST MONEY?   No

   HOW WELL DOES IT WORK?   ★★★★

....WHAT DOES IT DEVELOP?   Revisits, Participation

As you'll learn in Chapters 3 and 4, it is very important to know what your competitors are doing and what actions you need to take to always stay one step ahead.

With your Website, do you want to be a leader or a follower? To become the best Website in your subject field, you must be better than your competitors. This means identifying the strengths of all your competitors and bringing those strengths together into one location. It also means having your own unique aspect that puts you a step ahead.

The Web is like a wide-open land in which empires are trying to take control. All the elements of a war movie are there—enemies, allies, greed, honor, bravery, and betrayal. The smart Websites try to stay out of direct battles and slowly build a huge empire while making many allies.

Part of building your huge empire involves preparing of a detailed analysis of all your competitors. It involves dissecting what is best about each of your competitors and then bringing the best of all worlds into one site with your own personal touch and uniqueness. Study great sites. What makes them great? Why do people visit? What do you like about them? Now make a site that is much better.

Don't be left two steps behind when it's much better to be two steps ahead.

WEB MARKETING IDEA Ask Your Visitors to Link to You

DOES IT COST MONEY?   No

HOW WELL DOES IT WORK? ★★★

.....WHAT DOES IT DEVELOP?   Initial Contact

There's a good chance that many of your visitors have their own Websites—which may not be about the same thing your Website is about, but that doesn't matter. An opportunity is waiting for you to get extra traffic. Since you have no way of determining which of your visitors are Webmasters and which aren't, the pages of your Website present a perfect marketing opportunity for you.

There are four different methods you should use in asking your visitors to link to you:

1. Ask from each Web page. As discussed in Web Marketing Idea #33, on each of your key Web pages, especially your home page, you will want to put a simple request for Webmasters to link to you. Near the bottom of your Web page, state your request and list your URL. To get further use out of this tip, create some banners and allow Webmasters to take them for posting on their Website! In the second image for Web Marketing Idea #33, I stated, "Feel free to also grab a banner by **clicking here**. Thank you for your support!" When a person clicks on "clicking here," he or she is taken to a page with various Animation Artist banners (see image) to select from to place on his or her Website with a link back to *Animation Artist Magazine.*

2. Ask from your email newsletters. Use your email newsletter to also place a personal request for Webmasters to link to your Website.

3. Ask in editorials. If writing editorial messages is part of your Website content, be sure to drop a request now and then for Webmasters to link to your site.

4. As discussed in Web Marketing Idea #46, use visuals to encourage action. Create a unique animated GIF that would appeal to Webmasters for a link.

Don't get too carried away with link requests, but at the same time make requests with some level of consistency. Another Webmaster may not link to your Website the first time it is suggested, but may on the 27th time.

WEB MARKETING IDEA   Ask Your Visitors to Bookmark
                                       Your Web Page

    DOES IT COST MONEY?   No

    HOW WELL DOES IT WORK?   ★★★

 ....WHAT DOES IT DEVELOP?   Revisits

In Web Marketing Idea #44, I discussed asking visitors to link to your Website. You can also use your Web pages to remind visitors to bookmark your home page. If a visitor bookmarks your page, chances of that individual returning will greatly increase. For *Animation Artist Magazine,* we make our bookmark request a high priority. As shown in the following image, when a person comes to *Animation Artist Magazine*'s home page, he or she is greeted with our logo and slogan, and then a request (in red) to bookmark the page: "Be sure to bookmark this page for fast access." We made a request ("Bookmark this page") and we gave a reason ("for fast access"). Similarly, you may want to say, "Be sure to bookmark this page for the latest news," or "Bookmark this page to quickly access our latest updates." Web Marketing Idea #46 shares another strategy: using visuals to encourage action. Following that, Web Marketing Idea #47 gives you a great tip on making your bookmark link stand out in a person's bookmark files.

Be sure to bookmark this page for fast access.

WEB MARKETING IDEA Use Visuals to Encourage
Reader Action

    DOES IT COST MONEY?   No

    HOW WELL DOES IT WORK? ★★★

    WHAT DOES IT DEVELOP?   Revisits

While text requests for reader action ("Bookmark this page," "Click here to make this your home page," and so on) work fine, you'll discover that using an image to request the action will get a lot more attention. In fact, a link request on one part of your page and an image on another, making the same request, can be very effective as long as your Website doesn't begin to look "cluttered" with such requests.

I usually reserve image bookmark requests for pages that get a lot of traffic at *Animation Artist Magazine*. This includes the home page, upcoming animated films, the main interviews page, and the tutorials page. For the image, my wife (the better artist in the family) drew a bookmark in Adobe Illustrator. She then added the words, "Stay Informed: Bookmark this page" (see image). In a matter of ten minutes, I had a good image to upload.

This idea can be applied to other requests you make of your visitors, such as Web Marketing Idea #34, "Help Make Your Website Their Home Page." Use the visuals to draw interest to the action you are requesting. You could get two to three times the response you'd get with just a link request!

WEB MARKETING IDEA Create a Favorites Icon

DOES IT COST MONEY?   No

HOW WELL DOES IT WORK?   ★★★

WHAT DOES IT DEVELOP?   Revisits

Internet Explorer 5.0 has a nifty new feature in which a Webmaster can determine what icon will be shown in a person's Favorites (bookmarks) folder when that person bookmarks his or her Website. This is a great way to attract extra attention to your Web page. When a person bookmarks a Web page, the Internet Explorer default icon (of a blue *e* on a blank page) normally appears next to the bookmark. But with this trick, the default icon won't show when a person bookmarks your Web page—your icon will show!

If you've ever done a detailed analysis of your Website statistics, you've probably noticed, under Errors, that one of the errors is that *favicon.ico* is missing. That's because when a person using Internet Explorer 5.0 tries to bookmark a Website, the browser first checks to see whether you have an icon saved to use. If not, it puts its default Internet Explorer icon next to your bookmark, and you see on your log files the error that it couldn't be accessed.

Here's how to create your own Favorites icon (16 × 16 pixels):

1. Go to **www.favicon.com**.
2. Near the top of the page you'll see "Click Here to try the Favicon Icon Generator." Click there and a Java applet will load (see image, which shows a large version of my finished icon).
3. You can now create your image.
4. When you're done, click File, then Save.
5. You will next be prompted to enter an email address to which the image will be forwarded (saved as *favicon.ico*).
6. Upload this image to your root directory (as *favicon.ico*) and you're done!
7. Bookmark your page, then view the bookmark list to see your new icon.

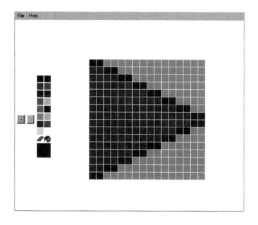

WEB MARKETING IDEA Write Content Articles for
                                       Other Websites

DOES IT COST MONEY?   No

HOW WELL DOES IT WORK?   ★★★

....WHAT DOES IT DEVELOP?   Initial Contact

Another great way to boost new traffic to your Website is by writing content for other Websites and using your bio space, at the end, to promote your own Website.

The number one thing that successful sites have is a lot of content. Yes, content is king, and as such it presents you with a great opportunity to turn the needs of others into traffic for yourself.

1. Start by writing a series of short articles. For example, my specialty is in Website marketing, so I might write articles on "20 Ways to Effectively Brand Your Website," "10 Methods for Creating Great Slogans," and so on.

2. After you have the articles written, submit the articles to high-traffic Websites that are always looking for good content. You'll be granting them the rights to republish the articles as long as the bio and copyright information remains untouched and unedited.

3. Don't submit all the articles at once! Space them out and submit different ones to different Websites. Rotate them and add new ones into the rotation. After they've rotated to all the Websites for a while, add them to your own. Waiting to add the articles to your site gives those to whom you've submitted the article a greater reason to publish it—the information will be fresh and hopefully original.

Do this on a consistent basis, because not only will it drive traffic to your Website, but it will also help brand you as a leader in your industry. Be as informative and helpful as possible in your articles. *Do not copy the work of anyone else.* Think outside the box—be original. Use your experiences and learning to relate great content to others.

WEB MARKETING IDEA   Offer Your Content for Republishing

DOES IT COST MONEY?   No

HOW WELL DOES IT WORK?   ★★★

WHAT DOES IT DEVELOP?   Initial Contact

In addition to Web Marketing Idea #48, another great idea that relates to providing content to others is allowing some articles, interviews, and features on your site to be republished by another Website. In exchange, you are credited for the article and a link is provided to your Website.

The process for this tip is simple:

1. Identify which articles, interviews, and so on you don't mind another Website republishing.

2. Create a listing of article titles, URLs, and a short description of each.

3. Create a statement that will appear at the end of each article. For example, "This article appears courtesy of *Animation Artist Magazine*—**www.animation artist.com**. Visit *Animation Artist Magazine* for other great articles! This article is © copyright 2000 by Animation Artist Magazine. All Rights Reserved. It is republished here with permission."

4. Send out an email to other Webmasters who might be interested in your material. Give a short welcome and tell them you are granting them permission to republish certain articles, interviews, and the like from your Website, provided that the statement you've attached is added to the end of each article. Then provide the list of URLs for Webmasters to obtain the material.

This type of cooperation between Webmasters is a win-win-win situation. First, the person you provide the tip to wins because of the valuable information you've provided for his or her Website. Second, you win because you will get traffic from the listing at the bottom of the article. Third, you win again because the content originally appeared on your Website and is still there (versus Web Marketing Idea #48, where the information doesn't appear on your site immediately).

WEB MARKETING IDEA Hold a Visitor Appreciation Day

DOES IT COST MONEY?   Yes

HOW WELL DOES IT WORK?   ★★★

....WHAT DOES IT DEVELOP?   Initial Contact, Revisits, Loyalty & Trust

Setting aside one day a year (perhaps your Website's anniversary) to honor your visitors is a great way to build an exciting event while thanking those who make your Website a success. It is an event you should plan for year-round, with the goal of making it truly a day unlike any other on your Website. And why is it unlike any other day? The answer is because you are paying special tribute to your visitors.

Look at this idea as an "online fair." Remember the small fair that used to come to your town, or the one that your school would plan for a special day every year? That's the kind of experience you want to recreate online for your visitor on this special day. It is a day of fun, contests, games, and celebration.

Here are some ideas for your Visitor Appreciation Day:

1. Redecorate major areas of your Website to take on a celebration theme.

2. Stretch a banner across your front page that says "Visitor Appreciation Day."

3. Add a series of one-day contests to your Website with prizes. These can include trivia contests, scavenger hunts through your Website, drawings, and so on. If you're bold, you can have some contests that have a new winner every hour, and post winner names throughout the day. If you're also celebrating your anniversary, you can have an interesting facts page on one page and trivia questions about those facts in another area of your Website.

4. Secure some great online games for your event. If you know of a Website that produces some great games, you may be able to talk the Webmaster into co-branding a page for your one-day event. It's a great way for you to add some fun to your Website, while the other Webmaster gets promotion as the game provider.

5. Add some fun music to different areas. While music is generally a no-no for Web pages, that tradition can be broken with fun, carnival-like music, on your Visitor Appreciation Day.

The goal is to create a fun and unique atmosphere where there are a lot of new things for visitors to explore and have fun with—including major discounts or free one-day coupons if you are a shopping site. Do heavy promotion of this event, including a press release the day before.

WEB MARKETING IDEA   Market Your Website within
                                          Your Website

   DOES IT COST MONEY?   No

   HOW WELL DOES IT WORK?   ★★★

....WHAT DOES IT DEVELOP?   Revisits, Participation

One of the best marketing media for revisits and participation comes from marketing from within your own Website. Because you have no guarantees as to where a visitor will enter your Website, you need to be prepared on every page to direct traffic the way you want it to flow. If a person enters through your Contacts page, how do you interest him or her in going to your home page?

Here are four marketing ideas that will help you effectively market your Website within your own Website:

1. **Create banners.** You may not have any advertising right now on your Website, but that doesn't mean *you* still can't advertise! Create a series of banners that promote various aspects of your Website.

2. **Use your logo.** In Web Marketing Idea #13 I talked about the importance of branding every Web page on your Website. Always make sure that your logo, which appears on every page, is linked directly to your home page.

3. **Provide text links.** At the bottom of every page, put a "Return to Home Page" link to your home page. Of course, you would customize it (for example, "Return to *Animation Artist Magazine*'s Home Page").

4. **Post teasers.** Inserting text and GIF teasers here and there is a great way to get a person to go from one area to another. For example, in an interview I conducted with one artist, I can put a teaser to "click here for an interview with [another artist]."

It's important to keep in mind that when a person doesn't know where to go, he or she usually decides to leave your Website. If, however, you give that person great choices to select from on all your pages, then chances are he or she will remain much longer. Study your log files carefully (Web Marketing Idea #26). What is the #1 page people are exiting from to go to other Websites? Work on that page to try to keep your visitors within your Website.

WEB MARKETING IDEA Give Visitors a Reason
                                          to Come Back

  DOES IT COST MONEY?   No

  HOW WELL DOES IT WORK?   ★★★

  ....WHAT DOES IT DEVELOP? Revisits, Loyalty and Trust

You want your visitors to return to your Website on a daily basis. In order for that to happen, you need to give them reasons to come back every day. By promoting reasons they should return, you should see a dramatic increase in the number of return visits from one person.

"Great," you say. "So how do I do that?"

The next several Web marketing ideas cover specific marketing techniques to get visitors to return on a daily basis. This includes adding more interactivity to your Website, daily insights into the subject matter you create, reviews, and so on. But that's not the only way to give visitors a reason to come back. Here are three other ways:

1. **Use teasers.** The front page of your Website is an excellent place to post teasers about upcoming updates on your Website. For example, if you did an interview with a popular personality, then be sure to use teasers on your front page for a couple of days leading to the publishing of the interview (for example, "Interview with John Doe—November 24, 1999").

2. **Use e-zine sneak peeks.** Your email newsletter is a great avenue to give visitors a "sneak peek" at something new you are preparing to update. Hold on to features, interviews, and the like until you can first do a promotion in your email newsletter. Publish the date the material will be on your Website, and your visitor count in that area will increase on that day.

3. **Use countdowns for big events.** On September 22, 1999, *Animation Artist Magazine* added five major new areas to its Website on one day. The amount of new material warranted an "event" status. Eight days prior to the launch of this new area we put up a countdown clock and an animated Java Applet that stated, "On September 22 . . . A New Adventure Will Begin! Animation Artist Magazine. 8 Days and Counting." Every day we'd change the applet to read a day less: "7 days and counting," and so on. We had spent four months preparing the expansion of *Animation Artist Magazine* and wanted to make sure that on September 22 everyone showed up for the big day. *Warning:* Use countdowns only for major events. They build curiosity and will get you visitors, but if what you show visitors is a joke, they'll laugh at any future countdowns you conduct. Use this method only on rare occasions. We do it only about once every year or every other year.

Give your readers a reason to come back every day and they will! If your updates are frequent enough, they may even make your home page their starting page!

WEB MARKETING IDEA   Add a Greeting Card Service
                                            to Your Website

    DOES IT COST MONEY?   No
    HOW WELL DOES IT WORK?   ★★★
....WHAT DOES IT DEVELOP?   Initial Contact, Revisits, Participation

Adding a nice greeting card service to your Website is a great way to increase participation on your Website and get new contacts via the recipients of the greeting cards
(who must come to your Website to see the card). Best of all, it's not a hard thing to
add to your Website!

To use a greeting card service (also known as *Web postcards*), you go to a Website
to select a card you would like "sent" to a friend. You choose a picture to go with the
card, then type in a message and the recipient's email address. When the recipient
receives the email, there is a URL where he or she can go to "pick up" the card. As you
can see, a thriving greeting card section on your Website could potentially bring a lot
of extra visitors who would be introduced to your site when picking up a greeting card.

Promote the service and add new images to your greeting card collection on a regular basis. It will be a fun benefit to your regulars, particularly if the images you use
somehow relate to the theme of your Website.

Here are a few places where you can get your own greeting card program for your
Website:

Free:
WebGrams 1—www.vanbrunt.com/webgrams/

Free:
Postcard Direct—www.ginini.com.au/tools/postcard-direct/
(Sends postcard directly to recipient. Be sure to read the license agreement.)

Small Fee:
Jason's Postcards—www.aestheticsurgerycenter.com/scripts/postcard/
(allows user to upload his or her own image)

WEB MARKETING IDEA Create and Market Separate
Entrance Pages

DOES IT COST MONEY? No

HOW WELL DOES IT WORK? ★★★

....WHAT DOES IT DEVELOP? Initial Contact

Because each search engine applies a different mechanism for how Websites are ranked, you will find it strategically wise to create four or five different "entrance pages" to your Website.

Separate entrance pages can be created via your own domain name (for example, **www.animationartist.com/entrance1.html**) or through a number of the free Website services, such as Xoom and Geocities. Each entrance page is a temporary pit stop to guide the visitor to your main page.

The key with separate entrance pages is to make changes to your title and meta tags in order to differentiate the page from each of your other entrance pages. You then submit each page to search engines as if each one were a separate Website. By doing this, you maximize your chances of getting higher (and more) rankings on search engines.

While there's nothing ethically wrong with creating separate entrance pages (after all, each search engine ranks pages according to different parameters), it is ethically wrong to create an entrance page aimed at getting rankings on a keyword that has nothing to do with your Website. Always keep the information on your entrance pages relative to your Website.

You can have some fun with entrance pages. For example, one of our entrance pages is a 10-second flash animation that gives a quick welcome to the visitor, then automatically transports him or her to the main page (**www.animationartist.com**).

Monitor the results of all your entrance pages to see how each one is doing in each search engine. If one isn't doing well in any of the search engines, change some of your parameters or duplicate a couple of your keywords. Add some additional text to the entrance page with relevant information about what is on the main site. Since search engines often change their parameters, you'll want to keep on top of your rankings on a regular basis.

WEB MARKETING IDEA   Add an Interactive Play Area
                                        to Your Website

    DOES IT COST MONEY?   Yes

    HOW WELL DOES IT WORK?   ★★★

    ....WHAT DOES IT DEVELOP?   Revisits, Participation

Besides being content-rich, your Website can benefit from being very fun and interactive. In Chapter 1 we discussed the four main things that surfers want from the Web; number two was interactivity.

If your site is rich in content, you are delivering a very valuable service to your readers. Now imagine that a reader is on your site and wants to take a break from all the content you've been feeding him or her. Do you have an area for the person to visit, or will he or she have to go to another Website to have some fun?

On September 22, 1999, *Animation Artist Magazine* opened up an interactive area on its Website called "Animation Artist Playland." It was one of the best things we ever did. Now visitors come to our Website for the content and then stay for the fun.

So what types of things can you add to increase the interactivity on your Website?

1. **Trivia.** Most people love to be challenged by a good trivia game. Why not add a trivia game to your Website with a focus on the subject matter of your site?

2. **Games.** From arcade-style games to "bet-style" horse racing games (without really betting), there are a lot of games you can download from the Web to add interactivity to your Website. It will require some programming knowledge to install the games.

3. **Cursor interaction.** A number of Java scripts allow users to interact with them via the mouse cursor. For example, in the Flozoids script on the Animation Artist Website, a number of firefly-type creatures chase the user's cursor around the screen.

Do some in-depth research on the Web and you'll be able to find lots of great (and free) things to add to your Website to make it more interactive. Be sure to check **www.webmastertechniques.com/webmarketing/** for a list of some places you can get games, trivia, and other fun stuff.

WEB MARKETING IDEA Offer Chat Events, Such as
Live Interviews

DOES IT COST MONEY? Yes

HOW WELL DOES IT WORK? ★★★

....WHAT DOES IT DEVELOP? Initial Contact, Participation

Offering a live chat event with a well-known personality within your industry can be a great traffic driver to your Website. It can also help further establish you as a leading Website within your industry (as can a number of other ideas in this chapter, including Web Marketing Idea #57).

"It's a good idea," you might say, "but how do I get a well-known personality within my industry to agree to a chat?"

It may be much easier than you think. Be sure to read Chapter 6, "It Never Hurts to Ask," for tips on getting people to agree to assist you on a project or interview. Once you've secured a talented person that people will want to listen to, you need to market the chat. This includes releasing a press release, contacting Websites whose visitors may be interested in the chat, and doing wide publicity of the chat on your Website and in your email newsletter.

There are some free chat engines on the Web if you search around. The problem is that most of them are not feature-rich enough to deliver what you need for a live chat event. Here are two of the better options:

1. You could attempt to host the event on an already established chat community, such as **http://webchat.msn.com/chat/**.

2. You could pay a leasing fee for use of a chat room. Try the $49- to $99-a-month options at DigiChat—**www.digichat.com**.

WEB MARKETING IDEA Hold Online Seminars

DOES IT COST MONEY?   Yes

HOW WELL DOES IT WORK?   ★★★

WHAT DOES IT DEVELOP?   Initial Contact, Participation

Have you ever attended a seminar in real life because you were interested in the topic of the presentation? Seminars are popular throughout the world—very popular. So why not take advantage of that popularity on the Web?

If you are an expert in a particular field—such as the field that your Website deals with—offering online seminars can be a great way of not only attracting new visitors and increasing visitor participation, but also establishing your Website as a leader in its field.

There are five key elements to remember about online seminars:

1. **The distribution method.** Will your seminar be delivered with streaming video via RealVideo or QuickTime? Or perhaps you'll use a multimedia applet with slides, chat, and audio. Determining the distribution method is a vital component to knowing your delivery limitations, including how many people you can allow into the seminar at once.

2. **Being prepared.** A seminar should be strategically planned and outlined months in advance of the delivery. The information you deliver and the way you deliver it must "wow" the audience, as it will be a direct reflection of your Website since the two are associated!

3. **Registering in advance.** Keep your seminar class size limited and make sure that attendees register in advance. This also allows you to collect information on each attendee, including email addresses for follow-ups.

4. **Making the subject interesting.** If you want to attract attendees to your seminar, both the subject and title must be something interesting. If you were trying to get out of debt, would you be more likely to attend a seminar titled "Debt Reduction" or "101 Ways to Eliminate Your Debt in 30 Days"?

5. **Rehearsing in advance.** Make sure that you have at least two "live" online rehearsals prior to opening it to your first audience. You want to know well in advance what issues you might face and how to deal with those issues.

If you want people to sign up for your seminars, you need to launch a strong marketing campaign for the seminars and stress the *value* to the attendee. If you have a way of recording the seminar to archive it, do it! You never know when seminar archives may come in handy.

WEB MARKETING IDEA Offer Previews and Unbiased Reviews

DOES IT COST MONEY?   No

HOW WELL DOES IT WORK? ★★★

....WHAT DOES IT DEVELOP?   Revisits, Loyalty & Trust

If your Website is content-oriented, you may want to give serious consideration to forming a strategic "review crew" to regularly review products and books that relate to the industry you cover. When you provide unbiased reviews, your visitors will learn that you are a resource that they can trust. By having frequent reviews, you'll find visitors returning more often.

Make sure that each member of your review crew is very thorough in the review process. People are interested in details, not fluff. Secure several screen shots to include with each review. I'd recommend that reviews be no fewer than 1,500 words. A strategic rating system may also be helpful to your readers.

Once your Website becomes prestigious, you'll find it fairly easy to obtain review copies of new products. You'll need to research a contact name in the marketing/PR departments of the company whose product you're interested in reviewing. Strike up an acquaintance and introduce your Website to them. If your site is prestigious in the industry, chances are they've already heard of you.

Going hand-in-hand with the review concept is the offering of previews. Web surfers are always interested in the "latest and greatest." If you can get a reputation for delivering new product information quickly, you'll find revisits to your site on the rise.

WEB MARKETING IDEA   Offer a Daily Insight Aimed
                                               at Your Market

   DOES IT COST MONEY?   No

   HOW WELL DOES IT WORK?   ★★★

....WHAT DOES IT DEVELOP?   Revisits

One of *Animation Artist Magazine*'s most popular features is the Fact of the Day or Quote of the Day that deals specifically with animation. We give historical insight into techniques, animation methods, and quotes from historical animated films such as *Snow White and the Seven Dwarfs, Pinocchio, Peter Pan,* and so on. Because the well-researched information we provide is not very well known in today's marketplace, it becomes a "must check" aspect of our site, bringing people back on a daily basis.

Begin researching unique aspects of your industry's past and putting together interesting facts and quotes that can be used in a daily routine. If you would like the process automated, get a program such as a *random text generator* and plug in 365 Facts of the Day from your main page. Here are a couple of great places that offer random text generators:

Message of the Day:

www.planetcgi.com/message.html

Tip of the Moment:

www.cgi-factory.com/tip/index.shtml

Random Quotes:

www.plebius.org/scripts/perl/Random_Quotes/

Plug your research into one of these free programs and you'll have a great service for your visitors that runs itself!

WEB MARKETING IDEA   Publish and Stick to a
                                            Mission Statement

   DOES IT COST MONEY?   No

   HOW WELL DOES IT WORK? ★★★

...WHAT DOES IT DEVELOP?   Loyalty & Trust

Mission statements are important for every Website (and company), as they give a focus to all the employees while giving your visitors a sense of direction and purpose for your existence. Unlike your internal goal statement (see Chapter 1), which is private, your mission statement is publicly posted. Frame it and place it on your wall. Read it every day.

Here is the mission statement for *Animation Artist Magazine:*

Animation Artist Magazine is dedicated to bringing "the Spirit of Animation" to life on a daily basis through our focus on the artists, animators, directors, and stories that bring animated illusions to life.

Animation Artist Magazine is committed to providing a daily service of information, news, and content for 2D/3D artists and to those who have an interest in animation.

Animation Artist Magazine is dedicated to quality, content, and most importantly, to you. It is the mission of *Animation Artist Magazine* to provide you with the most complete resource of animation information anywhere.

"The Spirit of Animation" is what *Animation Artist* is all about.

Notice that the total length of the mission statement is only five sentences. A mission statement doesn't need to be long. It is a simple summary of the reason you exist. It shouldn't be hard to write as long as you have a clear picture of what your Website is all about. Write a mission statement, post it for everyone to see, read it every day, and make it come true.

WEB MARKETING IDEA Hold Online Focus Groups

DOES IT COST MONEY? No

HOW WELL DOES IT WORK? ★★★

....WHAT DOES IT DEVELOP? Revisits, Participation, Loyalty & Trust

Focus groups play a major role in everything that happens within our society. When I was doing video and TV productions in Oregon, I was once hired to videotape two focus groups that were commissioned by one of the candidates running for governor of Oregon. It was very interesting to see the tests being conducted on the male group and then the female group. Unknown to the focus group, a strategic group of people were sitting in an adjacent room watching the event live! When the friendly host excused herself to go to the restroom, she would go to the side room to get follow-up questions and advice from the strategists.

I really wasn't that impressed with the overall process because a lot of the questioning was along the line of "mud-slinging" phrases that would have the biggest impact. In addition, the audience never knew that they were there because of a specific governor candidate since the focus group was aimed at people's stand on certain issues and the impact of certain phrases. Regardless of my like or dislike for that particular process, the focus group was conducted because it works.

I encourage you, from time to time, to select a group of your visitors to participate in an online focus group. Unlike the situation I witnessed, however, keep the purpose of the focus group on better meeting the needs of your visitors. What do visitors like best about your site? What areas need improvement? If the visitor were the Webmaster, what would he or she do first? Run hypothetical situations by those in the focus group to get their reactions. Log the private chat session you have with the focus group and study it in great detail. After reviewing the focus group results, take action on the issues brought up most frequently. Do everything in your power to improve the experience of your Website visitor.

In order to see how genders and age groups differ in opinion, you may want to consider splitting your focus group sessions into gender and age categories. You may be very surprised at the results!

WEB MARKETING IDEA **62** Offer Free Trials and Testimonials

DOES IT COST MONEY?   No

HOW WELL DOES IT WORK? ★★★

....WHAT DOES IT DEVELOP? Participation, Loyalty & Trust

If one of your marketing goals is to get people to sign up for a members-only area on your Website, three things will help you achieve that goal:

1. **Ask for testimonials from members.** When a person visits a Website and learns there is a members-only area, he or she has no idea what to really expect. You may say there's great stuff behind the locked door and that for $9.95 a month you'll unlock the door for him or her. That's not too convincing, however, because you're the salesperson in this person's mind. What you need to do is "bring people from the other side" to relate their experiences, through testimonials that you ask your members to give.

2. **Create a visitor tour.** Read Web Marketing Idea #74 on creating a video tour. It is a visual way of taking a person inside your Website.

3. **Offer free trial memberships.** Once a quarter on cable, a number of scrambled channels are unscrambled for a special "preview weekend" aimed at letting you see what great stuff you're missing by not being a subscriber. This same marketing strategy can be applied to members-only areas of Websites. Why not, once a month (or once a quarter), open up a section of your members-only area to the entire public for a preview of what they are missing? Preferably you want to make the areas you open to the public your *highly interactive* areas, because the more visitors participate during this free trial, the more likely they are to join.

The success of these three points will be reflected by how much time and energy you put into each. Be proactive in gathering testimonials, creating a killer visitor tour, and marketing your free trial memberships. And speaking of the free trial memberships, it is a good idea to have visitors "register" for the free trial with a name and email address. This gives you data you can use to market to your visitors in a follow-up email.

WEB MARKETING IDEA Run a Mailing List

DOES IT COST MONEY?   No

HOW WELL DOES IT WORK? ★★★

....WHAT DOES IT DEVELOP?   Revisits

In Web Marketing Idea #23, I talked about the importance of an email newsletter to your marketing efforts. There's another email idea that can also help drive a lot of traffic although it can be frustrating to handle—an email mailing list.

An email mailing list is much like a forum, except all communication between members occurs via email. With a mailing list, you can have hundreds of people communicating on a daily basis on a variety of subjects related to the purpose of your mailing list. Best of all the same services mentioned in Web Marketing Idea #23—ListBot, ONElist, Topica—each let you run mailing lists too.

The value of a mailing list to your marketing efforts comes through taglines and prestige:

1. **Taglines.** As the administrator of the list, you get to place a tagline on every message that goes to the list. It is an excellent way to continue promoting your Website.

2. **Prestige.** If your mailing list gets to the point that it is considered *the* list to be on by leaders in the subject it covers, then your Website will share in that professional appearance.

Before you rush off and start a mailing list, you should be aware that there are a few problems that come with running one:

1. **Flames.** Many times on mailing lists a group of people will begin *flaming* each other (putting others down), which brings down the quality of your list.

2. **Signal-to-noise ratio.** Some people feel that a mailing list is the equivalent of a chat channel and therefore send out dozens of messages a day on topics not relevant to your subject emphasis. As the problem gets worse, many regulars will start unsubscribing and the complaint level will rise.

Be prepared to put a lot of administrative and moderative effort into a mailing list if you decide to start one. Make sure you have strict rules and that those rules are enforced. Once you let your guard down it is hard to recover. Be prepared to be flamed yourself, too, when someone doesn't agree with something you do. Whatever happens, do not flame back. Kill your enemies with kindness. It works nearly every time, and people will see you as a better person because of it.

WEB MARKETING IDEA Send Birthday Greetings
(with drawing)

DOES IT COST MONEY? Yes

HOW WELL DOES IT WORK? ★★★

WHAT DOES IT DEVELOP? Revisits, Participation, Loyalty & Trust

One of the most sacred days of the year (and for some, the most dreaded) is a person's birthday. It's a time to celebrate your birth and the progress you've made throughout the years. It's also a great opportunity for you to be more interactive with your visitors and to help "celebrate" that special day. How can you achieve this? By offering a birthday drawing!

Here's how to create a birthday greeting program on your Website:

1. Create a special "Birthdays" page on your Website. This page must be updated *every single day* of the year.

2. Add some unique elements to this page, such as a program that gives a "This Day in History" type of report.

3. Produce a signup form for a person to send you his or her name, email address, mailing address, and birthday (year not required).

4. Every morning, post the names of your visitors whose birthday is that specific day. Congratulate each one. You'll also want to hold a drawing of all the names for that day and send the winner a birthday prize. The prize should be something simple, cost-effective, and neat. After all, you'll be mailing out 365 of these a year!

5. Bold the name of the winner in the list of birthdays with an explanation lower on the page of what the person in bold type has won and "how you can sign up."

6. Send a special email greeting to every person on your birthday list for that day. Be sure your email is *personalized*! In addition, send a congratulatory email to the person who won the drawing.

This type of interactive page can become very popular on a Website, especially when you begin to add new features such as This Day in History, where a person can find out significant things that happened on his or her date of birth in history. You could have a different inspirational quote every day—"Birthday Quote of the Day." The possibilities are endless and the personalization will do wonders for your image, as long as you are consistent with your updates and prize delivery.

WEB MARKETING IDEA Start an Affiliate Program

    DOES IT COST MONEY?   Yes
    HOW WELL DOES IT WORK?   ★★★
....WHAT DOES IT DEVELOP?   Initial Contact, Participation

There are tens of thousands of affiliate programs on the Web. The startling growth has occurred for one major reason—*it works*. However, there are just as many affiliate program failure stories as there are success stories. This mostly comes from mismanagement on the part of the Webmaster offering the program. If you decide to offer an affiliate program, you need to be a success story. Otherwise, your credibility could be lost—and that is something you never want to lose when dealing with other people.

Think long and hard before deciding to offer an affiliate program. There's not only a lot of management involved, but in most cases it will cost you a lot of money if money is one of the awards that your affiliates receive. If your money isn't managed right, you may suddenly find yourself owing tens of thousands of dollars to affiliates, with no money to pay them (because it went to other bills or purposes).

Affiliate programs can be offered for almost any purpose—to sell something, to register visitors for something, and to increase traffic to your Website. There are dozens of possibilities. Be creative. An affiliate program can be extremely useful if it is managed right. After all, an affiliate program made Amazon.com "Earth's largest bookstore."

Luckily there are programs to help Webmasters manage affiliate programs. One such program is Affiliate Programs Manager; find out more by going to **www.worksnet .com/apmmain.htm**. Check **www.webmastertechniques.com/webmarketing/** for a list of other affiliate program management systems.

WEB MARKETING IDEA 66   Offer Online Gift Certificates
                                              (limited-time)

    DOES IT COST MONEY?   Yes

    HOW WELL DOES IT WORK?   ★★★

    ....WHAT DOES IT DEVELOP? Revisits, Participation

Online gift certificates and limited offers are a good way to increase participation, revisits, and even sales. It's a great way to get a temporary boost in traffic that will hopefully lead to a stronger long-term relationship.

Amazon.com uses gift certificates to attract new business and repeat business. In the past year, I have received three $10 gift certificates from them via email. The certificates have an expiration date, which requires me to use them usually within a two-week period.

Certificates can be used for a variety of purposes—sales, access to membership areas, and special promotional items. There are different ways you can deliver your certificates, including via your email newsletter or even an oversized online banner.

One of the most important aspects of your certificate campaign is that your certificate must have a deadline (one to two weeks from the offer date) so that all action is immediate. Certificates are short-term solutions. Also, if you don't want the offer going to unlimited numbers of people, then don't put it on your Website!

Give a lot of thought to the purpose, timing, and execution of a certificate campaign before starting it. How many certificates will you offer? How will they be redeemed? Do you have enough inventory (if that's what the certificate is for) to fulfill all redemptions? What is the purpose of offering the certificates? How will you turn the short-term results into long-term possibilities? Certificates will work great if planned and executed with great care and thought.

WEB MARKETING IDEA   Create an Online Brochure

  DOES IT COST MONEY?   No
  HOW WELL DOES IT WORK?   ★★★
....WHAT DOES IT DEVELOP?   Revisits, Loyalty & Trust

Unfortunately many people overlook the great marketing value of electronic brochures. Brochures are a great marketing medium in the offline world and can be recreated online with many additional bonuses.

I picture an online brochure as part of a focused offline/online marketing effort. You create two versions of the same brochure for a product or service. One is the printed version that you physically hand to people. The other is an online version that brings elements of your offline brochure to life.

When I talk about an online brochure, I'm not talking about the Adobe Acrobat brochures that some Websites force you to download in order to view. I'm talking about a brochure that is built into your Web page design with life. It's a type of brochure that a reader can click on and the flaps open to reveal what's inside. The pictures can become larger or actually come to life. You can add sounds and animate your logo. You can even make the contact information interactive. There are dozens of creative possibilities.

For maximum effectiveness, match the layout and content of both versions of your brochure. The key is that your online brochure holds the interactive elements. It's like movie studios that add extra bonuses to DVD movies. Perhaps a person clicks on an image and it loads a movie based on that image. When a person clicks for contact information, it can bring up a form that can be instantly filled out. There are many creative ways to present your products and services through this medium (which is a subsection of your Website). The dual branding (offline and online) also helps strengthen your image.

WEB MARKETING IDEA Offer a Free Lottery on Your Website

DOES IT COST MONEY?   Yes

HOW WELL DOES IT WORK? ★★★

WHAT DOES IT DEVELOP?   Initial Contact, Revisits, Participation

If you want to get a lot of visitors to your Website in a short time and don't mind that many will just be "passing through," you may want to consider investing in a free lottery.

Free lotteries are becoming hot on the Internet. Some very alert companies have recognized this and have devised a new marketing medium using free lotteries. They allow Websites to "purchase" a free lottery to be offered on your Website for one week. As part of the deal, the lottery people drive the traffic to your site to use it.

Here's how the program works:

1. You sign up to be a "sponsor" ($79.95) of a weekly lotto in which those who play can win up to $5,000.

2. As a sponsor you are allowed to give free lotto tickets to your visitors so that they can play the online lotto for free. You are named sponsor for a week and are given a five-line classified ad in the lottery email newsletter.

3. As an online sponsor, people are required to come to your site in order to play that week's lottery. You are guaranteed traffic of at least 1,250 for the week.

The main group behind this is Free Money Lotto. For more information on the Free Money Lotto, visit **www.freemoneylotto.com/pages/60000/**. Even if you don't sign up to offer a free lottery on your site, you will be able to play the free lottery there for your chance at $5,000.

WEB MARKETING IDEA   Build Your Mailing List by Making
:   a Free Offer
:   DOES IT COST MONEY?   Yes
:   HOW WELL DOES IT WORK?   ★★★
:....WHAT DOES IT DEVELOP?   Revisits, Participation

One day I was doing a search on the Web for Disney products when I came across an interesting Website called Phil Sears Collectibles (**www.phil-sears.com**) that offered an impressive array of cool Disney collectibles for sale. As I went deeper into the pages, one of the items shown for sale was four 1968 Walt Disney six-cent stamps that were issued by the post office. You could buy the four stamps for $19.95. It was what appeared next that made me approvingly nod my head up and down, with a smile, over the Webmaster's ability to "think outside the box" when it comes to Web marketing.

After the four-stamp listing was a "FREE OFFER" to get one Walt Disney stamp for free in exchange for my mailing address. Here's exactly what it said:

> I sell these stamps in blocks of four at $19.95 plus shipping, but I will send you one of these historic, 30-year-old stamps absolutely free, just to add your name to my mailing list. This offer is open to anyone who has not contacted me before. Simply email me with the address you want the stamp shipped to and put the words "Free Disney Stamp" in the subject area. That's all! I'll send the stamp immediately, and let you know in the future when I add new, fun stuff to this Website. Limit 1 per household, while supply lasts.

I refer to this as *genius marketing*. For one thing, the Webmaster didn't put the offer on the front page. He put it about twelves pages deep into his Website, knowing that those who went that far truly had an interest in what he was selling. Then he placed the free stamp offer just after the $19.95-for-four-stamps listing. So now the reader sees a value. I emailed Phil my mailing address and had my free Disney stamp four days later. He had my address, I had my stamp—a win-win situation!

Just because your Website is on the information superhighway doesn't mean that you should ignore the side roads (offline opportunities). Using your Website to build your direct mail database of targeted individuals is definitely smart marketing.

WEB MARKETING IDEA Remind Visitors When Your
⋮   Website Has Been Updated
⋮   DOES IT COST MONEY?   No
⋮   HOW WELL DOES IT WORK?   ★★★
⋮....WHAT DOES IT DEVELOP?   Revisits

Many programs will send out reminders to individuals when your Website (or a specific page in your Website) has been updated. One such program is located at **www.netmind.com** (check **www.webmastertechniques.com/webmarketing/** for other similar programs).

NetMind puts out a program called Mind-it, "a uniquely powerful free service that increases visitor retention and improves customer loyalty, by bringing visitors back to your Web site on an ongoing basis." When you sign up for the program, you are given buttons to place on your Website that encourage your visitors to sign up to be notified whenever that page is updated. You simply place HTML code on your Website and Mind-it does the rest. When your page is updated, it sends out an email to everyone on the list letting them know. The result is more traffic on days you update your site (a great encouragement to do more updates)!

You can also remind visitors when your Website has been updated through a CGI script that places a button on your main page that states: "What's Changed in the Last 7 Days" (the dates are customizable). When a user clicks on it, a list of all pages updated throughout your site comes up. The user can then click on a link to go to the update of his or her choice.

A program you can use for these types of updates is Jawhatschanged. You can grab it for free from **www.ufbs.co.uk/jason/perl/jawhatschanged.html**.

Make sure that you are alerting your visitors via your newsletter, an update email service, and your Website as to recent changes. This will keep a steady flow of traffic coming to your Website . . . assuming there have been changes, of course!

WEB MARKETING IDEA   Add a News Feed to Your Website

    DOES IT COST MONEY?   Yes and No
    HOW WELL DOES IT WORK? ★★★
....WHAT DOES IT DEVELOP?   Revisits

One area of the Web that has really blossomed is the delivery of news. There are dozens of major news sites on the Web (for example, **www.usatoday.com**, **www.cnn.com**, and **www.abcnews.com**) and every one is getting hundreds of thousands of visitors. The Internet has become one of the most preferred media to get the latest news.

This presents some new marketing opportunities for you. No, you don't need to go out and hire 28 reporters on full salary, with benefits, to get your feeds. Many programs on the Web will help you link directly into news feeds from major news sources. This does not mean that you get the actual news stories; what you get is headlines that are automatically updated on your Website. When a visitor clicks on a headline, it takes him or her directly to the news story on the source provider's site.

Doesn't this drive traffic away from your Website? Yes, it does. It also drives traffic *to* your Website because your visitor knows that your site provides great news links in addition to your regular content.

I once ran a technology news page (one page) that was updated every single day with links (and descriptions) of interesting technology stories from around the Web. I was getting up to 650 visitors a day just for linking to interesting news stories on other Websites! So the potential of bringing in extra traffic to your Website is there.

There are two ways you can apply this idea. One is to manually go out and look for interesting stories and link to them on a daily basis (as I did). The other is to sign up for a service that gives you news feeds for your Website. I would recommend a service that links to multiple stories from multiple Websites. This will make your page more valuable than if all the stories were coming from one Website.

An example of a free news ticker can be found at **www.7am.com/ticker/**. One that is more elaborate and costs money can be found at **http://anaconda.net/ap _clip_demo.shtml**. Check **www.webmastertechniques.com/webmarketing/** for more links.

WEB MARKETING IDEA Buy an Ad in an Email Newsletter

DOES IT COST MONEY?   Yes

HOW WELL DOES IT WORK? ★★★

....WHAT DOES IT DEVELOP?   Initial Contact

Ads in email newsletters are not only much cheaper than purchasing a banner ad, but in some cases they are even more effective! Here are five reasons why:

1. **Email ads can't be filtered out.** Some of the hottest selling software on the market today is programs that filter out banner ads on Websites. This means that even though you are paying for every impression, some people are not seeing your ad at all! With email advertising, your ad cannot be removed.

2. **Most email newsletter ads are archived; banner ads aren't.** Most Websites keep a public archive of all past email newsletters. This means that weeks, months, even years after your ad appeared it will still be marketing for you. Banner ads, on the other hand, run for a specific time, then disappear—unless you pay more money to keep them going.

3. **You have better message delivery with email newsletter ads.** With most email newsletter ads, you are given more room to describe your product or service. This allows you to be more effective in your marketing message.

4. **You have a more targeted audience.** If a person takes the time to sign up for an email newsletter, you know that he or she is truly interested in what the newsletter is about. Every single person on that newsletter list is a highly targeted prospective customer. Your ad dollars aren't being wasted.

5. **Email newsletter ads don't rotate.** Most banner ads are set in rotation, so your message isn't before the eye of every visitor. Under the rotation method, it is possible for one visitor to see your ad several times over the course of a number of visits, and yet another visitor may not see your ad at all. With email newsletter advertising, your ad is stationary—everyone on the newsletter list will see it.

I have yet to see a detailed study on whether banner ads or email newsletter ads have a higher click-through ratio per person, but I'd be willing to bet that email is much higher—possibly double that of banner advertising. I've found this true in my own experience and hope that a larger study by an independent source will confirm it. In addition, email newsletter advertising is much cheaper than banner ads, and you can clearly see which is the more effective medium (in most cases). Of course, it never hurts to try both (if you have the budget), because banner ads are much more visual than email newsletter ads.

Visit Websites that you feel have a strong target audience for your Website. Sign up for their newsletter, analyze it, and if you feel it is effective then inquire about the number of people who receive it and the prices for an ad. Then do it if the price is right!

WEB MARKETING IDEA   Spread Your Pages Out for More
                                                Search Engine Hits

    DOES IT COST MONEY?   No

    HOW WELL DOES IT WORK? ★★★

....WHAT DOES IT DEVELOP?   Initial Contact

Do you offer original news on your Website? Most Webmasters archive dozens of news stories on one page, effectively creating a "book on a page" scenario. I've found that this type of archiving creates a missed opportunity—more search engine listings. By splitting your stories into solo pages or grouping them daily/weekly, you can effectively create new opportunities for visitors. Here's how:

1. Split your past archives into many separate pages—either by daily updates or weekly updates.

2. Next, go to each page and write down keywords from stories. For example, if DogsDaily (Web Marketing Idea #18) does a news article about Pomeranians and kennel cough, the Webmaster would list the keywords "Pomeranian" and "kennel cough" in his or her list. Compile a separate list for every page.

3. Create meta tags! Refer to Web Marketing Idea #3 for more information.

4. Submit your main archive page (which links to the many pages you created) to all the search engines and directories.

By following these four steps you will be able to index hundreds of new keywords in the search engines and directories to give you many more results in people's searches. This will bring you more visitors. Be sure to follow Web Marketing Ideas #51 and #52 to keep visitors within your site and returning!

WEB MARKETING IDEA   Create a Visitor Tour of Your
Website

DOES IT COST MONEY?   Yes and No

HOW WELL DOES IT WORK? ★★★

WHAT DOES IT DEVELOP?   Revisits, Participation, Loyalty & Trust

Creating a high-quality tour of your Website is a great way to give your visitors a more detailed look at what you offer while increasing the professional appearance of your Website.

At the minimum, a visitor tour needs to combine images of your Website with text. Ideally it will also have narration and music. For more elaborate productions, you can add video and animation. Your visitor tour should be synchronized to present a pleasing look at all the major elements your Website offers to visitors (and regulars).

Scripting and bringing together the creative elements for your Website tours will need to come from your inspiration. Software, however, can assist you in the execution. The more elaborate your production, the more it will cost. Here are some solutions:

> **Free:**
> Slide Viewer—www.ginini.com.au/tools/slideviewer/
>
> **Middle Range:**
> e-Show—www.alive.com
>
> **High End:**
> Emblaze OnDemand—www.emblaze.com/index.html

For grabbing pictures of your Website, I recommend a program called SnagIt, located at **www.snagit.com**.

When you've completed your visitor tour, test it on all major browsers and computer platforms to make sure it works. Then put it up on your Website!

WEB MARKETING IDEA   Add a Calendar of Events
to Your Website

DOES IT COST MONEY?   Yes and No

HOW WELL DOES IT WORK?   ★★★

WHAT DOES IT DEVELOP?   Revisits

Creating a calendar of events to keep your users informed of activities within the industry you cover is a great resource for obtaining revisits. The great news is that a number of calendar programs are available on the Web to aid you in your quest. Here are a few:

Free Calendar: by Matt Kruse
www.mattkruse.com/scripts/calendar/index.html

Medium-Priced Calendar: Lozinski's Calendar (approximately $50)
http://users.erols.com/lozinski/calendar/calendar.html

Higher-Priced Calendar: EventCalendar Version 1.1 (approximately $80)
www.cgi-world.com/calendar.html

Some calendar programs allow you to let users post events if they register. Unless you want an "open calendar" for the world to post whatever, disable this feature. Some calendar systems may allow you to pass on user names and passwords to people you *do* want updating the calendar.

Keep the calendar updated often and well in advance. Fill it with great information to make it a true asset to your Website. Have a link where visitors can email you to suggest events to be listed that relate to what your Website covers.

WEB MARKETING IDEA Offer Free Downloads

DOES IT COST MONEY?   No
HOW WELL DOES IT WORK?   ★★★
....WHAT DOES IT DEVELOP?   Revisits

As discussed in the first chapter, one of the top four reasons that people surf the Web is for free stuff, including free software or downloadable treats such as movie trailers. Why not offer some free downloads from your Website?

On the Web you will find numerous programs called *freeware* and *shareware*. A number of these programs may relate directly to the industry you cover on the Web. Contact the authors of these programs and request permission to redistribute their products via your Website. Then create a download area where visitors can easily obtain products.

The drawback to this idea is the high bandwidth that constant downloading creates. Most Web servers have a limit on the amount of bandwidth you can offer. For example, when Warner Bros. sent us the trailer for Pokémon to put on our *Animation Artist Magazine* Website, we saw our bandwidth rise to over ten times its normal rate. Our ISP told us that in order to be guaranteed good performance when using up that much bandwidth, we'd have to pay an extra $200–700 a month!

If you plan on offering downloads to your visitors, be sure to carefully select an ISP that will give you great service and a very high (or unlimited—read the terms of service) bandwidth rate so that it doesn't come back to haunt you.

Now here's an interesting twist on the same idea (two for the price of one)—create your own freeware, build your banner ad into it, then distribute it free from your Website and allow others to distribute it for free. If you don't know how to program, find someone who can throw together a nifty little application aimed at your industry for a fair price. Once it is done, get it out to all the free download sites you can. Users will get a great application and you'll be marketing to them through the program.

WEB MARKETING IDEA   Add Instant Messaging

    DOES IT COST MONEY?   Yes
    HOW WELL DOES IT WORK?   ★★★
 ....WHAT DOES IT DEVELOP?   Initial Contact, Revisits, Loyalty & Trust

Chances are that you or many people you know are using AOL's Instant Messenger service to chat with other people. It's a great concept—but finding a user name is virtually impossible because of the millions of people that use Instant Messenger on a daily basis. So why not start your own instant messaging service for your Website visitors to discuss your Website's subject matter with others who are in the same field of work or who have similar interests?

I was inspired about the concept of adding an instant messaging system *just for our Website visitors* when I came across a company, eShare Technologies, that offers a program called Connections. According to the company's Website, *"eShare Connections gives you the power to customize your own instant messenger and offer it to your site's community of users. Faster and less cumbersome than email, eShare Connections comes loaded with handy user features. Online users can search for and communicate with each other in real-time, bookmark their favorite URLs, store conversation notes—even enable sounds to alert them when friends have logged on."*

You can get more information on this instant messaging product at **www.eshare .com/products/connections/index.html**.

At the time of this writing, I have yet to see another company that offers customized instant messaging services just for individual Websites. If you know of any others, please let me know via **joetracy@earthlink.net** so that I can post it at **www.webmastertechniques.com/webmarketing/**.

WEB MARKETING IDEA **78** Announce Your Website

DOES IT COST MONEY?   No

HOW WELL DOES IT WORK? ★★

....WHAT DOES IT DEVELOP?   Initial Contact

So you have a new Website. Now what?

Dozens of Websites on the Internet specialize in announcing and promoting new Websites. If you're just starting up, spend some time submitting your information to these places.

Here are three places where you can start submitting your new Website:

1. **Starting Point—www.stpt.com/submit/submit.asp**

2. **What's New Too—www.whatsnewtoo.com/submit.html**

3. **Brand New Sites—www.brandnewsites.com/form.htm**

You will also want to make sure you are announced on any email newsletters that announce new Websites. Here are two to check out:

1. **Net-Announce—www.erspros.com/net-announce/content.phtml**

2. **NewPageList—http://web-star.com/newpage/newpage.html**
(very selective)

You can also announce your Website to relevant newsgroups (be careful, as some may consider this spam even though it is a legitimate announcement). Be sure to clearly label your subject header as "New Website Announcement." You may want to be more specific (for example, "New Dog-Related Website Announcement"). Do not post your announcement in a newsgroup unrelated to the major subject coverage of your Website.

Remember that before you submit to search engines, "What's New" sites, or directories, you need to make sure all of your meta tags, titles, and so on are properly set up, as discussed earlier in this chapter.

WEB MARKETING IDEA   Free For All Links

    DOES IT COST MONEY?   No
    HOW WELL DOES IT WORK?   ★★
....WHAT IT DEVELOPS: Initial Contact

Free For All Links is a way of getting your Website listed on sites that allow anyone to list their Web pages. This is great because it can get you on thousands of pages fairly quickly. However, the problem with Free For All Links is that as more people add links, yours moves further down on the list until it disappears. With the advent of submission services, links tend to disappear pretty quickly. Also, because hundreds of links are listed on these pages, your link will be fighting for recognition.

There's no real secret to Free For All Links. As long as you are consistent and can get your link noticed, you will get okay results. The key is to find as many mass submission sites and programs as possible. Then, on a daily basis, you schedule a different section of your Website to be promoted.

My recommendation is to set up a weekly schedule; every day of the week you promote a different aspect of your Website. This gets you in the habit of doing it every day and keeps your promotion level on these sites high. But you need to use some specific offensive and defensive tactics when it comes to Free For All Links, which I explain in Chapter 3, "Offensive Marketing Techniques." Read it before you submit or you'll be in for a big surprise when thousands of advertisements appear in your email box!

There are two ways you can find places that accept mass submissions for free. The first way is to spend hours (possibly days) doing detailed searches and bookmarking what you find. The second (and preferred) way is to go to the *Web Marketing Applied* Member Only area (free for all *Web Marketing Applied* owners) and visit the Free For All Links Submission section. I've linked directly to the submission sites that I use on a daily basis. You can get to those links by going to **www.webmastertechniques.com/ webmarketing/**.

WEB MARKETING IDEA Make Your Own FFA Page

DOES IT COST MONEY?   No

HOW WELL DOES IT WORK?   ★★

....WHAT DOES IT DEVELOP?   Initial Contact

By making your own Free For All Links (FFA) page, you acquire the power of the autoresponder. An FFA page is like a links page, except anyone can automatically post a link and see it instantly appear. Every time someone posts a link to your FFA page, the autoresponder (with your message) automatically sends an email to that individual. If you have hundreds of people a day signing up for your Free For All Links, you are getting your message to hundreds of people a day . . . sort of.

As discussed in Chapter 4, a lot of people who do mass postings are figuring out ways around the autoresponder. One method is creating email filters. Still, many people will get your message. Some will read it, some won't. But there may be enough value in those that read it to offer the service from your Website.

Hundreds of Websites allow you to easily build your own FFA page. Most let you do it for free. Why? For some it's because they get the advertising space on your FFA page. For others it's because it adds more pages to their multisubmit service, where they charge clients money to submit to thousands of FFA pages.

The other route to go is to set up your own FFA page without going through another service. Check out these five FFA page setup links, then decide for yourself:

1. Link-O-Matic—www.linkomatic.com/getyours.cgi

2. Cliff's Free Links Script—www.shavenferret.com/scripts/links/

3. LinkFree—http://scripts.blcassoc.com/free_links.html

4. FFA Links—http://megafreebies.hypermart.net (download from menu on left)

5. CougaLinks 3.0—www.cgiuk.com/cougalinks/

WEB MARKETING IDEA   Get Involved with Web Rings

    DOES IT COST MONEY?   Yes and No
    HOW WELL DOES IT WORK?   ★★
....WHAT DOES IT DEVELOP?   Initial Contact

Web rings are a good tool for getting people to your Website who are interested in a specific subject. The idea works even better when you are the one who started the Web ring!

In short, a Web ring consists of many sites linked together that deal with a specific subject. Each person involved in a Web ring places some HTML on his or her page that shows the Web ring control panel. The Web ring panel allows visitors to go to the next Website in the Web ring, go to the previous site, or get a listing of all the sites. If you are the one who started it, you get a double bonus because people go to *your* site to sign up and you get to name the Web ring. If you do start one, be sure to promote it extensively to sites that would qualify to be a part of it, because it does you no good just sitting on your Web page.

Are you ready to look into starting your own Web ring? If so, here's a list of four places where you can get a Web ring program:

1. WebZONE—www.simonstan.demon.co.uk/webzone/ (small fee for commercial use)

2. RingWorld—www.trxx.co.uk/products/ringworld.html ($50)

3. Ring Master—www.interactive-web.net/freeware/ringmaster.shtml (nice and free)

4. RobRing—www.robplanet.com/cgi/robring/ (free)

WEB MARKETING IDEA **82**   Participate in a Banner
Exchange Program

   DOES IT COST MONEY?   No

   HOW WELL DOES IT WORK?   ★★

....WHAT DOES IT DEVELOP?   Initial Contact

Banner exchange programs are hot on the Web because they don't cost any money; you're simply exchanging banners with other Webmasters through an organized effort. While this method of traffic driving sounds great, most programs have some fundamental problems, which is why this idea received only a two-star rating:

1. **You don't get an equal exchange rate.** For example, many of the programs show your banner only once for every two times you show someone else's banner. So for every 10,000 banner views you provide to others, you get only 5,000 banner views in exchange.

2. **Most programs don't target your ads.** Making sure your advertising efforts reach the right people is an important part of your marketing efforts. Unfortunately, most banner exchange programs don't take this into account. Let's say that your Website promotes exercise programs for senior citizens. You're probably not going to get much traffic from your banner displays on the "Teen Talk" Website.

Even with these two drawbacks, many people have reported some form of success with this type of marketing, which is why it is among our 101 ideas.

If you decide to pursue this type of program, give it your all because the more banners you display, the more displays you will get in return.

When you're ready to sign up with a program, check out the following four:

1. LinkExchange Banner Network—http://adnetwork.linkexchange.com/

2. Resource Marketing—http://resource-marketing.com/tb.shtml

3. SmartClicks—www.smartage.com/smartclicks/index.html

4. BannerSwap—www.bannerswap.com/

WEB MARKETING IDEA   Apply for Web Awards

DOES IT COST MONEY?   No

HOW WELL DOES IT WORK?   ★★

....WHAT DOES IT DEVELOP?   Initial Contact, possibly Loyalty & Trust

If you have a really good Website, you can begin to build additional traffic to it through applying for Web awards. Thousands of Websites give away awards to other Websites. Some awards are great and others are downright corny.

By applying for (and winning) respectable awards, you can both increase initial contact and build loyalty and trust from your Website visitors. Winning awards from the *Los Angeles Times, USA Today,* and the like are very prestigious. Yet winning and displaying an award from "Fifi's Nose Pick of the Day" could have an opposite effect!

The key to winning awards is to have an innovative Website and to be ready for the judges. Read the criteria before submitting your Website and make sure you exceed the standards. What makes your Website shine?

There are a couple of great benefits to increasing traffic by applying for Web awards. The first is that you are *guaranteed a visit by a judge.* Who knows, that judge may like your site so much that he or she will become a regular visitor! Another benefit is that if you win, the award site links to you. This will seldom lead to a ton of traffic (unless you get listed on a big award site, such as *USA Today*'s Hot Sites or the *Los Angeles Times* Pick of the Day). Even so, every initial contact is an opportunity to turn that person into a regular visitor.

So you're ready to apply for an award, but don't know where to start? Try these three places:

1. **Webmaster Techniques Magazine—www.webmastertechniques.com**

2. **Award Sites—www.focusa.com/awardsites/introduction.htm**

3. **Ultimate Award Submit—www.market-tek.com/awardsite.html**

Now if you're positive you have the best Website in the world and want to go for a more "official" award, then you can dish out $85 to apply for awards such as the International Web Page Awards. Check out their Website at **www.websiteawards.com**.

WEB MARKETING IDEA Keep Track of Who Is Linking to You

DOES IT COST MONEY?   No

HOW WELL DOES IT WORK? ★★

WHAT DOES IT DEVELOP?   Initial Contact, Loyalty & Trust

Did you know that you can find out who is linking to you through an interesting search engine technique? By finding out how many people are linking to your Website, you can get an idea of how effective some of your programs are doing. You can also look up competitor sites using this same method, then submit a link request to all sites they are on that you are not on yet!

Here's how to keep track of who is linking to you:

1. Go to **www.altavista.com** and/or **www.infoseek.com**.

2. Type in (without the quotes)—"link:http://www.yoursite.com" (for example, link:http://www.animationartist.com).

3. Click Search.

A list of all the sites linked to you will now come up! You can click on the subject headers to go to each page that has your link on it. If you're really feeling inspired, you can take time out to write each Webmaster a thank-you note for their link or to update them on any new projects your Website is involved with.

Keep in mind that if you are a regular submitter to FFA pages (Web Marketing Idea #79), a lot of the link returns may be FFA pages that were indexed on a day your link happened to be up.

Want to track your competitors? Follow the three steps, except put their Website address in step 2.

WEB MARKETING IDEA **85**   Form a Discussion Forum

DOES IT COST MONEY?   No

HOW WELL DOES IT WORK?   ★★

WHAT DOES IT DEVELOP?   Initial Contact, Loyalty & Trust

Many "build your own community" Websites allow visitors to create and market their own Web forums and communities. You can turn this into a marketing medium to further establish your Website's area of expertise while gaining new visitors to your site.

The main benefit you obtain through creating a forum (or community) on another Website is that you are placed in that site's forum/community directory. Suddenly you are reaching a whole new set of potential visitors to your Website. If your forum is strong enough in the category it is listed under, you also become further established as a leading voice in that marketplace.

You'll need to market your community, much like your Website, in order to build a user base. It will be time-consuming, but it can also be a lot of fun and a decent traffic-driving mechanism. If you have a stronger community at your Website, you can use this one to help "direct traffic."

Check out these locations for places you can start discussion forums or communities:

1. PowWow—ww2.tribal.com/communities/

2. Deja—www.deja.com

3. MSN Web Communities—http://communities.msn.com/home/

WEB MARKETING IDEA **86**   Translate Your Website into
                                    Another Language

DOES IT COST MONEY?   No

HOW WELL DOES IT WORK?   ★★

....WHAT DOES IT DEVELOP?   Revisits

Did you know that in just a few clicks your visitors can translate your entire Website into another language? You can even do it for fun to see what it looks like. You can also make it easy for visitors to do the translation so that you start reaching a bigger audience. This can greatly increase your appeal in other countries.

Here are step-by-step instructions for adding translations, courtesy of AltaVista, to your Website.

Step #1: Go to `http://babelfish.altavista.digital.com/content/faq.htm`.

Step #2: Scroll down to the question, "Can my page link to your site?"

Step #3: Enter the URL you want translated into the text box, then select from the scroll-down menu what translation you want.

Step #4: Click the Translate button (see image).

Step #5: Copy the URL that the page goes to and use this as the link from your page to the translation menu. When a person clicks on the link, he or she will be taken to a page that sets your URL and language preference as the default. When the person clicks Translate, he or she will get the translated page.

Can my page link to your site?

Yes, feel free to link to "http://babelfish.altavista.com/" as much as you like.
If you want a url to appear in the translation box, enter the url you want in the following box, choose the language, click translate and use the url of the resulting page:

```
www.animationartist.com
```

```
English to French  ▼    Translate
```

WEB MARKETING IDEA (87)   Combine Services into
                           a Navigation Bar

   DOES IT COST MONEY?   No

   HOW WELL DOES IT WORK?   ★★

   ...WHAT DOES IT DEVELOP?   Revisits

You can combine three cool marketing services into one (see image) through a simple navigation bar provided by a company called Send-A-Link. It's a pretty cool concept that I hope other companies will provide. If you don't mind having a small icon to Send-A-Link shown on the bar, then I'd recommend you give this one a try. Here's why:

1. The bar has an "Add This Page to Favorites" link that automates the task of bookmarking your page for the visitor. All he or she must do is click and confirm.

2. The bar has a "Share It with a Friend" link that allows your visitor to shoot an email off to a friend saying how great your Website is (you hope).

3. The bar has a "Make It Your Homepage" link that automates the task of making your Web page the visitor's homepage.

There you have it—three great marketing tools on one navigation bar (most work only under Internet Explorer 4.0 or higher). I would like to see the Webmaster make a version that a user can "buy" without the link to Send-A-Link (something like $5 per navigation bar) and to have more options in which to select. It's a great concept with a lot of great potential.

You can grab the navigation bar from **www.send-a-link.com**.

WEB MARKETING IDEA Purchase Banner Ads
on Other Websites

DOES IT COST MONEY?   Yes

HOW WELL DOES IT WORK? ★★

....WHAT DOES IT DEVELOP?   Initial Contact

This Web Marketing Idea is a real hot spot for me. As a Webmaster I want to sell banner ads to other companies, but as a marketer I find that they rarely work, which is why most Websites charge "per impression" instead of "per click." Consider the following two points:

1. There are popular programs on the market that strip out 468×60 banners so that Web surfers don't have to see ads when surfing the Web.

2. Many users have learned to effectively "ignore" Web banners. Few will rarely, if ever, click on one.

In order for a banner campaign to be effective, it must be combined with other premiums. Therefore, if you decide to negotiate with another company for advertising space, make sure they know you want a few bonuses thrown in, such as the following:

1. A mention in their newsletter with a link to your Website.

2. The option to provide an odd-sized banner.

3. A different location, if possible. Try to see if you can get space on the right-hand side of the page near the top. If you can get in a fresh new place with an odd-sized banner, chances are you will overcome the two pitfalls (ad being stripped out and users ignoring it).

If you decide to offer advertising on your Website, be sure to put together killer package options (this is discussed in detail in *Web Profits Applied*). Consider allowing advertisers to interact more with your Website. Sometimes USA Today—**www.usatoday .com**—does this very effectively.

Remember that banner ads are negotiable—so if you're going to purchase ads, don't settle for the first price you see. Try to get a better rate, with more options included. Also consider looking for smaller, more targeted Websites that may not have advertising. You can most likely get great packages at close to nothing. The Web is a wide-open marketplace. Use it to your advantage.

WEB MARKETING IDEA   Add "Tell a Friend" to Your Website

DOES IT COST MONEY?   No

HOW WELL DOES IT WORK?   ★

WHAT DOES IT DEVELOP?   Initial Contact

Chances are that you've seen a "tell a friend about this Website" program on many Websites that you visit. While very few people seem to be actually using these services, some do and that's why you may want to consider it for your Website. Word of mouth is important in spreading the word about your site. If a person really likes your Website, he or she will most likely use your "tell a friend" script as a courtesy to let a few other people know about it. The script provides a convenience and reminder to your visitors.

Here is a list of places that provide "tell a friend" scripts for you to use on your Web pages. If you don't know CGI, you may have to ask your Web hosting provider to install the script for you.

1. MasterRecommend—www.willmaster.com/MasterRecommend/

2. Tell-A-Friend—http://cgizone.stormerwebdesign.com/tellafriend.html

3. EasyRefer—http://getperl.virtualave.net/easyrefer/

4. ScreamRefer—http://screamsoft.hypermart.net/ScreamRefer/

5. Grab-A-Friend—www.webmasters-pub.com/scripts/cgi/friend/1.1/

WEB MARKETING IDEA Add the Ability for Visitors
to Email Your Pages

DOES IT COST MONEY?   Yes

HOW WELL DOES IT WORK? ★

....WHAT DOES IT DEVELOP? Initial Contact

Instead of having a person email a message to someone telling them about your site, you can give visitors the option of emailing an entire page!

A nifty program called "Mail-This-Page," put out by CGI City, allows you to place a simple form on your Web page for visitors to be able to mail that page to a friend. What's even better is that the script allows you to decide what part of the page you want sent! To avoid clogging the recipient's email with a large file, the program strips the HTML and sends only the text. It does a pretty good job at it too.

You've probably seen similar scripts on news sites. It's a good way to get some added publicity since it clearly documents what Website the material was sent from. The top of the email states, "I am sending you a copy of the page I read at . . ." followed by the URL.

You can find the "Mail-This-Page" script at **http://icthus.net/CGI-City/ scripts _mailthispage.shtml**. It costs $30 to purchase. I have yet to find a free equivalent to this script, but if I do I will post it at **www.webmastertechniques .com/webmarketing/**.

WEB MARKETING IDEA Buy Email Mailing Lists
:   for Email Blasts
:   DOES IT COST MONEY?   Yes
:   HOW WELL DOES IT WORK?   ★
:....WHAT DOES IT DEVELOP?   Initial Contact, Angry People
                                (in some cases)

Here's a major sore spot for me and I almost refused to put it in the list of 101 tips (see the questions and answers at the end of this chapter for more information).

Let me put it straight to you: **people hate spam.** Spam is most associated with email. In fact, I receive approximately 20 spam messages a day. States such as Washington are passing tough laws against spam. Even so, that seems to do little to stop the flow of email spam that is littering the information superhighway.

Out of this comes companies that claim to have "targeted lists" of individuals who have agreed to receive spam . . . er . . . advertisements from advertisers. How many "sign up here for free email advertisement" lists have you signed up for recently?

Names for these lists are gathered in different ways. Some are by questionnaires you fill out (remember checking boxes next to your "interests"?). Others are from email lists or contests you signed up for. Some are even from FFA lists that you may have never personally visited because you used a program to blast out your FFA requests.

Is email effective for direct Web advertising? The answer appears to be a hesitant yes. There are still enough people who read email advertisements and respond to them to keep the demand high for such services. If you don't mind making some enemies on the way, then you may want to consider this method. If you do, be sure to select a very reputable firm to handle your email blasts. Because I stay far away from this type of advertising, I have no recommendations on which firm to select.

WEB MARKETING IDEA (92) Add and Promote Your Own FAQ

```
DOES IT COST MONEY?      No
HOW WELL DOES IT WORK?   ★
....WHAT DOES IT DEVELOP? Loyalty & Trust
```

If you want to help build loyalty and trust on your Website, put together an extensive FAQ (Frequently Asked Questions, pronounced "fack") that answers visitor questions in great detail. It is a quick way of addressing the most frequent questions you are asked, while allowing you to give more depth and reasoning to certain questions.

Here are three reasons to have a FAQ on your Website:

1. It answers questions before they are emailed to you.

2. It lets visitors know you are active in addressing their needs, requests, and suggestions.

3. It helps direct visitors to appropriate places for more detailed information.

Even though it is referred to as Frequently Asked Questions, you can put any questions (even if they've never been asked) and answers in your FAQ. If you want to publicly address something, then add it to your FAQ. Make your FAQ accessible from the menu on your front page or on your "About this Site" page. The easier it is for people to find, the better chance they'll look there before emailing you.

Be very respectful in your FAQs. I've actually seen some FAQs with an exchange similar to this one:

Q: Why don't you update your Website more often?

A: Because it's my site and I can update it whenever I want.

Q: Are you going to add more graphics to your site?

A: No, why should I?

Questions and answers like these are a great way to lose visitors and secure a bad reputation. Treat each question with respect, care, and a helpful answer. For example:

Q: Why isn't there more coverage of products on your Website?

A: I give strong consideration to reader requests, suggestions, and complaints. I have received that same request from others and am working on a solution to bring more product coverage to the site. Thank you for your request and keep an eye out, as your voice has been heard!

If you make a promise in an answer (such as the one directly above), keep it! And the sooner you do, the better. Then remove the question, because it has been physically addressed in the expansion of your Website. Make it as easy as possible for visitors to find answers to questions.

WEB MARKETING IDEA   Add a Suggestion Box
.   to Your Home Page
.
.   DOES IT COST MONEY?   No
.
.   HOW WELL DOES IT WORK?   ★
.....WHAT DOES IT DEVELOP?   Participation, Loyalty & Trust

If you are serious about improving your Website and meeting the needs of your read-ers, you need to give them an easy way to contact you. One idea is to add a suggestion box to the front page of your Website.

Here's how the suggestion box works:

1. You create a "form" page that is very easy for the person to fill out. It should simply ask for the person's name, email address, subject, and suggestion.

2. On the front page of your Website, add an image of a suggestion box (an ani-mated one preferred) with the words, "Help enhance this Website—send us your suggestions! Click here."

3. Link the box picture and the "Click here" text to your form. The person then can easily fill out the form, click the "Submit" button, and be done.

4. Direct the user back to the home page or to a "thank you" page. When your user clicks Submit, you will want to make sure that it automatically takes that person back to the front page or to a special "thank you for your suggestion" Web page.

Short on participation in suggestions? Why not offer a monthly drawing? Every month, hold a drawing of all suggestions received. The suggestion drawn earns the per-son who submitted it a free T-shirt with your Website logo on it (or some other prize).

If you are not familiar with forms or how to get them to work, then at least link the suggestion box to an email address so that the individual can quickly send you an email with his or her suggestion.

WEB MARKETING IDEA Create an Online Video Commercial

DOES IT COST MONEY?   Yes

HOW WELL DOES IT WORK? ★

....WHAT DOES IT DEVELOP?   Initial Contact

You've seen 30-second commercials on TV and on the radio, so why not the Web? The Internet is a good distribution outlet for creative commercials. Because the concept is so rare, you could actually get people to watch them "just for the fun of it." In fact, some places such as Taco Bell replay their TV commercials online!

There are two main ways to use Web video commercials:

1. Use it in your banner advertising—"Click here to see a cool 30-second video commercial." Many will be curious enough to click (until the concept becomes overused).

2. Place the ads on your Website for your own visitors to see. If you have the ability to create fun, cool, and creative video commercials, you may find that they draw a lot of interest from your own users. Why not do some further branding by placing downloadable or live-stream commercials on your own site?

There are also a group of Websites starting to spring up that will place your video commercial or Internet infomercial on their Website with "live" playback. So if you don't have the ability to stream video from your site, you may want to hunt down others that do.

A regular boring commercial won't cut it on the Web. Study great TV commercials that are humorous and effective, then come up with your own concept to achieve the same results. Enter your commercial into awards programs, if you can add "Winner of the [Insert Name] Award" with the commercial, you'll see the viewings increase.

WEB MARKETING IDEA   Theme Your Site for the Holidays—
                                              Stay in the Spirit

   DOES IT COST MONEY?   No

   HOW WELL DOES IT WORK?   ★

....WHAT DOES IT DEVELOP?   Revisits, Participation (if theme
                              includes "fun" things)

Stay in the spirit of the holidays by adding themes to your Website as holidays approach. Not only does it bring a more festive spirit to your Website, but it can also give your site a "fresh" temporary look. For you, it can also be a lot of fun. Unfortunately, most of the key holidays for doing Website themes appear in the last 62 days of the year. This includes Halloween, Thanksgiving, Christmas, and New Year's. You could combine Christmas and New Year's into one.

Whatever holidays you select, have fun with them! Add some extra festivities during certain holiday seasons. For Christmas, you may want to add some inspirational Christmas stories. For Thanksgiving you may want to add "21 Reasons We're Thankful for You." You can also slightly alter your logo around holidays. Why not add some snow to your logo for Christmas? Add a wreath to your front page. How about some Christmas lights draped across the top of your page?

The possibilities for doing a specialized theme are nearly endless. You may decide to celebrate only one theme a year. For example, Disneyland and Universal Studios do a complete makeover of their theme parks for Christmas. Nearly everything is re-themed. Even "It's a Small World" undergoes extensive retouches (including different songs) for a Christmas theme. Why not turn your Website into a "winter wonderland"?

So where do you find great material for your themes? For one, hundreds of Websites give away free icons (do a Web search for "free icons"). Also, most software stores sell packages of 300,000+ icons for all occasions. Many contain animations and animated GIFs. Consider creating your own icons! Most important, have a lot of fun with it and make sure that all your pages are themed.

WEB MARKETING IDEA Sign Guest Books on Other Sites

DOES IT COST MONEY?   No

HOW WELL DOES IT WORK?   ★

WHAT DOES IT DEVELOP?   Initial Contact

The great thing about guest books is that they always have a place for you to list your URL. In many ways, it's like a free link and greetings combined. Here's how to turn other people's guest books into extra publicity for your Website:

Step #1: Do a search for Websites that deal with categories similar to yours.

Step #2: Go to each site and see whether it contains a guest book (usually on the home page).

Step #3: When you find a site that has a guest book, click to enter the guest book.

Step #4: Realize that some guest book administrators disable the function to show your URL even though they allow you to enter it. Therefore you'll want to also include the URL in the text of your message. Enter your information, then your message. Be sincere in what you say. You should probably take a look around and find something particular you like about the site to comment on. Then create your message: "Hi from Animation Artist Magazine—**www.animationartist.com**— I really like the animated GIFs you created from the Tarzan movie—looks great! Keep up the good work."

Anyone who signs the guest book after you will see your URL and may make a trip over to your Website.

Now let's turn the tables. Should you have a guest book on your Website? It's a good question. I don't put guest books on my sites, but at times I have been tempted (particularly for movie fan sites). It's nice just to have comments from your visitors and to get a peek at who is dropping in now and then.

WEB MARKETING IDEA   Join an Established Online Mall

DOES IT COST MONEY?   Yes

HOW WELL DOES IT WORK? ★

WHAT DOES IT DEVELOP?   Initial Contact

If you sell a number of items on your Website, you may want to gain some added publicity through joining other established shopping programs. For example, Yahoo!, the #1 visited site on the Web, offers a program called Yahoo! Shopping that allows you to build your own mall and offer up to 50 items for $100 a month ($300 a month for up to 1,000 items). The key is that you get the Yahoo! name behind you and you are marketed on the Yahoo! Shopping directory.

If you decide to start a store through a shopping area such as Yahoo! Shopping, be sure to put a very strong focus on customer service and to participate in any service programs that can identify you as a top customer service company. For example, Yahoo! Shopping runs a "Top Rated Store" program in which stores getting more than 95 percent positive customer ratings are given a special icon that recognizes them as a leader in customer service. The result is more sales and a higher loyalty and trust of your store.

In addition, you will want to launch a marketing campaign just for your Yahoo! Shopping store. Be sure to cross-promote it with your Website. Don't get started until you are prepared with a number of items to sell, as $100 a month is a lot to spend for an online mall rental space.

WEB MARKETING IDEA Place Classified Ads Online

DOES IT COST MONEY?   No

HOW WELL DOES IT WORK?   ★

....WHAT DOES IT DEVELOP?   Initial Contact

Classified ads do for online stores (and sales) what FFA links do for Websites. There are a lot of places to post classified ads (as with FFA links), you'll get a lot of junk mail (as with FFA links), and traffic will be minor (also as with FFA links). But a visitor is a visitor, right? Something must be right about classified ads, because it is predicted to be a near $2 billion industry by 2001, according to Jupiter Communications. In fact, there's even an annual event dedicated to classified ads called the Online Classifieds Industry Symposium!

Classified ads on the Web allow you to sell items much as with classified ads in newspapers. The only difference is that posting classified ads to thousands of sites on the Web is free (in most cases).

If you're ready to start blasting your classified ad out, here are some sites to do it at:

1. AdlandPro—www.adlandpro.com
2. Chris Rudolph's Free Classifieds—www.wizardsoftheweb.com/ partners/paths/classads.shtml
3. Yahoo Classifieds—http://classifieds.yahoo.com

Check www.webmastertechniques.com/webmarketing/ for more sites.

If you want to try something very different, how about multimedia classified ads? Warning—this one will cost some money, but may be worth checking out: www.classifind.com/

WEB MARKETING IDEA   Add a Chat Room to Your Website

DOES IT COST MONEY?   Yes and No

HOW WELL DOES IT WORK? ★

....WHAT DOES IT DEVELOP?   Revisits, Participation

If your Website already gets respectable traffic, you may want to consider adding a chat room to your site to increase participation and revisits.

Chat rooms can be a little tricky. First you must decide whether the chat room will be moderated. If it's moderated, you have to deal with enforcing rules and having people publicly disagree with you on the issue of "censorship." If it's not moderated, you have to deal with the potential that a few people can drive everyone away.

In order for your chat room to be successful and thrive, it's probably not wise to start one on your Website until you have at least 800 unique visitors a day. You'll want to launch a strong promotion when you're ready to add this service.

So where do you get a good chat room program? Try looking at some of these:

1. DigiChat—www.digichat.com (average fee)

2. The Palace—www.thepalace.com (average fee—great avatar style)

3. Multichat—www.multichat.com (free)

4. Lithic Personal Chatware—www.lithic.com/java/
   PersonalChatware.html (free for personal and educational use)

WEB MARKETING IDEA   Sponsor Net Events, Such
                                                           as Live Chat Interviews

   DOES IT COST MONEY?   Yes

   HOW WELL DOES IT WORK?   ★

....WHAT DOES IT DEVELOP?   Initial Contact

A number of Websites are starting to host live chat interviews. Interestingly enough, some Webmasters are getting high-profile personalities to participate in such events, even though their Website may be relatively small. This not only presents a great opportunity for them, but for you too (as a sponsor).

As you surf the Web, keep an eye out for sponsorship opportunities. If you see that a Website within your market is going to do a rather impressive event, such as a live chat with a figure known well within your industry, contact that Webmaster and ask if you can "sponsor" the event. Sponsorship of the event includes getting your logo on the person's Website, being identified at the beginning and end of the event as the sponsor, and possibly even having a banner or button displayed through the whole event. You'll also want to request that your logo be placed with any archived transcripts of the event.

If you don't want to pay for a sponsorship, you may want to try to barter for it. In exchange for marketing services (in which you actively market the event on your site and throughout the Web), you get the sponsorship package—a win-win situation. If the person doesn't have any sponsorship packages, make one up and name the price you'd be willing to pay. Your goal is to help the event succeed while creating a strong campaign to make those at the event aware of your Web presence. You may even want to work out an arrangement in which a follow-up event is held on your site immediately following the main event.

WEB MARKETING IDEA Build Your Own Online Radio Station

DOES IT COST MONEY?   Yes and No

HOW WELL DOES IT WORK?   ★ to ★★★★★ (depending on execution)

WHAT DOES IT DEVELOP?   Initial Contact, Revisits

The Web has opened opportunities for people that were never available to the general public. Where else can you create your own Web TV show and air it to a potential audience of millions?

How would you like your own online radio station? With the speed at which technology is moving, it is becoming easier for Webmasters to be able to offer radio stations to users.

Here are a few things to keep in mind when building your own radio station:

1. **Professional music is not free.** Unless you're signed up through another service providing music from professional singers and musicians, you won't be able to broadcast songs without proper licensing arrangements. The two biggest providers of the licensing arrangements are ASCAP (**www.ascap.com/ascap.html**) and BMI (**www.bmi.com**). It is very important that broadcasts of other people's work on your station are properly licensed. The good news is that you can get a license (BMI has forms you can download and fill out). The bad news is that it will cost you some money (the upfront fee alone is $500).

2. **Content.** What will you air over your station? What will make it stand out from other stations? If you can't afford a professional music option, what will you do to fill air time? You need to spend a great deal of your planning in outlining detailed content for your station.

3. **Hours.** What hours will you be open to the public? Do you have enough content to fill those hours? Will you be live or recorded?

4. **Advertising.** How will you advertise your radio station and attract a large audience? How will you use your radio station to advertise your Website?

Ready to get started? Check out these Websites for further instructions and tools to make your radio station a reality:

1. MP3Spy—**www.mp3spy.com/what/** and **www.shoutcast.com**
2. Imagine Radio—**www.imagineradio.com**

To see how *Animation Artist Magazine* runs its radio station, check out **www.animationradio.com**.

WEB MARKETING IDEA Always Give More Than Is Expected

    DOES IT COST MONEY?   No

    HOW WELL DOES IT WORK? ★★★★★

....WHAT DOES IT DEVELOP? Loyalty & Trust

One thing I've learned through my years in business is that if you always give the customer more than he or she expects, you build a much stronger connection.

I used to own a video/TV production business. Our mission was not only to deliver top quality products, but also to deliver more than was expected. For example, one of our clients was a huge church that put on a large Christmas program every year that thousands of people would attend. When we were hired to do the job, we agreed upon a price that included live filming of the event, with a tape and several copies delivered to the client. After finalizing the arrangements, we asked to be able to attend the final rehearsals in order to "practice." We emphasized there was no charge for this, as we wanted to make sure everything was working correctly. What we really did was film "behind-the-scenes" footage. We got shots of final sets being designed, the live orchestra rehearsing, people getting ready, the director giving encouraging words, and so on. After filming the live production, we took the master tape back to our studio and edited a nice 10-minute "behind-the-scenes" segment and tagged it to the end of the tape. The client was shocked by this free gesture, and every year thereafter we were hired to film the event.

We also did other little things in our video business to give the customer extra things that showed we appreciated their business—things like providing video copies on nice blue-colored hard-shell VHS tapes with a nice plastic sleeve (versus cardboard). Customers notice these things, and it makes them more loyal to you.

Learn to deliver more on the Web than your visitors expect. For example, if someone points out to you an error on your Website, send that person a T-shirt as a thank-you (make sure you don't have very many errors or you may go broke!). Don't overhype new areas you are preparing to open. It is much better to have visitors under-expecting than overexpecting.

Suppose an individual writes you with a request regarding your Website. Why not spend the following day building a huge aspect of your site based on that person's request (if it's a good one) and then open it to the public within 24 hours? Send an email—"Thank you for your request—I gave it priority attention and you can view the results at **www.hereitis.com**."

QUESTIONS AND ANSWERS

QUESTION: How can I afford the marketing techniques that cost money?

ANSWER: It is important that you never spend more money on your Website than you are bringing in. So the key is to begin with the free marketing techniques discussed in this chapter. As you drive people to your Website and they use your affiliate programs (see **www.web mastertechniques.com** for a full list of affiliate programs) or purchase from you, there will soon be a cash flow coming in. As mentioned in Idea #39, take 20 percent of the amount of money you bring in and put it into an account specifically for the purpose of marketing your Website. Be sure to read my next book, *Web Profits Applied,* for information on maximizing the income potential of your Website.

QUESTION: Why didn't I see direct email in your list of 101 marketing techniques?

ANSWER: I lightly touched on this in Idea #91. Mass marketing via email has become the biggest form of spamming on the Internet. It is hated so much by Internet surfers that some states are implementing laws against unsolicited email messages. These laws include heavy fines. My philosophy is that you should always be as ethical and honorable as possible in your Web marketing. Don't give people a reason to hate you and your Website before they've even visited it! Reserve email marketing for your email newsletters (which people sign up for first). If you still want to try this medium, you may want to search for companies that have permission to email advertisements to a targeted group of email members, as mentioned in Idea #91.

QUESTION: Why didn't I see any offline ideas mentioned, such as business cards and newspaper ads?

ANSWER: I've devoted an entire chapter just to those ideas! Check out Chapter 7, "Continuing the Marketing Efforts Offline."

QUESTION: Are there more techniques than the 101 listed?

ANSWER: Yes, there are—potentially hundreds more. Every day I discover a new way to do further marketing for initial contact, revisits, participation, or loyalty and trust. Your ability to find or invent these techniques and organize them in your strategic marketing plan will be a great contribution to your success. Throughout the rest of this book you'll even find some new techniques not discussed in this chapter. By networking with other Webmasters in places such as **www.web mastertechniques.com**, you'll be able to gain more valuable marketing insight.

QUESTION: Help! One of the links listed in this chapter now leads to a "File Not Found" error message!

ANSWER: You will find direct links to every URL mentioned in this chapter at **www.webmastertechniques.com/webmarketing/**. I will update any links that become outdated there.

QUESTION: In Web Marketing Idea #11, you mentioned various marketing slogans for Websites. What slogans did you come up with for your Websites?

ANSWER: We designed slogans for three of our Websites: Animation Artist Magazine, Webmaster Techniques, and The Creativity Factory. Here's what we came up with:

Animation Artist Magazine—"The Spirit of Animation"

Webmaster Techniques Magazine—"Defining Your Website's Success"

The Creativity Factory—"Where Creative Concepts Are Hatched"

QUESTION: I like the idea of adding holiday themes to your Website. How about April Fool's Day?

ANSWER: April Fool's Day is a great opportunity to have some fun on your Website. Just make sure people know which information is bogus (part of your April Fool's theme).

QUESTION: I already have a forum (Web Marketing Idea #37) but I can't get any-one to post to it. Any suggestions?

ANSWER: It can be quite embarrassing to open up a Web forum (particularly if you've paid money for it) only to get zero posts. The simple fact is that this is happening to hundreds of Webmasters right now and many are scratching their heads asking, "Why aren't people post-ing?" It's a legitimate question and hopefully some of the ideas I'm presenting to you in the following seven areas will be of great assis-tance:

1. **How many people visit your home page on a daily basis?** It is very important that you drive up your home page traffic to over 750 unique visitors a day before even thinking about a forum. You may even want to wait until you get a higher number. You need a strong base of regular visitors in which to pro-mote the forum. This includes a newsletter list with a respectable subscription base (600+).

2. **What are you doing to promote the forum within your site?** If you go to **www.animationartist.com** you'll notice that on the front page (top middle) we pull a quote from our forum *every day* and post it. It's both relative con-tent and an advertisement. If the quote is a really good discussion starter, the number of registrations (and posts) instantly increases as people respond to the quote in the forum.

3. **Are you forcing visitors to register?** Some visitors don't like the registration process of forums. Personally, I prefer to have visitors register. Yet when you're just starting out, you may want to eliminate forcing your visitors to register and let them freely post. This will help increase the initial participation in the forum.

4. **Where are your banner ads?** A forum should be treated as if it is its own Web-site. This means registering it with search engines and promoting it separately from your main site. It also means that you should create banner ads promot-ing your forum and spread those banners throughout your site.

5. **How hard is the process of posting?** When you first open a forum, it may be very confusing to visitors as to what process they follow to simply post a mes-sage. So make sure you are prepared in advance with step-by-step instructions that a user can easily print and follow to get signed up and posting.

6. **Have you told your friends and family about your forum?** Your friends and family can be a great help in starting some initial interesting topics and con-versations that will bring the involvement of others.

7. **How many rooms do you have?** Some Webmasters make the initial mistake of having too many forum rooms to start with. It's much better to start with one to three forum rooms and then expand as your forum grows. Since all your posts will be in one or two rooms, it will look like a much better interactive place than if all the posts were spread through several forums.

In addition to these seven steps, you may want to consider offering a monthly prize. At the Voices in Animation forum on the Animation Artist Website, we hold a random drawing once a month from a list of all who have posted that month. The winner receives a free Animation Artist T-shirt. Offering prizes can help encourage some extra posts.

Now that you have your Web Marketing Ideas down, let's get more into the offensive and defensive techniques in marketing your Website.

3 Offensive Marketing Techniques

The battle has begun! As commander in chief, it is your job to devise an offensive battle plan that will position your Website as the leader in its class. This means creating and executing offensive techniques that will get you recognized as number one.

There are most likely *hundreds* of other Websites that cover the same category as your Website. This means that you have *hundreds* of obstacles you must overcome to reach your final goal. Interestingly enough, it also means that you have *hundreds* of potential allies to assist you in reaching your final goal!

132

Before continuing, go to your local office-supply store and purchase a one-to-two-inch binder and some looseleaf paper. Now label this book something like "Website Wars: Offensive Battle Plan." As you go through this chapter, begin to establish an offensive campaign. Make detailed notes and include all these in your binder. This will become your "war room manual" and will serve as a great guide in your efforts to be number one.

To win the Website wars, you must do seven things:

1. Determine your offensive goals.
2. Define your plan of attack.
3. Select the right leaders to carry out the offensive maneuvers.
4. Form alliances.
5. Execute the attack.
6. Evaluate your progress and stay alert.
7. Press on until the battle is won.

You also need a strong defense, which we'll discuss in the next chapter. Right now, let's focus on breaking down the seven methods for winning the Website wars.

Step #1: Determine Your Offensive Goals

The first step in winning the Website wars is to determine your offensive goals. What exactly do you want to achieve with your Website? Where do you want to be in relation to your competitors? What specific goals do you see as critical to your success?

Determine Offensive Goals
What exactly do you want to achieve with your Website? Where do you want to be in relation to your competitors?

The offensive goals you create must be realistic goals. For example, if you are one person trying to start an online bookstore, "to topple Amazon.com and be king of the bookstores within two months" is not a realistic goal. That would be the equivalent of a small country such as Kuwait trying to attack a large country such as China or the United States. At this point Kuwait doesn't have the resources to execute such a battle. The same applies when you are first starting out on the Web. You will build your resources and ammunition over time. If you try to take over the world in one swing, you will spread your forces too thin and possibly suffer a humiliating defeat.

In Chapter 2, I mentioned a hypothetical Dogs Daily Website. Now let's say you're the Webmaster of **www.dogsdaily.com** and that the Website is dedicated to daily news, features, and shopping—all dealing with dogs. Since you've just started your Website, you are getting little to no traffic. Your biggest competitor is a Website called Dog Fair—**www.dogfair.com** (this URL was available as of late September 1999)—which is a daily celebration of fun interactions humans have with their dogs. Dog Fair already has thousands of pages, lots of advertisers, and a staff of twelve people, and it receives 2,000 unique visitors a day. Your Dogs Daily Website has six pages, no advertisers, and one person updating it (you), and it is receiving five unique visitors a day. Your goal, of course, is to become better than Dog Fair. However, you are far from having the resources to make that a reality any time soon. So what should your offensive goals be in a situation like this? *Start with short-term offensive goals first.* Here are six offensive goals that Dogs Daily might have:

1. **Identify possible allies and form strategic relationships.** What benefits could you gain from forming strategic relationships with other Websites in similar categories? Choose your allies carefully and never stab them in the back. You are still bound to a code of honor. Any alliances you form are the equivalent of "friendships." Keep it that way at all times. Discover the mutual benefits and work to strengthen your relationship with select Websites. For example, Dogs Daily may see some benefit in teaming up with **www.dogfood4sale.com** (this URL was available as of late September 1999). You may form an alliance wherein you sell their dog food exclusively and in exchange become their official content provider, with them sending traffic your way for the latest Dogs Daily news. They get more business and you get more visitors. Maybe they have a physical product they put out too (Yummies Dog Food). There's another opportunity for you to get on their packaging. Think of specific things you want to gain from this alliance and pursue them. Be sure that you're strong enough to be able to make an attractive offer. And one final thing: If your ally ever stabs you in the back, then yes, it is okay to quietly "declare war."

2. **Create a stronger community and recruit help from that community in building a stronger foundation.** There is strength in numbers. The more loyal people in your community and the more allies you have, the easier your battles will become. Just look at how Amazon.com became so popular. They built a community of affiliates who, in turn, propelled Amazon.com to king of all online bookstores. Without the strong emphasis on affiliates (and sharing the reward), Amazon.com would not be where they are today. Always be loyal, respectful, and giving to the visitors and regulars who make up your community. Involve them more in what you do. You may find some active community participants who may make great reporters, writers, or associate Webmasters.

3. **Seek out ways of opening up new paths and marketing opportunities online.** Part of the strategy in war is to devise new methods to achieve results. Practice "thinking outside the box" to come up with some unique strategic marketing opportunities (some can be expanded from the list in Chapter 2). One truly innovative idea could do wonders for your efforts.

4. **Increase unique visitors to 400 a day within the next two months.** Setting realistic short-term goals in traffic count can be a good motivator to help you achieve those goals. Reward yourself when you achieve success.

5. **Identify competitors.** You need to know who your competitors are in order to properly plan your attack. And the more you know, the better you'll be able to plan.

6. **Build relationship alliances with smaller Websites.** One of Dogs Daily's offensive goals may be to begin forming relationships with the smaller dog Websites. Perhaps Dogs Daily could be the official "news provider" for these sites. The relationships will help strengthen the market position of Dogs Daily.

Once you determine these goals, you need to incorporate them into a "plan of attack." This is the actual strategy of how the goals will be accomplished, when they will be accomplished, and who will carry the goals out.

Step #2: Define Your Plan of Attack

Now you must define your plan of attack. This is the blueprint to how your goals will be achieved. What *methods* will you use to reach each of your goals? What backup plans will you have if one or more of the goals are failing?

In order to define your plan of attack, you must also know everything you can about your main competitors—those whom you are trying to defeat. This means doing detailed research of their Websites, statistics, patterns, strengths, weaknesses, and so on. To win a "war" against other Websites, you must always be one step ahead. If you're always one step behind, your battle will be lost.

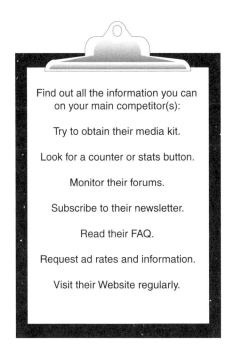

Find out all the information you can
on your main competitor(s):

Try to obtain their media kit.

Look for a counter or stats button.

Monitor their forums.

Subscribe to their newsletter.

Read their FAQ.

Request ad rates and information.

Visit their Website regularly.

So how exactly can you check your competitors? Try these seven methods:

1. **See if your competitor has a media kit on its Website.** A *media kit* contains detailed information about the Website's traffic and an outline of the prices the Website charges for advertising. A lot of bigger Websites have online media kits that anyone can access. Some of the more professional online media kits include elaborate graphs, detailed market research, tours, elaborate traffic information, future projections, and a complete breakdown of advertising costs.

2. **Look for a counter or statistics button on your competitor's site.** Many Websites have counters or statistics buttons. These counters can give you a lot of information about the traffic going to your competitor's Website. Start tracking the counter number every 24 hours to get an average idea of how many visits your competitor is getting a day. Also, you may want to try clicking on the counter or a statistics button, as it sometimes leads right to the detailed breakdown of Website traffic.

3. **Monitor their forums.** If your competitor has a forum, start monitoring it on a daily basis to see how busy it is and how many people are participating in it. Get an idea of the subjects people like to talk about and what their general comments are about the industry, their likes, and their dislikes.

4. **Subscribe to their newsletter.** Chances are that your competitor has a regular newsletter that goes out on a regular basis. Make sure you are subscribed to that newsletter in order to keep up to date on their activities.

5. **Look for an FAQ.** Many Websites have a FAQ page that gives out some details about the Website or why certain things are (or are not) done a certain way. Find the FAQ and print it out.

6. **Request advertising rates and information.** If you didn't find a media kit on your competitor's Website, try simply sending an email to the Webmaster (or have a friend do it) requesting advertising rates and Website statistic information. Who knows, if the rates are good enough you may want to consider advertising!

7. **Visit regularly.** Visit your competitor's site on a regular basis. Get a feel for how often it is updated. Determine its strengths and weaknesses. Work on a plan to expand on such strengths with your site and to turn your competitor's weaknesses into your strengths while still offering unique benefits.

Now you can compile all the information you gather into a detailed report on your competitor. As a smart commander in chief, you want to know more about the enemy than the enemy knows about itself!

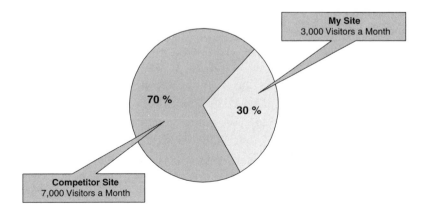

If you get visitor information on all your competitors, bring them all together, along with your numbers, and create a pie or bar chart that gives you a clear visual as to who the leaders are in your category. Now post that pie chart on your wall as a daily reminder of the work you have ahead of you.

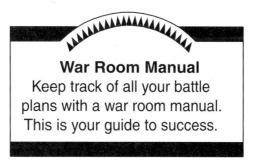

War Room Manual
Keep track of all your battle
plans with a war room manual.
This is your guide to success.

In your "war room manual," you should now have a list of your offensive goals and a detailed analysis of your competitors (including their traffic numbers, strengths, weaknesses, apparent strength of visitor loyalty, and so on). Now you must take all this information and actually define your plan of attack.

In defining your plan of attack, you want to make sure you attack the weaknesses of your competitor in an all-out assault to drive more of their traffic to your Website. At the same time, don't let down your defenses (see Chapter 4). Your campaign needs to be intense, consistent, and honorable. Never lose sight of your mission statement and always keep each of your visitors number one. If a front-line battle to drive traffic away from another site to your site results in a drop in customer service to your regular visitors, then you have already lost half the battle. This is the time for your customer service to be at an all-time high. After all, you want your new traffic to become regular visitors, right?

Target your offensive maneuvers at the weaknesses of the Website whose traffic you are trying to attract. See the question-and-answer section at the end of this chapter for a specific example. Ultimately you are trying to turn the weaknesses of your competitor into your strengths while holding on to your unique style and approach. This means implementing new ideas into your Website, new marketing methods, and a lot of energy. You are going after a targeted audience (visitors to your competitors' Websites), and you need to keep the offensive up a number of days (or weeks) to gain as many extra visitors as possible.

Reserve Plan
If a specific attack fails, you need to
have a reserve plan (reinforcements)
that can be instantly implemented.

Draw an outline of a country on a piece of paper. Place the name of your competitor's site on the country. Now label the areas in which the Website you are "attacking" is weak. Use your goals to attack these weaknesses and make them your strengths. You are creating a visual picture on how the battle will take place. Be sure to have a reserve plan in case your initial attack doesn't work.

Now it is time to select those who will help you carry out your plan.

Step #3: Select the Right Leaders to Carry Out the Offensive Maneuvers

To try to go into battle on your own is virtually insane. I use the word virtually because I do realize that there are some superhumans who can do the work of four or five people. For a successful battle, however, you need assistance in carrying out your plan. This may be assistance from friends, family, regular visitors, co-workers—anyone willing to give you a hand to succeed. Assemble a team of dedicated people who want to see your Website succeed—and when your Website does succeed, remember who helped you get to that point, and reward them.

My parents aren't what you consider "Internet savvy" yet. I bought their computer for them in 1998, set it up for them, and persuaded them to make the leap to the information superhighway. Now that they are connected, my mom lives, breathes, and sleeps email. She has even written emails to me saying, "send me something—anything," just so that she can receive another email. So to keep her busy while waiting for that next email message to arrive in her inbox, I prepared step-by-step instructions for submitting the Animation Artist Website to FFA blaster pages. I made a daily list: Sunday, Monday, Tuesday, Wednesday, Thursday, Friday, and Saturday. Under each day I put the instructions on which page to submit (a different section of the Website every day), exactly what to say, and so on. So now, every day, my parents are doing something to contribute to the success of Animation Artist, which in turn gives me the free time I need to focus on other marketing areas.

Team up with a group of talented people and you'll easily double or triple your offensive efforts and the chances of success.

Step #4: Form Alliances

As stated earlier, an ally is always better than an enemy. The earlier in the process you make the allies, the quicker your goals can be realized. You can have four main types of allies:

1. **Alliances with Websites that you would otherwise consider competitors.** This includes networking and building relationships with other Webmasters who serve the same industry as you. Your alliance may be as simple as a banner exchange or as elaborate as hosting the other person's Website under your site. Build as many of these alliances as possible. Do it by being genuinely friendly to other Webmasters and by initiating conversations about "teaming up."

2. **Alliances with people and places within the industry you cover.** Some of the best alliances you can have may not be with other Websites, but rather with companies within your industry that have agreed to some benefit such as *always giving you the news first.* It could also be an alliance in which they promote you in their print material, while you promote them on your Website. There are a lot of strategic possibilities here that you should look into.

3. **Alliances with noncompeting Websites that can give you a value-added service.** You may come across a Website that offers a service that your readers would greatly benefit from, even though it doesn't pertain to your industry (free email for your domain name, a calendar service, and so on). Try to build relationships and alliances with some of these key companies.

4. **Alliances with your regular visitors.** Another strategic alliance you can form is with some of your regular visitors. You need help updating your Website, right? They love your Website and the industry it serves,

right? Sounds like the potential for a great relationship. Recruit some of your regular visitors to help you with some difficult tasks. You may find some that would be willing to take over and regularly update a portion of your Website. Perhaps Helen Keller put it best when she said, "Alone we can do so little; together we can do so much."

REAL-LIFE EXAMPLE   www.animationartist.com

Four months after *Animation Artist Magazine* went online, we were contacted by the Webmaster of a much larger animation Website. The individual complimented us on the excellent job we were doing and invited us to "join forces." Basically, his Website would host ours for free if we became part of his network—a network that already contained dozens of other good animation Websites. We politely refused the offer because we knew that being cast under the other site would hamper the strong independent growth that we wanted to obtain. From day one we knew that this gentleman's particular Website was the one to beat. It isn't an easy task, however, because of all the strong alliances they had formed even before we started building our Website. Interestingly enough, we always keep open the option of a future alliance with this company. When you're a much stronger Website, you can negotiate better terms to the alliance. And there's nothing wrong with two superpowers merging. It happens all the time in the real world!

There's a very important thing to keep in mind when you make any decision about alliances, selling your Website (read my upcoming book, *Web Profits Applied*) and so on—*your customer*. It is your customers and your community that make your Website successful. Always put them first in the decisions you make, and they will put you first in return. One reason why Walt Disney was always so successful is that he never sacrificed family values for money. He always kept an intense focus at improving the experience for his customers, and the result was that customers flocked to his ventures! Ultimately your visitors will be your strongest soldiers and allies.

You can form many types of strategic partnerships with other Websites. Consult Web Marketing Idea #20 in Chapter 2 for a list of six.

Step #5: Execute the Attack

Once you have your strategy and battle plan prepared, it's time to execute it. As with real battles, you must put careful thought into how you execute your plan.

First, you must have a timeline. What will happen when? At what point do you consider your goal achieved? What backup plans (reinforcements) do you have in case your initial effort doesn't go as planned? You must outline all of this before executing your attack.

Also, before you attack, make sure that all your team members are in position and that the conditions are right for your offensive maneuvers. Make sure that all the services and marketing efforts you will introduce are complete. Make sure you are well rested and ready for the intense (and possibly long) campaign ahead. Battles are unpredictable. Some last for a day or two and others for years.

Ready? Now execute your plan. Put all your energy and focus into bringing your battle plan to life. Make sure that all your efforts are coordinated with those who are helping you. Keep any charts you've made handy to mark your progress (trust me, visuals always help the motivation because you physically *see* results).

Step #6: Evaluate Your Progress and Stay Alert

An essential element of your strategic battle comes from evaluating the progress you are making and adjusting your strategies accordingly.

Continuing with our Dogs Daily example, let's say that Dogs Daily introduces an online "Dog Beauty Pageant" that is much better organized, with better prizes and more unique features, than that of a competing Website. As part of the offensive, Dogs Daily distributes a press release through the professional wires (at up to $600 a pop) and relay posts on newsgroups, blasts to FFA sites, and so on. After two days of an intense marketing campaign, you find the results are not meeting your expectations. No one has picked up the press release, and the numbers of those checking out your new feature are lower than you expected. This has now become a battle that you are losing and you must mount another immediate offensive to help rescue it. Your new strategy may include making postcards of dogs that your visitors can email to friends (with an ad about your new service), sending a personal letter to some of the dog magazines (such as *Dog Fancy*), sending out a special announcement of the new service to your Website mailing list and requesting that your visitors "tell a friend" about it, and so on. As you can see, a new plan has been put into place (reinforcements if you will) to help aid that losing battle. Rescue it at all costs while still pressing forward on your other offensive maneuvers.

This is also a time to stay very alert. There's no doubt that within a day or two (if not sooner), your competitor(s) will notice your intensive marketing campaign and service additions. Most likely it will suddenly motivate him/her to get on the ball and start introducing new features, updates, etc. In essence, that Website may launch their own offensive to regain visitors they may be losing. *Be prepared!*

Are you subscribed to your competitor's newsletter? If not, make sure you are before your battle begins, because chances are that new competitor services, features, updates, etc. will first be announced in the newsletter. Make sure that you have a strong defense on your Website as discussed in the next chapter. Be very alert to every move that your competitor is making so that you can make proper adjustments to your battle plan in order to stay one step ahead.

Step #7: Press On Until the Battle Is Won

Some battles can be drawn out a long time (you've heard of the Hundred Years' year war, right?). Of course, you want to get your battle won as soon as possible so that you can get back to business as usual with the daily upkeep and marketing of your site.

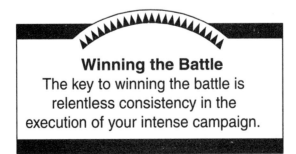

Winning the Battle
The key to winning the battle is relentless consistency in the execution of your intense campaign.

The key to winning the battle is relentless consistency in the execution of your intense campaign. If, at any time during the battle, you let down your guard (even for a single day), then you've created a wide open opportunity for your competitor. You must press on, every single day, until the battle is won. Consider this quote from P. T. Barnum: "Whatever you do, do it with all your might. Work at it, early and late, in season and out of season, not leaving a stone unturned, and never deferring for a single hour that which can be done just as well now." Apply the truth of that quote to the execution of your battle plan and press on until victory is yours.

QUESTIONS AND ANSWERS

QUESTION: What is the purpose of an offensive marketing campaign?

ANSWER: Offensive campaigns are usually reserved for periods of time in which you are trying to gain market share against another Website or simply trying to heavily promote some new products and services. The purpose is to give your Website a strong boost through an extraordinary and intense focus on reaching specific short-term goals. As in a battle, you don't stop until the goals are reached. Offensive marketing campaigns *do not* replace your normal marketing efforts. You should be marketing your Website *all the time,* regardless of whether it is part of an offensive marketing campaign

QUESTION: Are meta tags considered an offensive marketing technique?

ANSWER: Meta tags are the key to most search engine rankings, so yes, they are a very important long-term offensive strategy. Please read Web Marketing Idea #3 in Chapter 2 and then return here for additional information and techniques.

On May 26, 1998, SiteMetrics Corporation released the results of a detailed "Web Content Survey" of 40,000 commercial Websites. The results were quite surprising:

Of Interest...

Only 30% of all Websites use meta tags!

▶ Seventy percent of the Websites surveyed did not use meta tags.

▶ Only twenty-seven percent of the Websites surveyed included a description meta tag.

▶ Twenty-five percent of the Websites surveyed that used meta tags exceeded the recommended 200-character description length. One Website had a description that was 15,000 characters long!

If you want your Website to show up on search engines, *you must incorporate meta tags*. It is one of the single most important marketing strategies available to you. Under no circumstances should you ever submit your Web pages to a search engine before inserting meta tags on *every* page.

The most important of the meta tags is the keyword meta tag. This is what search engines use (in addition to other methods) to help determine where you rank. Give careful thought to the keyword choices you make.

Here are some steps to help guide you in determining your keywords:

Step #1: Grab a dictionary and thesaurus to find variations of words that could describe the content of your Website.

Step #2: Go to your competitors' Websites and view their source code (on most browsers you can do this by right-clicking on the page and selecting View Source). Print these pages and study the meta tags your competitors use.

Step #3: From steps 1 and 2, compile a list of keywords or phrases people may use to search for your Website.

Step #4: Once you have your list of keywords and phrases, determine the importance of each one. You will place your most important keywords and phrases first.

Step #5: Create your keyword meta tag by following the example shown in Chapter 2 (Web Marketing Idea #3).

If you feel uncomfortable with the meta tag process and would like it to be more automated, try using the meta tag generator on the Webmaster Techniques Website—**www.webmastertechniques.com**.

Make sure that all of your meta tags, from keywords to descriptions, are highly targeted to bring results in certain searches. Build "entrance pages" (Chapter 2, Web Marketing Idea #54) and very strong titles (Chapter 2, Web Marketing Idea #2).

QUESTION: Would most of the marketing ideas in Chapter 2 be considered offensive marketing techniques?

ANSWER: Absolutely. They can be used as offensive marketing techniques (executed with a stronger intensity) or regular marketing techniques.

Keep in mind that launching an offensive doesn't always have to be with the purpose of defeating another Website. You could do so to ignite stronger growth or to remain on top of your category when others attack. In the fourth quarter of 1999, Amazon.com launched a major offensive to increase awareness before the big holiday shopping season; they executed a strategic plan that included the introduction (and intense marketing) of new services such as zShops and wireless shopping. Amazon.com is a perfect example of a company that knows how to form and execute strategic battle plans for specific goals.

In launching an offensive marketing maneuver on the Web, it is important to identify where you are now and where you want to be when it is all over. Then continue the offensive until you reach your goal. Keep in mind that your strategic implementation of carefully selected ideas will make the impact.

QUESTION: In the section on forming alliances, you mentioned the possibility of recruiting die-hard regulars to help you with Website updating. While that's a good idea, I don't want to hand out my FTP username and password to anyone else. And I surely don't want anyone else having access to the entire Website. So how do I handle this?

ANSWER: You bring up a valid concern. Luckily, that exact problem has been addressed online. There are CGI programs that allow you to assign a unique user name and password to anyone you wish along with "permissions" as to which Web pages he or she can update! Check any of these three programs:

1. **Elite Web Page Builder—http://elitehosts.com/scripts/main.html** (free)
2. **WebHome—http://webhome.cyberscript.net/** ($80—there is also a free version)
3. **Home Free—http://solutionscripts.com/vault/homefree/** ($200)

QUESTION: When is the best time to execute a battle plan?

ANSWER: The best time is when your enemy is least expecting it or is having a hard time keeping their Website updated. With the latter scenario, people will be looking for other avenues of information. This is the perfect opportunity for you to strike with your new services and enhanced, intense marketing efforts.

QUESTION: Should those helping me know the whole plan?

ANSWER: There is no need for anyone but you to know the entire strategy or even that you are executing a battle plan against another Website. The choice is up to you. What those helping you out do need to know is what you want them to do and when. You must then make sure it gets done at that time.

QUESTION: Can two competing Websites simply co-exist?

ANSWER: It is very likely that you have hundreds of competitors or potential competitors on the Web. If you're too passive, your Website won't go anywhere. If you're too aggressive, you risk the chance of alienating many of your customers.

If you don't care about advertising dollars or traffic, then by all means forget about "Website wars." At least make sure you have a strong defense (see Chapter 3) in case another site starts targeting your industry and your visitors.

So can two high-end competing Websites simply co-exist? Yes they can. Yet you may find it to your advantage to co-exist as an ally versus as a continuing competitor. You can also try to define your Website to bring a different appeal than your closest competitor, so that the two of you can effectively "share" traffic.

Keep in mind that an alliance helps all parties involved. You are sharing information and visitors and effectively networking. I would select a strong alliance over "Website wars" any day. Why? Because it benefits everyone involved. Instead of trying to find ways to interest visitors in visiting your site more than another, you're working together to discover ways of bringing more traffic to both sites.

QUESTION: How long do these battles last?

ANSWER: Just as in real life, there are times of peace and times of war. Your preference, of course, is peace as long as you are in the position you want your Website to be in. Competition on the Web is very intense; you must be prepared at all times to launch an all-out offensive (behind the scenes, not publicly) or counterstrike against another Website if necessary. This means strengthening areas your competitors are weak in, inviting their visitors to come and visit you, launching huge focused marketing efforts, and being prepared with a few surprises (such as new areas of your site that no one else was aware you have been working on). Campaigns go on until you have reached your objectives for the battle. Once that is done, you can enjoy the benefits your Website will reap while strengthening your defenses and preparing for the next battle. It's also a great time to establish more allies.

QUESTION: Can you give a specific example of an offensive goal and how it would be defined in a plan of attack?

ANSWER: Sure. Let's continue using Dogs Daily as our example. Say that Dogs Daily plans to launch a secret war campaign against a slightly bigger Website called ACE Dog (www.acedog.com; this URL was available as of late September 1999). An ACE Dog feature that seems to be popular is its "Dog Shows and Festivals" calendar. The problem that you see is that the ACE Dog calendar isn't updated often; when it is, there is just a one- or two-sentence description of the new event. So you set an offensive goal to create a much more powerful calendar called "The Dogs Daily Events and Dog Shows Calendar" updated daily with detailed information of dog events, phone numbers, TV coverage of events, and interviews with those planning the events. So now you must create the new calendar in advance of launching your offensive maneuvers. Be creative in making your calendar not only a lot more powerful, but a lot more original too. Why not let dog owners send in the name of their dog and the dog's birthday. You can add birthday wishes to your calendar too (a good Revisits and Loyalty & Trust marketing idea).

Once you are prepared to launch your calendar and any other aspects of your offensive goals, it is time to define the event in your attack plan. You know that the ACE Dog calendar is updated once a month with limited information. You want to introduce a much more powerful calendar, updated daily, with a goal of getting visitors from ACE Dog to become regular calendar visitors at Dogs Daily. So how will you do this? Here are step-by-step instructions:

Step #1: Identify when, in your battle plan, the event is going to occur. The launching of the Dogs Daily calendar to compete against the ACE Dog calendar is only one small aspect of the entire battle plan. You must determine exactly when, within the battle, the event will occur. Is it the *first* offensive maneuver? The *last* one? Second, third, fourth? You must have a purpose for the time that you launch it. Consider that your offensive will most likely continue for several weeks. The calendar is only one small part of the entire battle. It must be introduced, grab the intended audience, and be stable while all your other maneuvers (targeted press releases, joint ventures with allies, cool contests, interview with well-known industry leader, live Internet radio broadcasts, and so on) take place.

Step #2: Identify the purpose of the goal. In the case of the calendar, the purpose is to draw more people away from ACE Dog to Dogs Daily when they are looking for timely information on dog events.

Step #3: Identify the support mechanisms. How will your maneuver be supported? In the case of the calendar, support means getting the word out through a mass marketing effort. This means newsgroup announcements, a possible press release, FFA link blasts, announcements on ally Websites, banners on ally Websites, and targeted search engine keyword listings.

Step #4: Identify who will carry out the maneuver. Who is responsible for carrying out a specific duty? How are you following up with that person? Do you receive regular progress reports? If you are that person, you will need to make your own progress reports so that you know how effectively the execution of your plan is going.

QUESTION: What if I don't get the desired results from my offensive maneuvering?

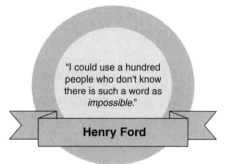

"I could use a hundred people who don't know there is such a word as *impossible*."

Henry Ford

ANSWER: Then it is time to regroup and try again. Evaluate what went right during your campaign and what went wrong. Also, don't dwell on failure. You win when you realize that reaching your goals is not impossible. Henry Ford realized this and even commented, "I could use a hundred people who don't know there is such a word as *impossible*." Eliminate the word *impossible* from your vocabulary. If you fail the first time, try again. Consistency makes winners; this has been proven time and again in the sports world. You don't win championships unless you are consistent through the whole season. Be consistent, diligent, positive, ethical, and patient in all your marketing efforts. Success *will* follow.

Most of all, learn from your failures and put them behind you. Move on. As Charles Kettering said, "You can't have a better tomorrow if you are thinking about yesterday all the time."

QUESTION: Is everything just about Website wars?

ANSWER: No, it isn't. Your survival on the Internet is determined by how well you market your Website and how well you handle your competitors (via the offensive marketing advice in this chapter). Ultimately, however, the *most important* aspect of your Website is *how you treat your visitors*. I cannot emphasize enough the importance of treating each of your visitors like a king or queen. Perhaps you can assume that each visitor who emails you is your boss; as with your boss, you will handle each request with promptness and detailed attention.

Always keep the human element as part of your Website. Never frustrate your visitors and always implement their requests (within reason). As long as you do this, you will retain a strong loyalty from those you have given your honest respect.

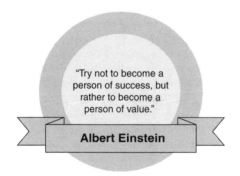

"Try not to become a person of success, but rather to become a person of value."

Albert Einstein

To emphasize this point, I turn to a quote from Albert Einstein: "Try not to become a person of success, but rather to become a person of value." This is the same philosophy that Walt Disney followed growing up; because he followed this philosophy of value first, success was a natural result.

Now raise your flag high and prepare to build a strong foundation and defense around your Website. After all, strong, fortified, and prepared armies are hard to attack and rarely get turned down when making alliance requests.

4 *Defensive Marketing Techniques*

A great offense, as outlined in Chapter 3, is only half of the battle your Website faces on the World Wide Web. Equally important is a strong defense. This chapter focuses on some defensive techniques (marketing and strategy) to help you protect your territory, keep your competitors guessing, enhance your marketing efforts, and develop a stronger loyalty with your visitors. You should apply these techniques to your Website regardless of whether you are in (or preparing for) a battle, as discussed in Chapter 3.

A strong defense is like a puzzle. If all the pieces are in place, you have a complete solution. Yet if one piece is missing, your puzzle is incomplete and weak.

Here are nine defensive techniques that will help you build a complete puzzle and strong defense. You should immediately apply these to your Website:

1. Select an excellent Website hosting company.
2. Keep your Website regularly updated.
3. Keep statistics information to yourself.
4. Don't spill the beans too soon.
5. Use filters on email.
6. Don't let your competitors jump ahead of you.
7. Protect your property.
8. Have a reason for linking to other Websites.
9. Keep visitors happy.

Select an Excellent Website Hosting Company

The first step in building a strong defense is to select an excellent Website hosting company. This is the company that will host your Website on their servers so that the rest of the world can access your site.

The Foundation of Your Website
The first step in building a strong defense is to select an excellent Website hosting company.

What does selecting a hosting company have to do with marketing, you may ask? The answer is *a lot*. Marketing isn't just about publicity. It's about making sure that things are properly in place to assist your campaigns. For example, selecting a poor hosting company could result in shabby service, which is then passed on to your users. Your users then don't return to your Website, and you lose business. Defensive marketing prevents this from the beginning so that you will have a stronger uptime with your site, making return visits more likely.

I've been on both sides of the tracks with this issue. A few years ago, I signed up one of my Websites under a service that turned out to be a complete nightmare. My Website was offline 25 percent of the time and whenever I emailed the Website hosting company and complained about the problems, I would get an email back saying that I should "stop complaining because it will just take longer to fix the problem." You can rest assured that I will never give this company (which is still in business, unfortunately) another penny.

Because there are hundreds of hosting companies to select from on the World Wide Web, I knew I had to somehow narrow my search to only high-quality Website hosting companies. Since all Website hosting companies make claims of "the best service," "superior quality," and so on, I had to go beyond claims.

What I found was the Web Host Guild, which serves the purpose of "setting an industry standard that [will] benefit all hosting companies and protects consumers as well. . . . Our mission statement is to protect consumers from unscrupulous hosts, and to help identify the honest, legitimate host companies that exist." It's a hard organization for hosting companies to get into because Website hosting companies must meet a strict "set of objectives, verifiable criteria for certifying Web host companies." These criteria include at least eight hours of live telephone support a day, 24-hour-a-day emergency service, guaranteed response time to technical support emails and emergency requests, and daily backups. Most of the companies listed with the Web Host Guild also have a 99.9 percent uptime guarantee.

The Web Host Guild is where my new search started and ended. I was able to examine some of the highest-quality Website hosting companies around and finalized on one. I haven't had any problems since. You can visit the Web Host Guild at **www.whg.org**.

The Website hosting company you select is the foundation of your Website. You must have a strong foundation upon which to build for the ultimate defensive stronghold.

Keep Your Website Regularly Updated

Your Website must be updated regularly (preferably daily or multiple times a day) so that your visitors are always coming back to your site and becoming a part of your community. The stronger your community, the harder it is for the enemy to infiltrate. Here is a four-step strategy:

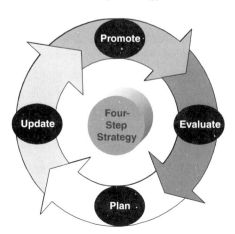

1. **Plan.** In the first stage, you plan out exactly what update is going to take place, who is doing the update, where it will go, and what types of marketing need to support that update (meta tags, announcements to targeted Websites, mention in your newsletter, and so on).

2. **Update.** The second stage consists of creating the update, spell-checking it, uploading it, and checking the URL to make sure it is working. Part of this process also consists of testing any links in the update to make sure all links work properly.

3. **Promote.** Once the update is made, the promotion begins! Every single update you do should have promotion ideas attached to it. This can be anything from some of the ideas in Chapter 2 to a "What's New" section on your front page. The important thing is to make sure people know about the update.

4. **Evaluate.** Finally, you must evaluate each update you make. Did it get the type of traffic you wanted? Did you get any responses to the update? Did the update achieve what you wanted it to? Did you market the update to its full potential?

The Key Ingredient
The one key ingredient that will keep visitors coming back to your Website day after day is fresh content.

The one key ingredient that will keep visitors coming back to your Website day after day is *fresh content.* The more content you put up and market on a daily basis, the better your results. You should begin to see a steady growth in the number of Website visitors (returning and new) as you implement this strategy on a consistent basis.

Plan, update, promote, and evaluate on a daily basis (or at least every weekday). Be consistent, as your visitors will come to expect updates by a certain time every day.

Keep Statistics Information to Yourself

If you are trying to build a professional presence on the Web, there is no reason for you to publicly broadcast your Website's statistics for the world to see. The only real purpose for displaying your Website statistics publicly is to inform your competitors of how much traffic you are receiving.

For you, the purpose of statistics is to help monitor how well your marketing efforts are working. It allows you to track how much traffic you're getting, where the traffic is coming from, what pages visitors are entering from, what pages visitors are exiting from, what browser visitors use the most, and so on. Statistics are a gold mine of information for your marketing evaluation and planning stages. Make sure those statistics don't go beyond you unless it is for an important reason.

Don't Spill the Beans Too Soon

By publicly laying out your upcoming plans for your Website, you are showing your competitors your battle plan, which gives them plenty of time to counterstrike.

Giving out your battle strategy
too early is a great way to
guarantee an early death
for your Website.

One of the competitors of a Website I run likes to mark his Website updates as "Versions." The opening of his Website was "Version 1.0." When the site was given a total face-lift with new features, it was "Version 2.0"—and so on. The Website is very attractive. It is well laid out, with a wealth of content and graphics. Overall it is an excellent Website competing for the same audience as one of my Websites. Unfortunately, this person doesn't have "strong defenses" on his site. For example, he lists *all his plans* for future new features up to six months in advance! He spends a lot of time trying to build up expectations for these areas before the areas are a reality. Furthermore, he uses the updating of these areas as an excuse for missing regular updates on his Website.

What this individual has done is laid out his whole battle plan before me. I know exactly what he is going to do and approximately when he is going to do it. Announcing his changes so far in advance gives his competitors an opportunity to quickly and easily beat him to the Web with the idea. Any competitor could take his idea, build it in a week, and be heavily promoting it and growing it months before it opens as part of "Version x.0."

There are two problems that create a weak defense for this individual (and anyone else who does what he does):

Two Great Ways to Disappoint Your Visitors:

1. **Announce features.**

2. **Build expectations.**

Problem #1—Announcing features. By announcing Website features months before they occur, this person has given all his competitors the information they need to build their strategies, battle plans, and counterstrikes. It's like having the leader of an enemy country as a spy for your country!

Problem #2—Building expectations. When announcing features, this individual heavily builds anticipation and expectations for these new areas. He talks about how they will be updated daily, will contain the best information in the field, and so on. What he has effectively done is build up his visitors for a disappointment. What if it *isn't* updated daily and *isn't* the best information in the field (especially now that competitors know about it)?

I used to be a high school teacher and the director of the high school drama team. Every year our drama group would put on a huge and elaborate production near the end of the year. The stage performances we did were all original and included a mixture of special effects, a strong story line, elaborate set designs, original songs, and original background scores. The first two years we did these productions, we launched huge marketing campaigns. As part of the campaigns we did heavy promotions on the "state-of-the-art" effects and set designs that would be part of the production. We continued to heavily promote all features we could think of as "elaborate" or "state-of-the-art."

When the play dates came for the productions, we packed the house. The productions went perfectly, but when people left there was no true enthusiasm for what had taken place. As I began to dig deeper into why people weren't going crazy over these productions, I discovered that *we had not met the expectations* that our elaborate marketing campaigns had described and built up. We had actually overmarketed the features, effectively creating a scenario in which no matter how good the performance went, people would be disappointed! You see this scenario frequently with movies such as *Godzilla* and *Star Wars: Episode One—The Phantom Menace.*

I learned from the experience of those first two years of performances. The third year, armed with this new knowledge, I completely changed my marketing strategy. Instead of hyping all the state-of-the-art effects, elaborate sets, and so on, we simply marketed the story line and the fact that it was an original story. We didn't mention anything about special effects or elaborate set designs. We purposely withheld information on key aspects of the production (such as live sword fights, 3D special effects incorporated into the stage play, and so on). We wanted these to be a surprise to the audience.

The results were astonishing! After the opening performance, everyone was raving about the play, the effects, and how it was such a great production. The second night of the performance we saw an amazing number of repeat visitors who came back "because the whole event was so great." The third night they were back again—each time with new friends. Because we had "underhyped" key aspects of the entire production, we exceeded the expectations of the audience. *You must do the same with your Website!*

Surprise your visitors on a regular basis. Don't always tell them what is around the corner. If a visitor points out a major error on your Website that no one else alerted you to, send him or her a free T-shirt, but don't advertise to the world that you did that. It is the little things that add up to a big production, and as long as you keep overdelivering to your visitors, you should see a much greater enthusiasm than had you built everything up in advance to a point where you couldn't meet their expectations.

Don't announce features for your competitors to get hold of, and don't make elaborate promises that build expectations well beyond what you can deliver. Instead, surprise your visitors often and always keep your competitors guessing as to what you'll deliver next.

**Don't put up a Web page
until it is complete.**

Another major sin of Web marketing is to announce your Website before it is fully functional. It is very frustrating for a visitor to go to a newly formed Website where ten of the twelve pages all say "Coming Soon." Avoid this like the plague. If you don't have it done, then don't put a page up for it. Frustrated visitors rarely return to a Website.

Use Filters on Email

Part of good marketing is being organized in your marketing efforts so that you don't waste time. One of the biggest time-consuming aspects of the Internet is email. Luckily, most major email software programs, such as Eudora and Outlook Express, allow you to create filters that help sort your email. Cutting down on junk mail and effectively sorting important messages will be a great time-saver and management tool. It will also help you with your FFA link strategy, as we'll discuss in a moment.

Use the filter features in your email program to sort your email into organized groups. In addition, use different email addresses on the "Contacts" page of your Website to help organize requests. For example, for advertising inquiries you may want to use `advertising@yoursitehere.com`. For problems visitors experience on your Website, they can email `problems@yoursitehere.com`. The key is to get all your email messages organized so that you don't have an inbox of 5,000 messages, some with replies and some without. Consult the Help area of your email program (use the index word "filter") for information on setting up filters with your email program.

One of the marketing ideas in Chapter 2 was blasting your URL out to thousands of FFA link pages. The only drawback to this tip is that you are required to provide a valid email address in exchange for the link. Then most FFA pages email you an advertisement. So blasting your link out to 15,000 FFA pages could result in you receiving 8,000+ emails, plus your email address would remain on some of these ad lists for the future. That could ruin your day real quick!

Luckily, creating an email filter is the answer. For *Animation Artist Magazine,* I created an email address just for FFA links: `ffa@animationartist.com`. I use this email address only for FFA links and no other purpose. Then, in my email account, I created a filter that sends anything coming to `ffa@animation artist.com` straight to the trash.

This concept works great and captures about 85 percent of the FFA emails. About 15 percent of emails from FFA sites were still making it to my main inbox, however. After analyzing the problem, I discovered that some FFA pages ignore the email address you enter for your FFA blast. Instead, they capture the email address from your browser and email that address! To solve this problem, I dusted off my copy of Netscape and set it up with the email address `ffa@animationartist.com`. Now I use Netscape simply to do all my FFA link blasts, and the result is that nearly all the FFA emails are filtered directly to the trash so that I don't have to wade through thousands of messages just to find messages from my visitors.

Make sure you have a defensive system in place before doing your FFA link blasts.

Don't Let Your Competitors Jump Ahead of You

Letting your competitors jump ahead of you puts you on the defensive automatically. Ideally, you always want to be on the offensive with a strong defense to make the job of your competitor much more difficult.

I'm familiar with two companies that recently went head-to-head in a specialized field. One company, Team A, had strong online marketing skills and a great team, but few offline marketing skills. The other, Team B, had great offline marketing resources, but little online knowledge. Team A had the team, skills, and money to start a major offensive. Team B also had the money, but spent all of its time in meetings trying to determine a direction that everyone could agree upon. Time didn't seem of an essence to Team B, which allowed Team A to quickly leave them in the dust. As long as Team A continues its offensive, while building a strong defense, there is practically no way that Team B will ever catch up to them.

I was asked to consult with Team B at one point. Team A already had an offensive jump and I knew there was virtually no way that Team B could catch them without some drastic measures. So I identified three key Websites already established in the industry and instructed Team B to immediately purchase these Websites (at a decent price) and incorporate them into its portal, which would instantly give Team B the boost, traffic, press coverage, and huge offensive counterstrike to "catch" Team A. So what happened? The idea went into meetings and never went anywhere. Today, Team B isn't even considered a serious player on the Web.

"Corporate politics" can kill a great Web venture. The Web is a fast-paced world. In order to keep up, you must spend more time updating your Website and less time untangling red tape or justifying everything in hourly meetings.

As a smart marketer, you must hold back the offensive maneuvers of a competitor at all costs, while creating carefully planned counterstrikes. You must also build a strong defense so that anything your competitor does has little effect on your traffic or community.

A good defense also comes from not provoking the enemy. Keep quiet and put all your focus on executing your strategy while building your offense and defense. When you see another Website executing offensive maneuvers against you, strengthen your defense, execute your counterstrike, and prepare to launch a full-scale attack with your offensive maneuvers. It's time for battle!

Protect Your Property

There are many people out there who think that any content on any Website is fair game to steal and republish on their own Website. Even some of your competitors may live by this misguided philosophy!

So the question becomes, what can you do to protect yourself?

1. **Copyright your information.** It is vital that you post a copyright notice on every page of your Website. This serves as an instant warning to anyone thinking of taking your information. Your copyright warning must include the copyright sign (a *c* with a circle around it) and specific copyright information. For example, "All content and graphics on this page are © Copyright 1999 by *Animation Artist Magazine* and may not be downloaded or reused for any purpose. All rights reserved."

2. **Disable right-click.** Use your own judgment on this tip. There is a Javascript function that can disable your visitor's ability to use the right-click feature on his or her mouse, which makes it more difficult (but not impossible) for someone to steal your images. I've used this sparingly on pages with a lot of original graphics. The problem is that some users use the right-click feature on their mouse to go back a page or for other legitimate reasons. So you must ask yourself whether protecting some of your images is worth inconveniencing your visitors. In most cases, the answer should be no. After all, you want to keep your visitors happy at all times. If you decide to try this feature out, however, I've

posted information on accessing it at **www.webmastertechniques.com/ webmarketing/**.

3. **Pursue stolen property.** If you find a Website illegally using content that was taken from one of your copyrighted pages, then pursue the issue. Send the Webmaster of that Website a friendly request to remove the copyrighted material from their Website. If that request is ignored or refused, then send the individual a cease-and-desist notice (see **www.webmastertechniques.com** for samples of cease-and-desist letters). If that is ignored, then consider possible legal action.

You need to make it clear on your Website that any content on your pages is copyrighted and cannot be reproduced without your permission. As the Web becomes more technologically advanced, you'll most likely see new products to assist Webmasters in the area of protecting your property.

Have a Reason for Linking to Other Websites

Providing links to other Websites is a quick way to move traffic away from your own Website, which almost defeats the purpose of any Website's existence. Therefore, make sure you have a very good reason for placing a link on your Website that sends your visitor away.

Imagine going into a pizza parlor and as you get ready to place your order, the cashier tells you, "Hey, there's a great pizza place just two blocks down the street that you may want to try out." How long would that company be in business if all they do is send people to other pizza places?

This is where defensive marketing plays a major role. Every link to another Website must have some sort of strategy behind it. Let's take our pizza example again. The situation would be much different if you went into the pizza parlor, placed your order, and received your pizza along with a coupon that sent you to a video store for a free rental. When you get your rental, your receipt contains a coupon for $4 off a large pizza at the pizza parlor. This is an example of effective networking and should be applied to your Website.

In Chapter 2, one of the marketing ideas I talked about was a banner-for-directory-listing exchange, in which a person places your Website banner on his or her home page, and in exchange you give them a 50-word listing in your Website's "Resource Directory." Now you're not just "sending away" traffic, but also receiving. You're effectively networking.

So what links, if any, are best to provide on your Website?

1. Links that go to a review on another site that is about your product or service.

2. Links that go to a write-up or press release on another site that is about your product, service, or Website.

3. Links that are done as part of an exchange (the person you are linking to has a banner or link to you on his or her Website).

4. Links that go to pages within any other Website you own.

5. Links that go to content on another Website with a strong value for your readers, but not competitive with your site. For example, at Animation Artist we linked to an animation contest sponsored by one of the major animation studios. Their site was not competitive, and we wanted to give our readers a chance to win a valuable prize.

Naturally, not all these rules will apply if the purpose of your Website is to be a link directory or search engine!

Keep Visitors Happy

Keeping your visitors happy should be your number one goal in marketing. Ultimately, your visitors will make you successful. Walt Disney knew this, which is why he was a man of principle and why he became so successful. Disney designed his parks and ideas around people (and visitor comfort) instead of money. With Walt Disney, the customer was always first. Because of this philosophy, the money naturally came. People wanted to spend money on Disney products and services because the experience was truly a joyful one.

Keep Visitors Happy
Keeping visitors happy should
be your number one goal
in marketing.

Your goal for your Website may be to make a lot of money. If you alter your goal to "provide the best customer service and visitor experience on the Web" for your category, you will discover that the money will naturally follow. As long as you don't get greedy, and you continue to meet the needs of your customers in a timely fashion, you will find that success will continue to grow.

Animation Artist Magazine once received an email from someone who was upset that we had not yet put up a movie trailer for a particular movie. There are many ways we could have responded to that email. We could have shot back excuses about time constraints, understaffing, and so on. We could have been upset in our response. But the way we responded was to simply say, "You are right. We will have that movie trailer up within the next 24 hours." That then became our number one priority and we had it up within eight hours. The follow-up response we got from the reader was an apology for the harshness of the original email and a thank-you for our quick response.

When you treat visitors with respect, give them a lot of information on a regular basis, and answer their needs and requests immediately, you will find that many will become loyal to your Website. For many, your Website will become their home page (the highest compliment you can get as a Webmaster), and they will spend most of their Internet time on your site. These are the types of "soldiers" that you want to have on your Website.

How else can you keep visitors happy?

1. Make your Website easy to navigate.
2. Keep all promises you make, deliver on those promises early, and deliver more than the visitor was expecting.

3. Get rid of old information from your front page. Keep the front page clean, fresh, and up-to-date on a daily basis.

4. Keep visitors informed of "What's New" on your Website.

5. Have fun interactive games, contests, and other activities. that relate to the theme of your Website.

QUESTIONS AND ANSWERS

QUESTION: I don't actually run my own Website. I've been hired to do marketing for another site. So suggestions such as "Update your Website regularly" don't apply directly to me. Any suggestions aimed at Website marketers who aren't Webmasters?

ANSWER: Yes. *Become a Webmaster.* In order for a Web marketer to have the maximum effectiveness, he or she must have experience as a solo Webmaster. If this means taking a hobby and turning it into a Website in your own free time, then so be it. The key is to get experience at what it is like to start a Website from scratch and try to get traffic there for the first time. As you deal with the challenges that regular Webmasters face, you'll learn ways to turn those challenges into opportunities that will carry over into your regular Web marketing job.

As the Internet marketing director for American Computer Experience, I have Websites that I run on my own time. It is an important element to staying in tune with Webmaster skills, Webmaster tools, Website experience, and interaction with visitors. These, in turn, help to further develop my Website marketing skills and help me learn more strategic ways of utilizing my marketing ideas.

As a Web marketer, the majority of ideas presented in this chapter should be your direct responsibility. Marketing is what defines a company, and the marketing department (you) needs to be actively involved in most aspects of the company. From monitoring Website statistics to helping plan and execute updates, you should be directly involved.

QUESTION: I realize that responding to reader inquiries quickly is very important, but I just get too many emails! Any ideas?

ANSWER: Here are five ideas to help you with this problem:

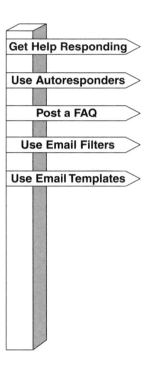

1. **Get help responding.** If you're overwhelmed, perhaps you can recruit a friend, family member, or very loyal regular to help you with the load.

2. **Use autoresponders.** An autoresponder is a message that is automatically sent to a person who emails an autoresponder address. You could set up different autoresponder categories on your Website that allow visitors to get more information simply by emailing a specific address. For example, you can have a "More Information" section of your Website. A visitor who goes there finds the statement, "Send an email to any of these addresses for an automated response with detailed information." Then there's a list of categories such as Advertising, Submitting Information, and so on. When the visitor sends an email to that address, he or she immediately receives an automated response with the detailed information! Check with your Web hosting company for more information on autoresponders. You can also get more information on autoresponders from **www.webmastertechniques.com**.

3. **Post a FAQ.** By posting a Frequently Asked Questions section to your Website, you can answer questions before they are asked.

4. **Use email filters.** As discussed earlier in this chapter, use email filters to help eliminate junk (and FFA) email so that you can focus on email messages that count.

5. **Use email templates.** Using email templates can help you give a personalized response quickly to people who email you with similar questions. Most email programs, such as Eudora and Outlook Express, allow you to build templates from scratch (called "stationery" in these two programs). Look in the Help file of your email program for information on easy construction and use of such templates. Another solution is to buy a template program. For example, a company called /n software has developed a specialized set of email templates for Microsoft Outlook. You can get more information on these from **www.emailtemplates.com**.

QUESTION: How about using an autoresponder that responds to keyword inquiries sent to my general email account?

ANSWER: Avoid this like the plague! Using an autoresponder is OK only if the person sending the email knows that he or she is sending for an autoresponder message. Setting up your autoresponder to look for keywords in messages and respond (as if from a human) is a very bad idea. I've run into many companies on the Web who do this, and time after time the autoresponse I get has nothing to do with the question I asked! This is nonpersonal and a great way to frustrate your visitors. Give all direct inquiries a personal response.

QUESTION: If I want to court advertisers, don't I have to publicly post my statistics?

ANSWER: That depends on how you seek out advertisers. If you want to try it through a publicly available online media kit, then the answer is yes, you do need to publicly post your statistics. If you are doing it through initiating calls or emails, then you can have the media kit in a password-secure area (giving the password only to those you want to have it) or in a form that can be emailed to prospective advertisers. That way you know exactly who can see your statistical information.

QUESTION: How can I track how well my marketing campaigns work to my home page?

ANSWER: Most people don't realize that there is a very easy method that marketers can use to track the effectiveness of marketing campaigns. Here's the secret:

Through the links you create, you can effectively track how much traffic is coming from your marketing efforts. Let's say you're launching a marketing campaign that includes using FFA links, a high-profile link/banner exchange with another Website, a link ad in an email newsletter, and heavy promotion from another one of your Websites. Each one will point to your home page URL, but you want to know exactly which marketing ideas work the best. The secret is in creating a "comment" line with your URLs.

Let's apply this scenario to *Animation Artist Magazine*. The home page URL is **www.animationartist.com**. But I'll never directly use this URL in my campaigns because it makes tracking harder to do. Here's how I'll do it:

1. FFA link promotion: **http://www.animationartist.com?index1**

2. Link/banner exchange: **http://www.animationartist.com?index2**

3. Email newsletter link: **http://www.animationartist.com?index3**

4. Link from second Website: **http://www.animationartist.com?index4**

No matter which link you click on, it will load **www.animationartist.com**. The key is that your statistics program will log the "?index1," "?index2," and so on, so that you know exactly how many people came from those sources. You can also use this idea to test various headlines to see which ones pull more traffic to your Website.

QUESTION: How easy is it to lose a visitor once he or she has become a regular?

ANSWER: It's fairly easy to lose a regular if there is an abrupt change in your routine. For example, I was once in charge of a daily technology news site for another company that received 600 to 1,000 or more visitors every day. When I left that position, the company didn't bother updating the page for weeks. All the loyalty I had spent months building with visitors was gone in the matter of a few weeks because there were no updates. In that period of time, regular visitors were able to find other places to meet their needs.

Consistency is the name of the game on the Internet just as it is in everyday life. In the 1999 baseball season, the San Diego Padres had a club record fourteen-game winning streak. That did little to help, because the Padres didn't play with any consistency and ended the season in second-to-last place in their division. Great winning streaks won't help your Website unless they happen on a regular basis—*every day,* if possible.

Now that you are armed with offensive and defensive marketing techniques, let's take a look, in the next chapter, at how to effectively market your Website's image.

5

Marketing Your Website's Image

Did you know that some Web portals, such as CNET, spend up to $100 million on Website branding? The reason is that building a Website's image through branding is a critical element to the long-term success of the Website. While I would never spend $100 million on branding, I do recommend that you dedicate a good chunk of your marketing budget and time to this technique.

Branding
is the image and experience you
provide to the public on a
consistent basis.

So what exactly is branding? In short, I describe branding as "the image and experience you provide to the public on a consistent basis." Branding is your identity—it is how you position your Website and how your Website positions itself. If your branding is unorganized and has mixed messages, the image a visitor has of your Website will be mixed. If your branding is strong and consistent, with a strong experience, it can drive visitor loyalty, trust, and revisits.

Your goal with branding is to get people to instantly identify your Website as the source to go to when they think of a particular category. When people are looking for animation information, I want them to think of *Animation Artist Magazine* as their first and only choice.

The most important element of branding is *consistency*. This means consistency in your look, your message, your delivery, your style, your identity, and the impressions you are making. It is a consistency you must maintain day after day, month after month, and year after year. By doing this, you begin to build a gap between yourself and all of your competitors—you begin to *position* your Website. The consistency of your message (and the delivery of your message) will make an impact over the long term.

Positioning Statements and Positioning Your Website

In a moment we are going to discuss seven branding techniques that you can use to begin increasing your Website's image. But before tackling specific branding techniques, you must first decide how you want to position your Website. For example, did you know that Kleenex is a brand of tissue? They have actually branded themselves so well that most people ask "Do you have a Kleenex?" instead of "Do you have a tissue?"

Position your Website as
number one in its category.

What is the positioning statement (see Chapter 9 to see how this differs from a mission statement and an internal goal statement) for your Website? For our Dogs Daily example, the positioning statement might be "Dogs Daily is the *leading provider* of daily *dog health news and information* for *dog owners.*" Now Dogs Daily must make that positioning statement a reality and get dog owners to truly recognize them as the leading provider of dog health news and information.

In many ways, your positioning statement is like your selling statement. Why should people go to your Website over your competitors? What makes your Website so special? Create a positioning statement for your Website that is two or three sentences long.

Your positioning statement is only the first step. You need to secure your Website as the number one leader in the category you are covering and fortify that position. The more unique your category, the better chance you have of pulling this off. For example, to position your new "Books for Me" Website as number one is impossible unless you have a billion dollars to spend to overtake giants such as Amazon.com and Barnes & Noble.

Once you have a good category defined in which you know you can reach the number one position, it's time to start applying long-term branding techniques that will help you reach and maintain a lead in the industry.

Specific Branding Techniques

Here are seven branding techniques you can use to begin branding your Website's image:

1. Select a good name.
2. Design a strong logo, slogan, and website.
3. Create a unique niche.
4. Post testimonials.
5. Promote trust.
6. Invest in customer relationships.
7. Master "the experience."

Select a Good Name

The first step in branding—before you even open your Website to the public—is to select the name and URL for your Website. This is a vital first step; the easier the name is to remember, the easier it will be for people to find you. An example of selecting a good name can be found in the online bookstore business. Which URL is easier to remember and type in: **www.amazon.com** or **www.barnesandnoble.com**? Not only is Amazon.com easier to remember, but there's a better chance you'll misspell barnesandnoble.com. Luckily, Barnes & Noble thought of this early on and snagged **www.barnesandnobel.com** too.

Make your name short and easy to remember. Also, strongly consider the .com part as a permanent part of your name. It will help the branding of the URL. For example, Amazon.com is always referred to as its official business name of Amazon.com. You never hear them refer to their name as just Amazon. The logos, T-shirts, and all branding say Amazon.com. It makes the URL all the easier to remember.

Another tip in selecting a name is to avoid the ever-confusing "-" (hyphen) when selecting a name. You rarely see a hyphen as part of a name in the real world; you should equally avoid it online.

Remember that the name you select doesn't have to be a word directly associated with your industry. For example, the word *Yahoo* had nothing to do with search directories until Yahoo! branded the name as a directory service. Yahoo! could have just as easily called itself something like Esearch or Isearch, but was able to very effectively brand its more unique idea—Yahoo! *Topica* is the name of a mailing list server (like ListBot and ONElist). The Topica people simply did an interesting play on words to come up with a simple but unique title for their service.

Did you know that *Happy Puppy* is the name, and URL, of a popular video game Website (**www.happypuppy.com**)? Remember, you can take any name you want and, through branding, make it mean something powerful.

Let's try a little experiment. I'm going to name four online categories. Write down the first company name that pops into your mind. We'll see whether your results are the same as mine.

In talking about the online experience, what company do you first think of when I say:

1. Books
2. Auctions
3. Toys
4. Search engine/directory

Chances are that your answers were Amazon.com, eBay, eToys, and Yahoo!. Through strong branding, these Websites have established themselves as the leaders in these categories and are the first names that most Web surfers think of when the categories are mentioned.

Now what is the category you plan on covering? Put all your efforts into branding your Website so that it is the first thing people think of when the category you cover is mentioned.

Design a Strong Logo, Slogan, and Website

In Chapter 2, we discussed the importance of a strong logo and slogan. It is your logo and slogan that most people will see first, possibly even before visiting your Website (in a banner ad, banner exchange, newspaper ad, and so on).

Branding is often associated with consistency. This means keeping your logo, your slogan, and the feel of your Website the same. Why, exactly, is this important? How does changing a logo or slogan harm branding? The answer is that as your Website remains steadfastly consistent, people become more comfortable with your site and what it offers. The trust begins to build. Any abrupt change can shake that foundation and for many Websites or companies making changes, the branding (which may have taken years to successfully build) has to start from scratch!

I'm familiar with a 3D software company that once decided to change its public look because it felt it needed a "new corporate identity." So much for branding. The logo changed, colors changed—everything.

This same company changes marketing directors every two to three years. A new marketing director comes in and wants to change the way everything was done. These directors have no concern for the branding and trust that has been built over the years. So the branding goes out the door because a new marketing director has his or her own way of doing things. The result is confusion for the consumer. In addition, the company has to start all over in building the strong identity it once possessed.

Build the strongest possible logo, slogan, online identity, colors, and so on from day one, then plan on using all those elements for the long haul. Enhancements to a particular look are fine, as long as those enhancements are not drastic.

Consider building your slogan into your logo (as Animation Artist has done) and be sure to always brand the name of your Website and your slogan in all promotional material, including the signature on your email messages, newsgroup posts, and so on. For example:

```
Sincerely,

Joe Tracy, Publisher
Animation Artist Magazine—"The Spirit of Animation"
http://www.animationartist.com
```

Create a Unique Niche

If your Website is not different from those of your competitors, why would people want to visit your site? It is important that you select one unique aspect of your Website and work really hard to develop that part of your site better than anyone else. That aspect of your site will be the driving force of new visitors, who then get the added benefit of all your other offerings.

The unique aspect of your Website must have a very strong offense and defense attached to it so that it cannot be easily duplicated on another site.

Some product Websites try to create a niche by giving detailed tips and tutorials on the products they sell. Some Websites even go as far as to publish results of independent tests, whether positive or negative. This helps build customer trust, because customers get the impression that the Website is truly concerned about the quality of the product that they are looking to purchase.

Let's take a quick look at three well-positioned Websites and what the unique niche of each serves:

Amazon.com (leader in book sales)—Niche: Strong affiliate program that no other bookstore can match. For consumers it has dozens of "Top 100" lists in various categories.

Disney.com (leader in "family/kids" Websites)—Niche: Highly interactive and visual. The experience comes across as a lot of "fun."

eToys.com (leader in toy sales online)—Niche: "The eToys Idea Center," which allows visitors to come up with instant ideas for gifts and toy purchases. Another niche that eToys has developed is the ability to search for toys by age categories.

Now let's switch gears a little. *Animation Artist Magazine* is currently in a battle to become the leading provider and destination for animation information. We are using a strong focus on interactivity (animation games, trivia, forums, contests, reader image reviews, and so on) as our niche. We also have a secondary niche of updating the Animation Artist Website every single day, including Saturdays, Sundays, and all holidays (including Christmas). *Every day* of the year, visitors can get new animation information.

What about our competitors? Each one also has a niche that we've identified. One of our strong competitors, who has been around much longer than us (which is an advantage of its own), uses networking as its niche. The competitor takes smaller animation Websites and hosts them under its Website's "umbrella" for free. Our other competitor (we've identified only two main competitors) has a niche of personalized editorializing. This means that you will frequently find his personal opinion (and diaries) throughout the Website, and you know everything about his personal life (including his birthday and other personal information). While this may seem somewhat egotistic, it actually works well for a certain group of people because they can identify with the Webmaster on many levels and also know that there is a human behind all the information.

Look in detail at all your competitors, then decide what you can offer that will make your Website much better and more original.

Post Testimonials

Testimonials go a long way to help establish your brand identity. The reason is that testimonials come from other visitors—your customers' peers. Such testimonials are unbiased and thus become an excellent branding tool for your message.

Create an area of your Website dedicated strictly to testimonials—comments readers have sent you in praise of your Website or the products and services you offer. On the page, be sure to include an easy form that others can fill out with their comments. If a person sends an email to you via your personal email box, you may want to first ask permission before publishing their statements. Most of the time they'll quickly say yes.

Testimonials are also great for other branding media. You can put testimonials in media kits, in press kits, and even in press releases. We find that using quotes from visitors in our press releases gives us more of a personalized (versus corporate) approach.

Promote Trust

Promoting trust is another essential item to effective branding. Here are four ways to help promote trust on your Website:

1. Publish a privacy statement, as discussed in Chapter 2.

2. List your contact information so that people can easily reach you (discussed later). Respond immediately to inquiries.

3. If you sell products, offer a money-back guarantee.

4. Always practice ethical marketing (refer to Chapter 1 for more information).

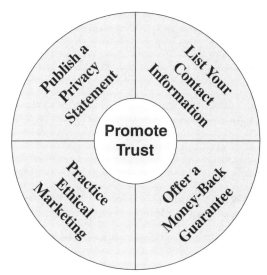

Ask yourself this question: "Why should a visitor trust my Website?" Now promote the answers you come up with while continuing to implement features that build trust.

Remember that trust is easy to lose. All it takes is for a visitor to have one bad experience and if the follow-up isn't handled right, you may lose that visitor forever.

I used to own a video productions business in Oregon called Studio Visions. We were a strong customer-oriented company doing TV commercials, corporate videos, and even duplications for the community. One day a woman brought in a tape to be duplicated that had a lot of bad signal problems. We did our best to eliminate these problems on the copy, and after viewing the results on our equipment, we decided we had succeeded. The woman dropped off her check and took the duplications.

The next day I received a telephone call from this woman, who was absolutely irate! No sooner had I said "Studio Visions, may I help you?" than she was yelling about how the video wasn't playing back right and she couldn't believe we did such lousy work and what terrible people we were for messing it up and on and on. She wouldn't even let me get a word in to try to figure out what the problem was! She was cussing and fuming, and while my anger was now building from her reaction, I kept it under control and calmly tried to figure out the problem with her—but she still wouldn't let me get a word in and hung up on me after her irate speech.

What would you do in a situation like this? I was upset at first, because not only had we never received a complaint on any duplications we had ever done (thousands), but this woman had been verbally abusive without even letting me try to help her resolve the situation.

Obviously, this woman's first experience with us had been a negative one. Letting it end that way was not an option. She now had no trust in our company or our service. It was my goal to change that with a follow-up.

I became deeply concerned about the event. We check every tape before it leaves, and her copies had left our offices in just as good a shape as her original. But obviously something was wrong, and the situation needed to be rectified immediately. Not wanting to deal with her on the phone, I sat down and wrote her a very polite letter. I explained our duplication procedure and our process of checking every tape multiple times, and apologized for any problems there might have been on her copies. I told her that our work was guaranteed, and therefore I was refunding her money (I enclosed a check for the full amount). I also told her that if she brought the tapes back to my office, we would view them and determine the problem, and I would redo her duplications *for free!* I made sure that the letter went *priority* in the same day's mail so that she would get it for sure the next day.

The next afternoon, the woman came into the office with the tapes, and the first thing she did was apologize to me. She said how sorry she was for the way she had acted and that she had had a very bad day and was extremely sorry that she had taken her frustrations out on me. She thanked me profusely for my professionalism and said that she was very impressed with my response to her outburst.

We went into the editing room and played the tapes on our professional editing decks and then in a $249 combination TV/VCR. In both places the duplications played back perfectly. I told her she could keep those copies or throw them away and that I'd work on making some more adjustments to her tapes and reduplicate them for free. That's exactly what I did, spending extra time and care in making sure that everything about the duplication was perfect. The final result was that a woman who for a moment had been our worst enemy was now our biggest ally and it was all because of the way we treated her. We not only turned her trust of our company around with our quick response, but we also gained a valuable customer willing to recommend our business to other people because of our customer service.

Earn and keep your visitors' trust from the beginning and instantly respond to any problems so that you don't lose that visitor forever.

Here's an example from the other side. When I was looking for an email service to offer to my Website visitors (yourname@animationartist.net), I came across one that looked very attractive. It allowed you to customize the look, and all ad banners were evenly split so that the company provided 50 percent of the ads and you provided the other 50 percent. The Website looked nice, and staff immediately responded to my inquiries. However, there was a red flag. The Website's forum was filled with messages from Webmasters having problems with their service. Most of the problems were related to server issues in which it was taking forever for users to access their email. The company kept promising that changes were coming, but the problems continued. Even though this company was having problems keeping up with the demand of its users, it kept doing mass advertising to sign up more Webmasters. Then it introduced a whole new line of services without first fixing the email problems!

When it came to decision-making time, I didn't trust this company with my business. It was my opinion that this company was interested only in building up a huge user base in order to take the company public and make millions of dollars. Even when service was terrible and complaints at an all-time high, the company continued to mass-advertise its email service. This happened even as current customers were posting in the forum to "please stop accepting new applications until your problems are fixed!"

This company has lost the trust of hundreds of Webmasters. Many will switch over to a competitor and never look back. Others will stick it out, believing that they are still gaining real value because this service is "free" for them.

When you stop putting the customer first, you lose the trust of your customer. Never let that happen—and if it does, correct the problem immediately.

Invest in Customer Relationships

Did you know that some companies have budgets for customer relationships? It's called a *relationship budget* and is built into the budgeting of many strong-branded companies. For some, it is based on a percentage of sales. For example, 5 percent of every sale of Brand X may go to further building a relationship with you so that you become more loyal to the company.

I consider investing in customer relationships one of the most important elements of long-term branding. Investing in customer relationships will help directly influence user loyalty to your product, service, or Website.

For example, one car company has fiercely loyal users that would make any car company envious. Not surprising, it is also a company that is a leader in customer relationship investing. That company is Saturn, which invests heavily in customer relationships. Saturn even hosts a periodic get-together for Saturn car owners called "Homecoming." It's a popular event, too—tens of thousands of Saturn car owners attended the last one in the summer of 1999!

You have to admire a company that has such strong loyalty that tens of thousands of their customers take time off work, some driving thousands of miles in their Saturn cars, to attend a huge event put together specifically for them by a car company! Saturn is definitely a prime example of a company that has mastered investing in customer relationships.

So far, the Internet has come across as a very impersonal medium where people just surf from one site to another with no considerations given to loyalty. You must change this.

"That's great," you may say, "but how can I invest in customer relationships online?"

Good question. So far the Internet has come across as a very impersonal medium where people just surf from one site to another with no considerations given to loyalty. You must change this. Just as Saturn is "a different kind of car company," you must be "a different kind of Website." Here are seven specific ideas:

1. When a person complains about something, *address the problem immediately.*

2. If a person points out a problem on your Website, *fix it within ten minutes of reading the message* and send a personalized thank-you to that person.

3. Give out a lot of contact information: phone, fax, email, and so on. *Make it as easy and convenient as possible for your Website visitors to contact you.*

4. *Nurture relationships.* If you find out a visitor has an interest similar to yours, chat about it with him or her. Be very personable and enjoy making new friendships with your Website visitors.

5. *Organize personalized online get-togethers* with personalities within your industry. This could be in the form of chats, forum presentations, a free course, and so on.

6. *Do long-term follow-up.* Animation Artist readers make frequent inquiries regarding various aspects of our Website. While we immediately address the inquiries, we put those that correlate with our long-term goals into a follow-up folder, so that we can keep users notified when these goals become a reality. So not only do users get an immediate response from us, but one to two months later we are in contact with them again with an update to their suggestion or concern.

7. *Arrange a physical meeting.* If your online community is strong enough, you may want to invest in a real get-together with guest speakers, food, festivities, and so on, specifically for your Website visitors.

Master "the Experience"

You have one of the best names in the industry, a great logo, a catchy slogan, a unique niche, and public testimonials, and you answer inquiries immediately. Those are all great branding techniques. However, none of those will be successful unless the user has a good experience on your Website. Perceptions are formed from the experience a person has when visiting your Website. If it's a great experience, then all the other branding techniques are going to work all the stronger.

One place where branding is very big is in the movie industry. Major motion picture studios know that if they can get you to think of a movie as an event (for example, *Star Wars*) rather than just a movie, they will get a lot of money from you. Just look at all the free publicity that *Star Wars: Episode One* received because it was perceived by many as the event of the decade. Other examples of movies that ran effective campaigns to capture this type of status were *Jurassic Park, Godzilla,* and *ID4* (*Independence Day*). Even if the movie was slammed by critics and moviegoers (for example, *Godzilla*), it still brought in $150 million or more (because it had reached "event" status), which is all the studios care about.

As a smart marketer, you care about the quality of the experience that a visitor has on your Website. From the time a visitor enters to the time a visitor leaves, you want that to be the best surfing experience the visitor has had for the entire day. Great information, interactive content, frequent updates, quick responses, contests, and so on all contribute to a solid experience. In essence, your Website should be a theme park of activities with the core being your "content zone," which gives the visitor the information he or she is looking for as quickly as possible. Make sure your pages load quickly and that it is easy to find information quickly.

Master the ability to provide a fun, solid, and informative experience to each visitor, and all of your branding will be more effective because of it.

There you have it—seven great ideas to help your branding efforts on the Web. Beware, however, because there is a "danger zone" in branding. That danger is when you break your consistency.

**Avoid danger zones, or years
of branding efforts can go
down the drain.**

The Danger Zone

It is possible to ruin all of your branding efforts in a short time period. The quickest way to do this is to suddenly change your message, style, logo, or slogan. I've seen company after company have to start from square one just because they thought it was "time for a change." Branding is not like a house, where you move furniture around because you are bored of the look. If you go moving furniture around all the time on your Website, you'll only confuse visitors, because they'll no longer know where to go and what to do.

Branding is a long-term process—long-term meaning years and decades. Every time your consistent message hits another person, you are branding an image. Once you change the message, you are starting all over because you're no longer reinforcing the same message, but rather starting a new one. For effective branding, this is a major no-no. Don't start new messages all the time, but rather reinforce the same message.

Another aspect of the danger zone is simply not delivering. If your Website promises "daily updates" and you sometimes go two or three days without an update, you are losing the interest (and patience) of your visitor. Your Website is no longer of value to regular visitors, and their habit of checking your Website daily will quickly disappear.

Avoid danger zones!

QUESTIONS AND ANSWERS

QUESTION: I've seen some Websites that put their logo in the bottom right-hand corner of the Web page and it stays there even when you scroll. Wouldn't this be a good form of branding?

ANSWER: No! Branding can actually become somewhat ineffective when you begin doing things that annoy your visitors. This includes making pop-up windows with your logo and doing what Geocities used to do, with the logo always on the screen even when you scroll. As discussed throughout this chapter, you can effectively brand your Website image without annoying your visitors.

Another example of negative branding is email spam. If you send unsolicited emails to people promoting (and "branding") your business, you'll end up with negative branding instead of positive. It's better to have no branding than consistent negative branding. At all costs, avoid things that annoy your visitors.

QUESTION: Does music represent a form of branding?

ANSWER: Absolutely! Recognizable jingles, music, and songs are an excellent form of branding. Some of the best branding comes from consistently using the same message and song. Remember these jingles?

1. **Kool-Aid**—"Here comes Kool-Aid, here comes Kool-Aid, he's gonna save the day . . ."
2. **Kit Kat Bars**—"Give me a break, give me a break; break me off a piece of that Kit Kat bar . . ."
3. **Almond Joy**—"Sometimes you feel like a nut, sometimes you don't . . ."

Catchy jingles and songs played over and over become branded in a person's mind. This is highly effective because years after your branding efforts have ended, people will still recall your tunes.

Even sound effects can be a form of branding. Every time I hear a car honk quickly twice, I still think of "AAMCO—double A (honk, honk), M-C-O."

Intel does a very effective job of branding a short musical effect. Every time you see the Intel Inside logo on a TV commercial, the branding sound effect accompanies it.

QUESTION: Every time I start a new program, another Website copies what I do. How am I supposed to develop a niche that way?

ANSWER: You must find something that you can do 100 percent better than your competitor. Now put half of your energy into further developing that area, while putting the other half of your energy into consistently adding other new areas and updates to your Website. Whatever your competitor copies, make sure you do it better as you continue to further develop your main niche area.

Ask yourself the question, "Why should someone visit my Website over my competitor's Website?" Find the answer and develop it more. Make it stronger. Whatever you do, don't bring any public attention to the other Website. Leaders should never publicly mention the name of a competitor. Always stay one step ahead. As long as your competitor is always copying you, you are the established leader and your competitor is the established follower. That's a pretty good position for you to be in.

QUESTION: In Chapter 2, banner advertising didn't rank very high on your list of marketing ideas. Isn't banner advertising a good form of branding?

ANSWER: Banner advertising appears to be much more effective at branding rather than getting click-throughs (unless you "trick" the user, as with the "Catch the Monkey" campaign). You may want to explore banner advertising to assist in your branding campaign. For example, if you use an advertising service such as ValueClick to host your banners (**www.valueclick.com**), you only pay for every click-through. Therefore all the times the banner is shown, but not clicked on, you aren't paying anything! This type of campaign could work well for branding.

QUESTION: Is branding something physical or mental?

ANSWER: In essence, branding is the whole experience that a visitor has with your company or Website. Messages, ads, slogans, interactions, relationships, and perceptions all combine to form an opinion in the mind of the visitor. Branding means educating visitors and building relationships. This is done through physical means such as email, design, and so on. The bottom line is consistency. Your job in branding is to make sure that the image portrayed is a positive and consistent one that establishes your Website as the ultimate leader in the category you cover.

One thing that can help your branding experience is getting top personalities within your industry to interact with your audience. You might be surprised at the number of people who would say yes to an interview or chat request. You'll never know, however, unless you ask. That's what the next chapter is about.

6   *It Never Hurts to Ask*

It is possible for you to get someone well known in your industry to participate in a function on your Website (interview, live chat, telling a story, and so on). The key is simply *to ask*.

"Is it that simple?" you may inquire. The answer is "Yes, it is that simple."

When I was associate publisher of a 3D print publication that went out to tens of thousands of animators, artists, and video producers, I was often asked by a man named Tim in San Diego to come to his small user group meetings to give a speech. Every single time he asked, I accepted.

But I wasn't the only one appearing as a guest speaker at these meetings where 25 to 70 user group members would show up. Guest speakers ranging from software developers to the CEO of a major 3D software company made appearances. Every month Tim had a new (and prominent) guest at his user group meeting.

By far, Tim ran one of the most active 3D user groups I had ever seen. No, it wasn't the biggest user group around, but it was the most active.

So what was Tim's secret? The big secret is that he would *call people and ask them* to come and address his user group. *That's it.* Meanwhile, dozens of other user groups wondered how Tim was able to constantly attract high-profile speakers week after week.

Ask and they will come.

You may wonder why a person would be interested in taking a big chunk of time out of his or her day or week to address such a small user group. Maybe this true-life example will help.

At one of Tim's user group meetings, the CEO and founder of a 3D software company had flown in from another state just to give a one-hour speech at Tim's request. The CEO didn't charge the group a dime. Why? Simply put, he cares about his end users. It didn't matter whether 5 or 50,000 people were present at the meeting. These people had put money into his company's products, and he wanted to show his appreciation by accepting an invitation to speak to a small group of his users. Sure, he could have been in a high-level meeting with vice-presidents of his company, but he wasn't. For that day and time, his focus was devoted 100 percent to a small group of people who built their lives around his company's products.

You might be surprised at the number of people who are like that CEO. Give them the opportunity and they will take it.

About Celebrities

Celebrities (for example, Hollywood actors and actresses) are in a different league from other high-profile people in the industry your Website covers. Celebrities are always on tight time schedules with strange shooting schedules (there are no nine-to-five jobs in the movie industry). Actors and actresses also have agents who handle all requests (at hefty fees). Even if you're lucky enough to get close to a celebrity, chances are that restrictions will be placed on you. For example, my wife and I were lucky enough to be on the set of *Home Improvement* (during a rehearsal run) and on the set of *The X-Files* (for the "Millennium" episode that aired December 5, 1999). In both cases we were given explicit instructions that we could not, for any reason, talk to any of the actors or actresses. Writers, directors, and crew were all fine to talk to, but the actors and actresses were off limits (unless they first spoke to us, as Earl Hindman did to a group of us on the *Home Improvement* set). So for the most part you'll find that celebrities are off limits. That doesn't mean you can't try, however. This is particularly true if you have a very strong entertainment Website. In that case, do a search for the celebrity's publicist and go for it. Remember that it never hurts to ask.

The high-profile people we are discussing in this chapter are people such as CEOs of major companies that relate to the industry you cover with your Website. Perhaps the person is a public speaker, writer, astronaut, specialist, air traffic controller, or other type of professional. Most people who are in high-profile jobs, but not necessarily in the public eye a lot, are prime candidates to ask for an interview or some other contribution because normally they love to share their experiences with other people, but rarely get the opportunity.

I was once asked by *StoryCrafting* magazine for an interview based on some screenplays I was writing and my coverage of the special effects industry in Hollywood. I was more than happy to oblige because I love to share with other people. I like to share tips, techniques, tutorials, thoughts, ideas, and opinions, as do many other people. The first step in getting the participation, however, is *to ask*.

Here are seven steps to aid you in contacting high-profile people:

1. Research the person whom you want to contact.
2. Be prepared.
3. Write an official request to the individual.
4. Follow up if you don't receive a response.
5. Plan the details of the event.
6. Execute the event.
7. Send a thank-you card to the person.

Step #1: Research the Person Whom You Want to Contact

The first step in contacting high-profile people is to determine whom you want to interview or ask to contribute an article (or other information) to your Website. You can obtain most of this information directly from Websites or by doing searches on the World Wide Web.

For example, I was once interested in interviewing animation writer Michael Reaves. So the first thing I did was conduct a search (you may have to use multiple search engines) for "Michael Reaves." Within the first ten listings I found a direct link to Michael Reaves's official home page. On the Website was an email address. From there I was able to email a request and secure an interview with him.

Not all searches will be as successful as the one I had with Michael Reaves. Therefore, you need to incorporate other research methods. For example, let's say that Michael Reaves didn't have his own Website. Then what?

One of the first obvious places to go is any Website on which the person may be mentioned. For example, let's say I'm interested in obtaining an interview with the president of Saturn, Cynthia Trudell, to talk about her company's philosophies. What steps would I take to locate her?

1. First I'd go to **www.saturn.com**. Upon my arrival, I discover there are three main areas that I can select from. The first is "A Different Kind of Company," the second is "A Different Kind of Car," and the third is "Research Center." My first stop would be "A Different Kind of Company" to see whether it has a personnel listing. Clicking on that

doesn't give me any options for personnel, but it does give me a customer service phone number. There's my first step in the right direction (it helps that it is an 800 number).

2. Now I would call the 800 number and explain who I am and what I'm looking for: "Hi, this is Joe Tracy and I'm the editor of *Webmaster Techniques Magazine*. I'm interested in arranging an interview with Cynthia Trudell, the president of Saturn. Can you point me in the right direction so that I can contact her?" Chances are that they will give me a phone number to the secretary for Cynthia Trudell. With luck, that will be my last stop.

If you still can't get to a person's phone number or email address, you may want to play the "email guessing game," which has worked for me on more than one occasion. For example, let's say I'm trying to contact the president of a company called XYXYZ. The president's name is John Doe. In contacting John Doe, I may "guess" at his email address. The three most obvious guesses, in order, would be jdoe@xyxyz.com, johndoe@xyxyz.com, or john.doe@xyxyz.com.

Stay persistent until you reach the person. If the company the person works for is customer-oriented, like Saturn, chances are that reaching someone high up in the company with your request will be fairly easy. If a company is very closed-minded and protective of higher-up personnel, then your task will be much more difficult, but not impossible. Three-fourths of the battle in securing an interview request is simply getting in contact with the person you want to interview.

BTW, it's not just CEOs and presidents that make interesting prospects for interviews. For example, when the animated movie *The Iron Giant* first came out, we targeted actual artists—people who worked on the film—for interviews. The movie's director, Brad Bird, had already been interviewed by dozens of other publications, so our angle was to go for the lesser-known people who might have more interesting stories. An example was interviewing Mark Whiting, who was the production designer. We also interviewed the head animator, a lead animator, and the artistic coordinator of the movie. It worked great, as our audience was given more of a complete overview of the process.

Interviews

Mark Whiting
The Production Designer for *The Iron Giant*

Mark Whiting served as the Production Designer on *The Iron Giant*, supplying the background and layout department with a quantity of artwork that would help illustrate the overall look of the film.

Step #2: Be Prepared

You know whom you want to contact; now you need to make sure that your Website is prepared for a visit from this person. One great thing about asking high-profile people to be involved in an event on your Website is that they will first check out your Website! Make sure that you are near the top of your category in providing excellent information, interactivity, branding, and so on. The more impressed a person is with your Website, the more likely he or she will grant your request. You may also gain a regular visitor with whom you may be able to form a strategic relationship.

You must also be prepared for the actual phone call you will make or the email you will write. This means knowing a lot of information about the company and the person. Although this is only your first contact, the amount of knowledge you exhibit could have an impact on the person's desire to take time out for your request. Research the company and the person, and have your notes ready.

In preparing for your call, you never know what you may find. For example, when I went to the Saturn Website to prepare for the examples in this chapter, one of the areas I went to was the FAQ page, which gave a lot of great information on the company.

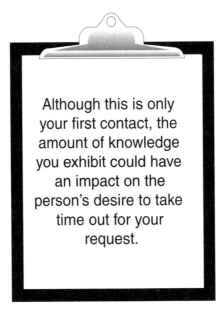

Although this is only your first contact, the amount of knowledge you exhibit could have an impact on the person's desire to take time out for your request.

Step #3: Write an Official Request to the Individual

Now it's time to make the official request. Although I've never contacted Cynthia Trudell or Saturn for any requests, let's assume that I want to interview her for *Webmaster Techniques Magazine*. Here is a sample of the email I would write:

```
Date: January 10, 2000

To: Cynthia Trudell, president of Saturn
From: Joe Tracy, editor of Webmaster Techniques
About: Interview Request

Dear Cynthia Trudell,

Congratulations on such a successful Homecoming this year! It looks
like you have, once again, shown that building relationships with
customers is the key to true business success. I've always admired
Saturn's philosophy of building strong relationships with employees
and customers. It does make a difference.
```

As the editor of Webmaster Techniques Magazine, I am always looking
for innovative people to interview. I consider the relationship-building
techniques you use at Saturn to be very innovative (especially since
such customer service is so rare these days) and would like to request
an interview with you. I think my readers can greatly benefit from
the Saturn philosophy, which I believe can be applied to Websites
with great success.

Webmaster Techniques Magazine is the leading provider of tools, tips,
and techniques for Webmasters who are trying to grow their Websites.
We receive over 2,000 unique visitors a day. An interview about
"The Saturn Philosophy" would be a great addition of top-of-the-line
information for our readers, and I thank you for giving an interview
your consideration.

You can contact me at 123-456-7890 or at joetracy@earthlink.net.
I'd be more than happy to provide you with a list of questions in
advance and to conduct the interview through the most convenient
method for you (for example, email or phone).

I look forward to hearing back from you at your earliest convenience.

Wishing you much continued success,

Joe Tracy, Editor
Webmaster Techniques Magazine
http://www.webmastertechniques.com

P.S. Congratulations on your excellent sponsorship of the Special
Olympics in 1999!

As you can see, I did my research before writing the email so that the message wasn't all one-sided. Yes, I am a firm believer in "the Saturn philosophy,"
which is why I would want an interview with Cynthia Trudell in the first place.
By doing further research I was able to start the letter with a comment that Cynthia Trudell would be interested in—Saturn's huge (and successful) Homecoming event. It immediately started us on common ground. Notice that my
actual request doesn't come until midway through the second paragraph. Establish common ground (Homecoming), praise something you like about the person or company (Saturn's philosophy), introduce your credentials (editor of
Webmaster Techniques Magazine), then make the request (interview).

Step #4: Follow Up If You Don't Receive a Response

Sometimes you won't get a response from the person you are trying to contact. Don't assume that it is because he or she is ignoring you. The person could be on vacation, may be very busy, or may not have received your email. Therefore if you haven't heard from the person within a week, you should send a friendly follow-up email (and double-check the email address). Include your original email in your follow-up email. Here's an example:

```
January 18, 2000

To: Cynthia Trudell, president of Saturn
From: Joe Tracy, editor of Webmaster Techniques
About: Interview Request

Dear Cynthia Trudell,

Last week I emailed you with a request to interview you for
Webmaster Techniques Magazine based on Saturn's excellent customer
service. Since I have not heard back from you regarding my request,
I fear that my original email may not have reached you. Please find
it directly below. Thank you for your time and for getting back to me
at your earliest convenience.

Joe Tracy
(paste original message here)
```

Notice that the follow-up email was very short and to the point. That's because I included the original message with the follow-up. I also didn't ask why she didn't respond, but rather said, "I fear that my original email may not have reached you." This makes a good neutral response without putting the recipient on the defensive. Also, it may be true that the person never got your first email! Emails do get lost. Finally, I stated, "Thank you for your time and for getting back to me at your earliest convenience." This statement is a friendly reminder to respond to my message.

If you still don't get a response, wait about two weeks and send another follow-up, as the person may be on vacation. Always include the original letter.

Keep in mind that you don't have to reach your contact via email. You can just as easily research the phone number for the person you are trying to reach.

Once you've made contact, it's a matter of receiving a yes or no. If you get a yes, that's great! Move on to the next tip. If you receive a no, then move on to the next person you'd like to interview. If you don't receive a response after three follow-up email letters, then the individual isn't worth your time anymore.

Step #5: Plan the Details of the Event

Once you get a confirmation, it is time to plan the details of the event. When will the event take place? Is it a live event or arranged in advance? Who are all the players involved? How will it be executed? The details of the event must be planned to go as smoothly as possible. And then there's the question of marketing. You should have a mini-campaign set up in advance. For example, if you will be doing a live chat, you would be wise to make sure it is heavily marketed. There's nothing more embarrassing than holding a "big" event and having only five people (including you and the person you are interviewing) show up.

For some types of events, such as an interview that takes place via email and then is formatted and posted to your Website at your convenience, the planning process isn't that difficult. But for something like a live chat, you need to be prepared for all potential problems. What if your guest doesn't show up? What if there are too many people? What if you get only one or two people? What if the chat server crashes? How will questions be asked of the guest? Is there a moderator? You must have backup plans for a lot of scenarios in order to make the event go as smoothly as possible.

Step #6: Execute the Event

Once the event has been thoroughly planned, it is time to execute it. You should have had a strong marketing campaign leading up to this point if it is an event that requires a large audience (such as a chat or seminar). For interviews you are just posting after conducting the interview via email or phone, your marketing campaign will start once the interview is publicly posted.

Make sure you stay in contact with your guest leading up to the event. Keep him or her informed so that there is no confusion. Make the process as easy as possible.

Step #7: Send a Thank-You Card to the Person

The proper thing to do once an interview (or event) is complete is to send a thank-you card to the person via "snail mail." Handwrite your thank-you note (it's more personal) and hand-address the envelope. Building relationships shouldn't stop with your visitors, but should apply to anyone involved with your Website ventures.

QUESTIONS AND ANSWERS

QUESTION: Can these strategies apply to areas other than getting high-profile people to address my Website visitors?

ANSWER: Absolutely. For example, when *Animation Artist Magazine* released a press announcement about many of its expansions, we looked at various companies for the distribution of the release. One of those companies was Internet Wire, which was charging $225 to distribute a press release (that price has since gone up to $275). I emailed Internet Wire and asked whether we could get a special $150 rate since this was our first time using their service. Within twelve hours I had the response—"Sure." I saved Animation Artist $75 simply because *I asked* for a cheaper rate.

Here's another example. Let's say you come across a Website with an excellent feature story that would be perfect for your readers. Why not email the Webmaster and ask whether you can reprint it (which is better than just linking to the story). When I ask to republish an article from another Website, about 70 percent of the time I get a positive response. Usually the only requirement is to acknowledge where the article originated. Out of the other 30 percent, some don't respond, some say no, and a few say to link to the article directly. I ignore the 30 percent and focus on the material gained from the 70 percent. You never know what can come from the 70 percent, either. For example, the initial inquiry (and granted permission) could lead to a strategic partnership or networking agreement!

QUESTION: What if I'm doing "email guessing" and get no response?

ANSWER: Chances are that if your first guess is wrong, the email will be bounced back. However, that isn't always the case. Therefore, if you don't hear from the person after one follow-up (to your first email address), then try the second email address and finally the third one. If all three fail, then find a "Webmaster" email address on the official Website and send the letter to the Webmaster with the title "Attention (Person's Name Here)," and with luck it will be forwarded.

We've been discussing a lot of great online marketing techniques over the past several chapters. Now let's move on to offline marketing techniques, which will have a major impact on the success of your Website when incorporated into your Strategic Website Marketing Plan.

7 Continuing Your Marketing Efforts Offline

Many people thought the Internet would bring an end to many long-time communication media such as newspapers, magazines, and—some predicted—even television. What really happened is that traditional media became a preferred marketing tool for the Internet! Turn on the TV and you can't miss an ad for an Internet Website. Open up your newspaper and you'll find URLs all over the place, quoted in stories and ads. Open up a magazine and there are full-page color ads for a specific

URL. To make matters more interesting, print magazines are being born from the Internet. You can now get *Yahoo! Internet Life* magazine, *eBay Magazine,* and dozens of others. Even radio stations are now reaching a wider audience by broadcasting live via the Internet.

This should tell you something very important—*traditional media are essential to an effective marketing campaign.* What I just said is so urgent that I'm going to say it one more time: *Traditional media are essential to an effective marketing campaign.*

There's a reason why you hear Amazon.com commercials on the radio, see news stations promoting their URLs, and see full-page magazine ads solely promoting a Website. The reason is that mixing offline marketing efforts with online marketing efforts can double, triple, or even quadruple the results of your marketing campaign.

The next several pages are dedicated to 28 specific offline marketing ideas that you can implement to further advertise your Website. So if you add these new ideas to the 101 ideas in Chapter 2, you have a total of 129 total Website marketing ideas!

The headers for each idea are as follows:

Offline Web Marketing Idea—The title of the idea.

How much does it cost?—One dollar sign (**$**) = inexpensive; five dollar signs (**$$$$$**) = very expensive.

What does it develop?—All four options from Chapter 2 are available (Initial Contact, Revisits, Participation, Loyalty & Trust).

You'll notice that a lot of the offline ideas work toward loyalty and trust, making these ideas all the more important. This is because the offline marketing ideas, with established and more expensive media, are strong in branding.

OFFLINE WEB MARKETING IDEA

    Send Announcements

    HOW MUCH DOES IT COST? $$–$$$
....WHAT DOES IT DEVELOP?   Initial Contact

You have a new Website. The first thing you should do is send announcements out to any list of customers you have. For example, if you run a fitness center and just opened up an online fitness Website, you should send out an announcement of your new Website, via direct mail, to all of your customers.

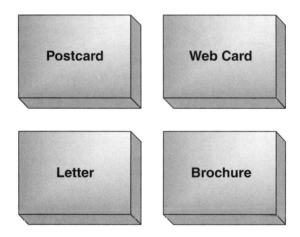

There are four main ways to send your announcement:

1. Send a postcard with notice of your new Website.
2. Send a Web Card (see Offline Web Marketing Idea #9).
3. Send a letter from the company owner, president, or CEO.
4. Design and mail an announcement brochure.

The cost of this tip depends on which method you select (I prefer Web Cards or letters) and how many people will receive your direct mail announcement.

If you want to go all-out, you can design a specific welcome brochure that introduces your Website to your customer. See Offline Web Marketing Idea #5 for more information on brochures.

Be sure that you have something great to show your customers before sending out the announcement! Also, if you are selling things online (products, memberships, and so on) be sure to include a promotional coupon, as discussed in Offline Web Marketing Idea #17.

OFFLINE WEB MARKETING IDEA

Use Your Car to Advertise

HOW MUCH DOES IT COST? $$$ (not including the car)
WHAT DOES IT DEVELOP?   Initial Contact

Many days, when walking to work, I would pass one of those new and stylish Volkswagen Beetles. This one, however, was different (see pictures). This Beetle was not providing just transportation for the driver, but also the traffic to his Website (**www .makeitwork.net**)! It could possibly even be a nice tax deduction.

When I saw this car, I knew that it had to go into my *Web Marketing Applied* book. The way the Website is presented on the car gives it added style and adds to the power of the message that potentially hundreds of people see *every day*.

I contacted the CEO of Make It Work, Eric David Greenspan, and he told me that the cost to have the URL added to the Beetle (as seen in the pictures) was only $400. It is not painted on the Beetle, but rather done by vinyl cut-and-paste. It is removable and doesn't affect the finish if he ever removes it. You can get it done at a sign service bureau.

Greenspan says that the Beetle has not only attracted a lot of attention, but also resulted in several opportunities. Now his company has three Beetles advertising the Make It Work Websites!

OFFLINE WEB MARKETING IDEA 3

Create, Sell, and Give Away T-Shirts

HOW MUCH DOES IT COST? $$

WHAT DOES IT DEVELOP?   Initial Contact, Loyalty & Trust

Many people love to collect and wear T-shirts, so what better T-shirt to wear than yours? T-shirts are great items because you can sell them, give them away, award them as prizes, and use them as part of your public relations efforts. Furthermore, T-shirts aren't that expensive ($7–10 a shirt). It's a small price to pay for assistance in branding and building loyalty and trust.

T-shirts were the very first thing we had made for *Animation Artist Magazine*. However, we don't sell them. The only way people can get them is through our participation contests. For example, we gave away a T-shirt to each of the first three people who posted 50 messages in our new forum. We have a mailing list drawing every month to award a T-shirt.

We also use T-shirts as "thank you" gifts or "I'm sorry" gifts. For example, a woman once handwrote us a two-page letter because she had a complaint about something on our Website. In today's technologically advanced society, it is rare to see a detailed hand-written letter. So we wrote a letter back to address her issue and sent her a T-shirt. After all the effort she went through to relay her feelings, the least we could do was award her with a "thank you" gift of a T-shirt. Don't advertise that you do this, however, or you might start receiving lots of "complaint" letters!

Shop around and find a good T-shirt place to have T-shirts made on a regular basis. Be sure to find out all the costs involved, including the set-up fees (usually $25–55).

OFFLINE WEB MARKETING IDEA

  Attend and Exhibit at Trade Shows

  HOW MUCH DOES IT COST? $$$$$
....WHAT DOES IT DEVELOP?   Initial Contact, Loyalty & Trust

Trade shows are an excellent place to meet people and form alliances. They are a very powerful marketing force, which is why tens of thousands of trade shows are held throughout the nation every year. Consider these two findings by the Center for Exhibition Industry Research:

1. More than nine out of ten attendees rate exhibitions as the number one most useful source for purchasing information, because they can examine and evaluate competing products all in one location.

2. Exhibitions are more effective in achieving sales and marketing objectives than business-to-business advertising, direct mail, and telemarketing.

Trade shows give you the opportunity to obtain leads and prospects (for visits, networking, and advertising), build your Website's image, and meet visitors who are already visiting your Website on a regular basis.

The problem with trade shows is that they are generally expensive (especially for Webmasters) and can take a big chunk out of your marketing budget. There are a lot of expenses, including the booth itself, union set-up fees, staffing, promotional gifts, marketing your presence at the trade show. Even so, more and more booths promoting Websites are popping up at trade shows. It is an effective one-on-one personalized medium. In addition, the chance to form new allies is very good.

Even if you don't exhibit at a trade show, be sure to attend all trade shows related to your field. Take a lot of business cards, wear a T-shirt publicizing your Website, meet a lot of people, and gather a lot of material. You will find it well worth your time, and an investment that will help both your short-term and long-term goals.

For more information on what trade shows are available, visit these two Websites:

1. Trade Show News Network—www.tsnn.com

2. TS Central—www.tscentral.com

OFFLINE WEB MARKETING IDEA

Create a Brochure

HOW MUCH DOES IT COST? $$$

....WHAT DOES IT DEVELOP? Initial Contact, Loyalty & Trust

A really nice brochure is an essential promotional item to present all the benefits and features of your Website. Unless you are trained in graphic design and copyediting, I would highly recommend that you have your brochure professionally created and published. Here are a few tips to maximize the marketing effectiveness of your brochure:

1. Put a heavy focus on the design of the brochure to make it as nice and eye-catching as possible. Be sure to provide lots of graphics to the people you hire to create your brochure.

2. Be clear on the features and benefits of your Website in your brochure. See the question-and-answer section at the end of this chapter for information on the difference between a feature and a benefit.

3. List contact information in your brochure. This includes your mailing address, phone number (if applicable), email address, fax number, and Website URL. Your Website URL should be mentioned in several places throughout your brochure, since that is the topic of the brochure! This is where a company name the same as your URL (for example, Amazon.com) comes in really handy—every time you mention your company, you are mentioning your URL!

4. Give reasons why a person should visit your Website. While writing your brochure copy, always ask yourself, "Would this influence someone to visit my Website?" Does your brochure copy clearly give reasons why a person should visit?

5. Use a call to action. Be sure to urge the reader in one or two places to visit your Website today (for example, "Visit *Animation Artist Magazine* today by going to **www.animationartist.com**"). Let the reader know what you want him or her to do.

6. Test the brochure first. Make up a dummy brochure before providing your copy to a professional company for designing. Give the dummy brochure to your friends and family, asking what they think—and more specifically, *what they would change or reword.* If you have customers, test it on some of them. Revise your brochure accordingly.

OFFLINE WEB MARKETING IDEA

Give Your Work to Others

HOW MUCH DOES IT COST?   FREE

WHAT DOES IT DEVELOP?   Initial Contact

There are 7,367 employees of the U.S. Veterans Administration whose salaries exceed $100,000 per year.

One of the people I work with has a friend, Daryl Cagle, who draws professional cartoons for newspapers (see cartoon). Daryl also has a Website, and one of the methods he uses to promote his Website is giving away his cartoons, for free, to select media as long as the URL for his Website is included in the credits. For example, I was allowed to republish the cartoon on this page for free as long as Daryl Cagle was given credit and the URL for his Website listed.

What do you have that you can give to others in exchange for promotion? If you produce TV commercials, you could do a public service announcement for a company in exchange for credit, and the listing of your Website URL, in their monthly newsletter. This also helps build you as a participant in charity and the community.

Come up with some creative ideas to exchange your services or product for publicity.

The cartoon on this page is reprinted with the permission of Daryl Cagle. You can find his Website of editorial cartoons at **www.cagle.com**.

OFFLINE WEB MARKETING IDEA

Newspaper and Magazine Ads

HOW MUCH DOES IT COST? $–$$$$$
WHAT DOES IT DEVELOP?   Initial Contact, Revisits, Loyalty & Trust

Advertising in print media such as newspapers and magazines is a good way to brand your Website, get new visitors, and get revisits—as long as you are consistent. Advertising campaigns via newspaper and magazine are rarely successful unless they consistently continue for a long duration. This is because the more times a person sees your ad, the more your name becomes embedded in his or her mind and the better chance that the person will pay your Website a visit.

Like a brochure, the ad must be very well designed for maximum efficiency. This may require hiring someone to do it for you. That, coupled with the price of magazine ads, could cost a pretty penny. This could force you to explore alternatives.

Most magazines have a "marketplace" section where buying a long-term ad is much cheaper. Likewise, most newspapers have an Internet advertising section that costs around $30 per listing (depending on the geographical location and distribution).

Look at magazines that will meet your target market, then call those magazines and ask for their media kit. This will give you details on the magazine's distribution prices. Having worked years in the magazine industry, I can assure you that the prices listed are very flexible. Remember Chapter 6, "It Never Hurts to Ask"? Be sure to negotiate a price that is much more favorable to you, and always ask for extras.

For example, when you get to a price that is agreeable to you, tell the sales rep, "I really like your magazine and the value it could bring to me. While the price is still a little steep for me, I will do it if you throw in a 486 × 60 banner ad on the news page of your Website." Many sales representatives usually have specific numbers they have to reach and are more than willing to bargain for "value-added services" in order to close the deal. Go for it.

OFFLINE WEB MARKETING IDEA

Use Your Talents

HOW MUCH DOES IT COST? FREE (you may even get paid!)

WHAT DOES IT DEVELOP?   Initial Contact, Loyalty & Trust

In 1992, I had the privilege of representing the United States in the WCTU speech championships held in Sweden. It was part of a year-long speech competition that required a lot of intense training in public speaking. My trainer was my college professor, Dr. James Chase, who always encouraged his classes to participate in such events. That encouragement led to many future opportunities in the area of public speaking that also paid off with free advertising.

Whenever I address a major gathering, there are usually three key places where I can plug a Website:

1. My written bio that appears on the program handed out to the audience ("Joe Tracy is the editor of *Webmaster Techniques Magazine* at **www.webmaster techniques.com**").

2. The bio information that the person introducing me reads to the audience.

3. Examples within my speech, as long as they are appropriate to the subject matter and enhance the message of the speech.

Since most places pay money and all expenses for speaking engagements, it is the equivalent of getting paid to do something I love while getting free advertising for my Websites.

Enhance your talents, then use them for occasions where you can provide a service to the public while getting free advertising for your Website in return. Make sure other people know about your talents, in order to open the door for invitations.

OFFLINE WEB MARKETING IDEA

Send Web Cards

HOW MUCH DOES IT COST? $$

WHAT DOES IT DEVELOP?   Initial Contact

Web Cards are a fairly recent unique marketing tool that is gaining in popularity. A Web Card is like an oversized postcard with a picture of the front page of your Website pictured on the front. You can then send these Web Cards to friends, family, customers, and potential clients. In addition, you can put a customized message on the front of the Web Card.

I was introduced to Web Cards when I stumbled across the URL **www.printing .com**. It happens to be owned by a company called Web Cards.

Domain Marketing Misstep—www.printing.com

While **www.printing.com** is a great URL, the primary purpose of the Website is Web Cards, which the site has been doing for quite a while. So it came as a surprise to me that the URL **www.webcards.com** remained open until September 19, 1999 (many months after **www.printing.com** had been doing Web Cards), when a person in France reserved it.

Be alert when it comes to domain names; if you have a good idea or product, be sure to immediately reserve the URL of the name of that idea or product. When I was writing this section, the first place I went to was **www.webcards.com**, before having to check my bookmarks to discover that the Web Cards location is **www.printing.com**.

I recommend that you go to **www.printing.com** and check out the Web Cards. There is even an address where you can send for free samples. In addition, you can download a brochure on Web Cards (smart marketing). There is even a "10 Best Ways to Use Web Cards" list.

OFFLINE WEB MARKETING IDEA

    Create a CD-ROM

    HOW MUCH DOES IT COST? $$
....WHAT DOES IT DEVELOP?   Initial Contact, Loyalty & Trust

The CD-ROM is the most underused marketing medium available today. A CD-ROM can bring out a wonderful multimedia experience for the user that can also be a strong branding effort for you.

The team that created the cover of this book is the epic software group (**www.epicsoftware.com**). This company specializes in creating multimedia CD-ROMs. Knowing the importance of a CD-ROM in marketing, the epic software group has created a "demo CD-ROM" that you can request from their Website.

Let's take a closer look at CD-ROMs for a second.

1. Nearly every computer sold has a CD-ROM drive.

2. Duplicating CD-ROMs costs around $1 each.

3. There are many cool CD-ROM packages for people who aren't programmers.

So why don't you have a company CD-ROM out in the marketplace? If you don't have the resources to do it yourself, find someone who does. Create a killer multimedia experience and start mass-distributing it. It can be an excellent tool to portray the benefits of your Website to potential visitors, advertisers, and investors.

Visit **www.webmastertechniques.com/webmarketing/** for a flash animation, courtesy of epic software group, on "10 Steps to Producing a Successful Multimedia CD-ROM Presentation."

OFFLINE WEB MARKETING IDEA 11

Use Business Cards and Stationery

HOW MUCH DOES IT COST? $$

WHAT DOES IT DEVELOP?   Initial Contact, Revisits, Loyalty & Trust

This idea is almost too obvious to list, except that most Websites don't have business cards and stationery!

Carry business cards with you at all times, handing them out to everyone you meet. In the business world, it is only proper to exchange business cards when going into meetings. It can be embarrassing to say, "I don't have one."

If you have company business cards, the company's Website URL and your email address must be listed on it. In many ways, a URL and your email address are more important than a phone number these days. You would probably never distribute a business card without a phone number; likewise you should never distribute it without a URL and email address.

Website-branded stationery and envelopes are also important, because you never know when you will have to send a snail-mail letter to another individual. In Offline Web Marketing Idea #3, I told you about a woman who handwrote us a letter. The only method we had to contact her was snail mail.

Always have a handy supply of Website-branded business cards, letterhead, and envelopes.

OFFLINE WEB MARKETING IDEA 12

Join Associations

HOW MUCH DOES IT COST? **$$**

....WHAT DOES IT DEVELOP?   **Initial Contact, Loyalty & Trust**

Joining associations is a great way to network—and, as a follow-up to the previous idea, many people exchange business cards there.

One of the first places you'll want to look at joining is your local chamber of commerce. It will cost you money to join, but if the group is active, the benefits you'll receive back are at least fivefold:

1. You'll be able to network with other local business leaders.

2. You'll be able to list your URL in the chamber of commerce directory.

3. You'll be able to suggest yourself as a speaker on certain topics for chamber of commerce meetings.

4. You may be given the opportunity to "sponsor" a meeting.

5. You'll be able to hand out a lot of business cards!

It is important to be involved as much as possible in community events, not out of a desire to market, market, and market, but rather out of a desire to "give back to the community." Marketing can't buy this type of sincerity.

Look into other associations to join, both inside and outside your community. Before you know it, you will have a team of strong allies to assist you and to participate with you in co-marketing opportunities.

OFFLINE WEB MARKETING IDEA

Offer a Local Seminar

HOW MUCH DOES IT COST? $$$

....WHAT DOES IT DEVELOP?   Initial Contact, Participation

If your Website covers a specialized market, you may be able to use local seminars to draw more interest to your Website. Of course, the purpose of the seminar isn't to promote your site. That's a side benefit. The purpose is to promote concepts and solutions that deal with a specialized market.

For example, let's take *Webmaster Techniques Magazine* as an example. There are a number of great seminars I can offer locally that would have ties to *Webmaster Techniques Magazine*. Here are three seminar topics I could cover:

1. Unleashing the power of Web marketing on your Website.

2. How to turn your Website into a community portal.

3. Twenty methods for ranking high in search engine results.

To hold a seminar, you have to keep a number of things in mind:

1. Where will it be held?

2. What day and time will it be?

3. Who will assist you in registering attendees and other activities?

4. How will you advertise and market the seminar?

5. What materials will you provide your guests?

6. Will it be free or cost money?

Attend a few seminars in your community before holding your own. If you're not a good presenter, get someone who is. On the materials you provide your guests, make sure the URL for your Website is listed at the bottom of every page. Include a write-up about your Website and how it can benefit the attendees.

OFFLINE WEB MARKETING IDEA

Create a Radio or TV Commercial

HOW MUCH DOES IT COST? $$–$$$$
....WHAT DOES IT DEVELOP?   Initial Contact, Loyalty & Trust

The cost of producing a radio or TV commercial could be cheaper than you think, depending on what type of market you are in. For example, some markets have Cable TV commercials as low as $8 per airing. Sure, you have to buy a package plan of 25+ commercials, but at $8 per airing, that's a great price. If you have a lot of money to put into TV commercials, look at your local network affiliates (CBS, ABC, NBC, Fox), which usually charge three- or four-figure prices *per commercial*. Remember what we learned in Chapter 6—these prices are negotiable *if you ask*.

Your TV commercial success will only be as good as the TV commercial you produce, so don't skimp on the quality of the TV commercial production. Ask to see many samples of a company's work before hiring them to do your commercial. Besides the actual production, also study things such as the quality of the sound and picture and how well the selected background music goes with the scene. Be sure to ask for a script and storyboard in advance of finalizing the filming. Show these to your friends and associates to get their opinions. Then let the crew work its magic to bring the production to life.

A production company may tell you that they can schedule the TV commercials for you at the same rate the stations charge. The reason they are eager to do this is because most will get a 15 percent cut of what you pay if you schedule through them. Use this to your advantage and tell them, "I understand you will get a 15 percent commission if I book through you. If we can negotiate the production fees a little, I'd be more than happy to do the booking through you."

You don't always have to go through a production company. Many TV stations and cable stations can also film a TV commercial for you.

Most radio stations also have reasonable prices. A lot are willing to also barter or bargain, depending on what you have to offer in return. Radio stations generally create the radio commercial for you, and some will do it for free, depending on how many commercial slots you purchase.

Whatever media you select for advertising, make sure they are part of a strategic plan so you are getting maximum exposure for a lengthy period of time. *Consistency* is the key.

OFFLINE WEB MARKETING IDEA

   Send Thank-You Cards with Your URL

   HOW MUCH DOES IT COST? $$
....WHAT DOES IT DEVELOP?   Initial Contact, Loyalty & Trust

Whenever you have concluded a service for a customer, be sure to follow up with a thank-you card. Also, be sure that your URL is listed on that thank-you card!

Few companies take the time to follow up their services with a thank-you card for the client. Yet such measures just help separate you from your competitors. In today's rush-rush society, customer service has been thrown away by many companies. To some, it is all about money and nothing else. That's why providing excellent customer service instantly sets you apart from the majority of other companies—because it is rare. Practice excellent customer service on a daily basis.

Thank-you cards aren't just for offline services. If you conduct an interview with someone for your Website or receive an article contribution, be sure to follow that up with a thank-you card to the person.

The idea of thank-you cards can also work in conjunction with Web Cards, as discussed in Offline Web Marketing Idea #9. You can have a picture of the front page of your Website with the words "Thank You" on the front of the card and a handwritten message on the back. It takes only a few moments of your time, but does what years worth of branding could never do.

OFFLINE WEB MARKETING IDEA 16

Offer Free Reports

HOW MUCH DOES IT COST? $$

....WHAT DOES IT DEVELOP?   Initial Contact, Loyalty & Trust

In Chapter 2, we discussed offering free reports to other Websites in order to publicize your URL. This idea doesn't have to be limited to the Web. Tens of thousands of newsletters are published on a regular basis that are desperate for material. Why not send free reports to some of these publications, with the only stipulation for printing being the listing of your URL in the credits?

Here's another idea: Why not create a free report that isn't offered on the Web, but is promoted on your Website to help you build your mailing list? Here's an example of what you'd stick on your Website:

FREE REPORT—50 Techniques for Branding Your Website

With today's tough competition on the Web, branding is becoming the key that sets one Website apart from another. Now there is a free report, "50 Techniques for Branding Your Website," that will provide you with the knowledge you need to gain a competitive edge on your competitor while building the loyalty and trust of your visitors. To receive this report, available only via snail mail, email your name and address to freereport@webmastertechniques.com.

There are literally dozens of ways, such as this technique, to use free reports to help build a database or further market your Website. For the record, the free report mentioned here does not exist (yet)—but stay tuned to www.webmastertechniques.com; you never know when other similar free reports may become available.

OFFLINE WEB MARKETING IDEA

Offer Promotional Coupons

HOW MUCH DOES IT COST? $$

WHAT DOES IT DEVELOP?   Initial Contact, Participation

If your Website sells products or memberships, you will want to give serious consideration to using offline promotional coupons to help drive traffic and participation.

Here's how an offline promotional coupon works:

1. You get a database of names and addresses that fits your target audience for your Website. This could include your offline customer list if you are a small-business owner.

2. Prepare a printed coupon that has a tempting offer (for example, "$20 off any purchase in our online store"). Make sure you have a code tracking system in place so that the coupons can be used only once!

3. Mail out the coupons along with your brochure and a personalized letter introducing your Website or service. In all mass promotions I've ever done, I have always hand-signed each letter in a different-colored pen. If someone on the receiving end is going to take the time to read my offer, then I can take the time to sign it! Besides, people can always tell whether a stamp was used for the signature (very impersonal, even if it is practical).

1. Track the usage and effectiveness of the campaign so that you can evaluate it for a possible wider audience. Use smaller markets to test different promotional ideas. When one hits that is hot, run with it.

OFFLINE WEB MARKETING IDEA

:   Conduct Focus Groups
:
:
:   HOW MUCH DOES IT COST? $$$
:....WHAT DOES IT DEVELOP?   Initial Contact, Participation

There is a reason politicians spend tens of thousands of dollars on regular focus groups. It is because *focus groups work* at arming you with vital information to reach a larger audience.

Focus groups are very delicate to put together, which is why there are large companies that charge tens of thousands of dollars to conduct just one focus group. These companies, however, take into account all vital information, such as demographics, background, location, and affiliations. They even provide the host for the focus groups, create the questionnaire or session with you, and so on. The whole process is based on in-depth research to give you an appropriate feel for mass opinion. Participants are also paid for their time.

Generally, focus groups are held in meeting rooms of local hotels. If you are ever asked to be in one, which is always filmed, and you see a cord going from the camera under the door, you will know that there are people in another room watching everything you say and do. The person conducting the focus group will then "take a break," but is actually going to the other room to retrieve any follow-up questions.

It is possible to put together your own focus group on a limited budget. I would highly recommend that you study up on focus groups in detail and how to determine exactly who should be a participant.

What type of things would you want to look for in a focus group of your own? Anything from "What keeps a person on a Website?" to "What would cause you to make a purchase from a smaller Website?" The possibilities are endless and the research is *yours*. Listen closely to the results of a focus group and make recommended changes so that you can better serve your customers and maximize your marketing.

OFFLINE WEB MARKETING IDEA

   Write Articles for Print Magazines

   HOW MUCH DOES IT COST?   FREE (you may even get paid!)
   ....WHAT DOES IT DEVELOP?   Initial Contact, Loyalty & Trust

A great way to get traffic to your Website, while branding the professionalism of your site, is to write some killer articles for print publications.

As a former editor and associate publisher of print magazines, I can tell you that editors are always looking for really strong talent. If you have a gift for writing and an in-depth knowledge of the field your Website covers, then start writing some print articles. Not only will you get paid money, but you can list your URL in your bio that most magazines put at the end of an article. Being published in a good magazine can do a number of things for you:

1. It will bring extra traffic to your Website.

2. It will establish you as a professional in the field.

3. It will bring in some extra cash that you can spend on your Website.

4. It could result in more opportunities.

When I was editor of a 3D magazine, I once received a tutorial from a new writer named Dave. The quality and depth of his tutorial astounded me. I printed it, then signed him to a contract for the magazine. After a year of writing for me, I asked him to do a book with me and another author. He ended up providing the bulk of the material, with huge tutorials of 150+ steps with dozens of photos. About eight months after the book came out, he was hired by Foundation Imaging, a premiere special effects facility producing animation work for top TV shows such as the *Star Trek* series.

It all started because Dave took the time to submit a killer tutorial; now he is fulfilling one of his life's dreams (to work on Hollywood projects). Put your heart and soul into your work and don't be afraid to submit it for possible publication.

Seek out magazines you are interested in via the Internet. Go to the magazine's Web site and look for submission rules. Strictly follow the submission guidelines and send your article off. If it gets rejected, don't give up. Many successful writers had dozens of articles rejected before reaching fame.

OFFLINE WEB MARKETING IDEA

    Sponsor an Event or Sports Team

    HOW MUCH DOES IT COST? $$$
....WHAT DOES IT DEVELOP?   Initial Contact, Loyalty & Trust

Many local groups are always looking for sponsors of different events. Most of the time, that sponsorship is in the form of money donated for a specific purpose. For example, many Little League teams look for uniform sponsors in exchange for your name on the back of the uniforms. Many schools are looking for companies to place yearbook ads. Why not your Website?

As you become more successful on the Web and apply the budget strategy (mentioned in Chapter 2) to create a marketing budget, you will have more opportunities to spend the marketing money. This is a great opportunity to farm out into your local community more by spending some of that money on local events, educational purposes, and sponsorships.

As a general rule of thumb you'll find that the more you spend, the more you will be solicited. So be sure to carefully plan in advance what you want to do so that you don't overspend on the local market and not enough on the Internet market.

Local sponsorship opportunities are everywhere. When I was doing video productions, we use to create videos for a school that raised money to pay for the videos by selling 30-second sponsorship ads in the videos. It was explained at the beginning of the video that the sponsors are what made the video possible, which created deeper respect for the sponsors rather than annoyance from the ads.

Yearbooks are a good place for Website advertisements that will be around for years. Video yearbooks are also a great source for multimedia sponsorships. As you go about your business throughout the community, become more alert to the opportunities around you. Also, use your contacts in the chamber of commerce to identify good possibilities.

OFFLINE WEB MARKETING IDEA

Participate in Movie Theater Slide Shows

HOW MUCH DOES IT COST? $$$
....WHAT DOES IT DEVELOP?   Initial Contact, Loyalty & Trust

Many movie theaters have found a great way to generate extra income—showing slide advertisements before a movie begins. Some theaters are very reasonable in their pricing, while others are outrageously high. Be sure to check with theater management for a full list of costs, and remember that you can always ask for a cheaper rate!

While participating with a slide advertisement can help your initial contact to a small degree, the real purpose is for branding. Selecting this technique should not be a random event. It must be part of your strategic plan to increase community awareness about your Website. So it might fit into a plan as follows:

Six-Week Branding Campaign

Cable TV Commercials
Local Country Station Radio Commercials
Local Rock Station Radio Commercials
Hosting of Chamber of Commerce Meeting
Listing in Newspaper Internet Guide
Slides in Local Movie Theaters

What you are doing is hitting everyone in your community with your identity at every possible opportunity. You are strategically branding your image as much as possible so that people begin to become more curious, to the point of action (going to your Website).

The theater may want to charge you a hefty price to create the slide for you. If this is the case, look around locally for someone to create it. Since your slide is being projected on a large screen, be sure to make your URL VERY LARGE (for extra emphasis). Be careful, however, to maintain consistency in the look of all your branding techniques and the general theme for the duration of the campaign.

OFFLINE WEB MARKETING IDEA 22

Take Out a Phone Book Advertisement

HOW MUCH DOES IT COST? $$

WHAT DOES IT DEVELOP?   Initial Contact

Many phone books now have an Internet directory section of the phone book. Be sure you are listed there if there is a local version and the price isn't too expensive. Also, the regular Yellow Pages area is another great advantage to companies who have ".com" as part of their business name (for example, Amazon.com) because you can list your company's name and URL in the same word.

If you are a small business that normally takes out a small ad in the Yellow Pages, remember that your URL and email address are just as vital as your phone number. Many people use the Internet to communicate, so make sure that both your URL and email address are worked into the design of your ad.

At some point you may be approached by someone who makes "Yellow Pages book covers" and wants to sell you an ad for these covers, which are distributed to "thousands of people and businesses." My advice: Don't do it. The first year I was approached with this idea, I did it. Having tracking methods in place for business, I can let you know that not one single person ever called us as the result of a Yellow Pages book cover ad.

Should you purchase color in your ad? That depends on how much you can afford and whether the phone book has worked well for you in the past. It's interesting, because on rare occasions some pages are filled with so many color ads that the black-only ad actually draws the most attention.

OFFLINE WEB MARKETING IDEA

   Give Radio Interviews

   HOW MUCH DOES IT COST? FREE to $

....WHAT DOES IT DEVELOP?   Initial Contact

Did you know that there are entire Websites, such as **www.radioguests.com**, that are dedicated to getting you on the radio? Being a radio guest can be an excellent boost to your Website. Before pursuing this as a unique marketing option for your Website, first answer the following questions:

1. What do you have to say that will be interesting to thousands of listeners?

2. How well do you communicate when put on the spot?

3. What are your credentials for speaking on a specific topic?

4. Can you deliver a strong message?

The type of guest desired for a radio show depends much on the show itself. Some radio shows are serious, and others are humorous, with stories that sound almost made-up.

Radio shows are interested in what interesting and valuable material you can provide to guests. This means less promotion of your Website and more substance for the listeners.

OFFLINE WEB MARKETING IDEA

    Write a Letter to the Editor

    HOW MUCH DOES IT COST? FREE

    WHAT DOES IT DEVELOP?   Initial Contact

Sharing your professional opinion in the Letters to the Editor section of a newspaper or magazine could get you some contact. However, the strength of your opinion could have a positive or negative branding effect. With that in mind, you may want to be careful with the topic you address in your letter, unless your goal is to create controversy.

The key is to get the URL of your Website listed. The best way to accomplish this is to use your URL as your business title; when you sign the letter, add your position title and URL (for example, "Joe Tracy, Publisher—animationartist.com"). This still isn't a guarantee that the URL won't be edited out, but should increase the chances that it remains.

Letters to the editor can have a strong short-term effect at bringing new traffic to your Website. Seek out a number of different avenues and look for interesting topics to expand upon with your expertise.

OFFLINE WEB MARKETING IDEA

Partner with an Offline Company

HOW MUCH DOES IT COST? FREE

WHAT DOES IT DEVELOP?   Initial Contact, Loyalty & Trust

In Chapters 2 and 3 we discussed the importance of networking with other online Websites—creating allies. That same advice is equally important for you to do offline. Find some great offline relationships that can benefit both parties. Look for some interesting networking options. For example:

> MapQuest provides online maps and online driving directions. They could form a great networking relationship with AAA, which provides printed maps to members. A joint venture could help promote both companies.

> The auction site eBay recently bought out a real-life auction company to start broadening its auction program to offline media.

> Even at *Animation Artist Magazine,* we have looked into possible networking relationships with a printed animation magazine. Readers could get the best of both worlds.

Keep an eye out for a good opportunity that can create equal value between your online venture and someone's offline venture.

OFFLINE WEB MARKETING IDEA 26

Create a Calendar

HOW MUCH DOES IT COST? $$
....WHAT DOES IT DEVELOP? Initial Contact, Loyalty & Trust

Calendars make popular gift ideas and are relatively inexpensive to create. So why not make a bunch with a focus on your industry? You can add your Website URL to every calendar page. Use catchy photos and interesting facts to make the calendar interesting, then start a mass distribution campaign around Christmas. Mail the calendar to your customers, those who help you on your Website, friends, family—everyone!

Let's say that you distributed 2,000 calendars and only 15 percent of the calendars you distributed were used on a regular basis. That's 300 people using your calendar every day and having your name and message consistently branded to them. In addition, you receive extra branding points for sending the calendars out as a surprise gift. Even if a person doesn't use it, he or she will be pleased that you thought of them.

The twelve-month calendars with pictures aren't your only option. You can also purchase large desk calendars that come in a custom-made holder. These are generally cheaper because the only part customized is the calendar holder. You can also find small desktop calendars that you can personalize.

If you want to search for your calendar solution online, go to your favorite search engine and type in "custom calendars."

OFFLINE WEB MARKETING IDEA

Take a Team to Charity Events

HOW MUCH DOES IT COST?   FREE

....WHAT DOES IT DEVELOP?   Initial Contact, Loyalty & Trust

Being involved in charity events on a regular basis is a great contribution to your community and an equally great development of loyalty and trust. For example, why not organize a number of your friends, family, and staff to participate in a specific charity walk-a-thon. Invite your Website visitors to come along. Have everyone wear your Website's T-shirt at the event or have T-shirts made specifically for the event (for example, "Animation Artist for March of Dimes").

Use the opportunity to create a press release. Even if none of the news media republish it, you will have it in your online press area and it will show that you are actively involved in community and charity efforts.

Another idea is to conduct a major event, with a team, where the proceeds go to charity. For example, take out a food or game booth at a school or community fair and donate 50 percent (or 100 percent) of the proceeds to a specific charity organization.

You'll find that doing something entertaining and fun, with proceeds going to charity, can increase your chance of getting press coverage.

OFFLINE WEB MARKETING IDEA 28

Advertise on Billboards

HOW MUCH DOES IT COST? $$$$$
....WHAT DOES IT DEVELOP?   Initial Contact

Billboards are huge and expensive, but they are great branding tools if you can afford the cost. Some billboards are unique enough that they generate tens of thousands of dollars in free press. Here's an example.

In early 1999, 24-Hour Fitness launched a billboard campaign that showed aliens arriving on Earth with the words, "When they come, they'll eat the fat ones first." The message, of course, was to "get in shape at 24-Hour Fitness." While the billboard was definitely unique and creative, it created a controversy for some people, who claimed it was making fun of fat people. The National Association to Advance Fat Acceptance (NAAFA) launched a demonstration against 24-Hour Fitness over the campaign. San Francisco (where the campaign began) supervisor Tom Ammiano proposed a new law, two days after protests began, to protect fat people under the city's antidiscrimination laws.

The demonstrations caused the press to focus on the issue, and pictures of the billboard started appearing in newspapers everywhere. For those who thought it was a very creative campaign, which seemed to be the majority, the message and branding were very strong and effective. The billboard ended up reaching millions of people throughout the world by pictures being republished in magazines and online.

Study billboard campaigns in depth before launching one. You must keep in mind that the average driver has only a few seconds to read a billboard. That means fewer words and more visual impact.

"JUST FOR FUN" OFFLINE WEB MARKETING IDEA

Solicit Customer Tattoos

HOW MUCH DOES IT COST? $$$

.... WHAT DOES IT DEVELOP?   Initial Contact, Revisits

Here's something different for you. One day I was watching the news and a story aired about a unique way one restaurant was literally "branding" its business. The business told its patrons that it would give a free lunch, every day, to anyone who would get the restaurant's logo tattooed on their body. The logo had to be clearly distinguishable, and in order to get the free lunch, the patron had to show the tattoo. The restaurant actually had a number of takers! People were being "branded" for free lunches. The marketing idea obviously worked well for this company, because it was an interesting enough story for the press to pick up and run with it. The business received tens of thousands of dollars in free advertising.

This story goes to show that there are new, unique ways of marketing out there. I'm not going to recommend that you start having your visitors tattoo your logo on them for free memberships, but I will recommend that you do some creative thinking when coming up with marketing ideas.

One of my Website projects for 2000 is a place I call "The Creativity Factory." Located at **www.creativityfactory.com**, it is a place I am working to build into a creative-thinking environment where people can create and celebrate new ideas. Creative marketing is one of the aspects of this venture. Sometimes it is the unique marketing that gives you the needed attention to make your Website soar.

QUESTIONS AND ANSWERS

QUESTION: In Offline Web Marketing Idea #1, you suggest sending announcements out to your customers. In my situation, however, I don't maintain mailing addresses of customers. So how can I send announcements?

ANSWER: If one way fails, you need to look for a creative alternative. For example, let's say that you manage a small souvenir store and you've just opened up a gift-idea Website. Why not pre-stuff announcements into the bags that you put customer purchases into? If a tip doesn't apply directly to you, try to think up a creative solution to still make the tip work!

QUESTION: In Offline Web Marketing Idea #2, you talk about adding a URL to your car. Will this work with any car?

ANSWER: Keep in mind that the quality and uniqueness of your car can affect the perception of the message. For example, if I'm driving a dented, beat-up 1982 car, the impact of having a URL on that car could be negative—unless the URL is something like **www.repairyourcar .com**. In that case it might be very effective. Generally, the nicer or more unique the car, the better the results will be.

You don't have to use the car finish for your URL either. As in the previous answer, try creative alternatives. How about putting the URL on your back window or maybe across the entire back of your bumper?

QUESTION: In Offline Web Marketing Idea #5, you talk about creating a brochure and mention the importance of being clear on the features and benefits. What is the difference between a feature and a benefit?

ANSWER: Great question! Features and benefits are often confused. In short, a feature is usually something *physical and descriptive,* while a benefit is something more *mental and meaningful*. For example, a *feature* of *Animation Artist Magazine* is that it is *updated every day of the week*, 365 days a year. A *benefit* of *Animation Artist Magazine* is that it is *convenient* for quickly finding recent animation news. To help further demonstrate the difference between features and benefits, here are some more examples:

Feature of M&Ms: They come in a candy shell.

Benefit of M&Ms: They melt in your mouth, not in your hands.

Feature of Brand X phone: The phone is cordless.

Benefit of Brand X phone: You can talk anywhere in the house.

Feature of Animation Radio (**www.animationradio.com**): Popular radio music available 24 hours a day via the Internet.

Benefit of Animation Radio: You can enjoy great music while you surf the Web.

Once you come up with a feature, simply ask yourself, "So what does that mean?" to get the benefit. If a feature of a bakery is "All donuts made fresh every day," then *what does that mean?* It means that "The donuts taste better." There is your benefit.

QUESTION: Can't focus group questions be slanted?

ANSWER: Yes, they can, which is why it is important to have a professional team create unbiased questions for you (or to make an extra effort to ensure that all your questions are unbiased). Biased questions are asked all the time, especially by media Websites. For example, on October 16, 1999, AOL asked:

"After five years and $47 million worth of investigations into various Clinton-related allegations ranging from Whitewater to the travel office firings to Monica Lewinsky, Kenneth Starr will step down next week from his role as independent counsel. Now you can pass judgment on him:

▶ Good luck, Ken. You fought tirelessly to expose corruption and wrongdoing.

▶ Good riddance. Your politically motivated witch-hunts have been expensive embarrassments.

▶ Who cares?

▶ Who's Ken Starr?"

The way the question is asked creates a slant for the most popular answer to be #2—"Good riddance"—because it puts the $47 million blame directly on Ken Starr. Likewise the question could have been set up to get "Good luck" as the most popular answer by phrasing it this way:

"Kenneth Starr will step down next week from his role as independent counsel. At the request of Janet Reno, Starr investigated President Clinton, who lied to America and investigators, resulting in the investigation having to go longer than planned and costing American taxpayers over $40 million. Ken is now leaving to spend more time with his family. What message would you like to send him?"

As you can see, the way you phrase the question can determine what the most popular answer will be. This does you no good as a marketer seeking unbiased research.

In our example, AOL could have made the question more unbiased by leaving judgments (for example, blame for the $47 million) out of the question. It should have simply asked:

"Ken Starr has resigned as independent counsel. Your message to him is:

▶ Good luck.

▶ Good riddance."

The rephrased question contains no biased phrases, such as "$47 million" or "pass judgment."

If you ever do questionnaires, focus groups, or surveys, always be careful how you phrase a question. If you want honest answers, don't insert biased words or phrases into the questions.

All of your online and offline Website marketing ideas must be supported with a strong public relations campaign for maximum success. In the next chapter, we'll take a closer look at the role of public relations in marketing.

8 The Role of Public Relations in Web Marketing

Public relations is the art of nurturing relationships with everyone around you (that is, press, visitors, and the community) through effective communication.

Many people confuse the roles of public relations and marketing, often viewing both as the same thing. Hopefully this chapter will not only give you a clear view of the difference, but will also help you use public relations to make your Website clearly stand out from others, because of its focus on visitor relations.

What is the difference between public relations and marketing?

Public Relations Defined
Public relations is the art of nurturing
relationships with everyone around you
(that is, press, visitors, and the community)
through effective communication.

1. Public relations is relationship-oriented, while marketing is *results-oriented*.
2. Public relations efforts aim for *positive public opinion,* while marketing efforts aim for *higher traffic or sales.*
3. The focus of public relations is on *public perceptions,* while the focus of marketing is on *the bottom line.*

Even though public relations and marketing have different goals, both use the same media. For example, a press release that goes to the local newspaper, describing a company's involvement with charity, is a public relations effort. Meanwhile, an ad sent to the same newspaper to promote the company's service is a clear marketing effort. Both use the same medium, but have different goals. For public relations, the goal is to *increase public awareness* and *positive vibes* toward the company. For marketing, the goal is to *obtain more business* for the company.

Our focus in this chapter is to analyze the following four areas of public relations in greater detail:

Press Relations | Visitor Relations
Community Relations | Relations Training

- ► Press relations (writing and distributing press releases)
- ► Visitor relations (building better visitor perceptions of your Website)
- ► Community relations (building local support for your efforts)
- ► Training for better relations (applying public relations to your daily life)

Press Relations

Press relations involves knowing who the press people are in your marketplace, submitting press releases and press kits to these key individuals, immediately answering any press inquiries, and building a sense of goodwill and openness between your company and press contacts. It also means subscribing to the media to whom you send press releases and knowing everything possible about the publications.

Your main contact with the press is through the distribution of press releases. The next several pages will discuss writing press releases, distributing releases, creating press kits, and a list titled "10 Ways to Turn Press People against You." Let's start with press releases.

All about Press Releases

A major function of public relations is the creation and distribution of press releases. Here is a sample press release that was put out by *Animation Artist Magazine* on October 19, 1999. After the press release, we'll break down the elements.

FOR IMMEDIATE RELEASE
October 19, 1999

Contact:
Joe Tracy, Publisher
Animation Artist Magazine
805-566-2994
jtracy@animationartist.com

New Screening Room Encourages Public Critique
of Animator and Student Images

(Santa Barbara) Animation Artist Online Magazine – **www.animation artist.com**—has unveiled an innovative online method for animators and students to have their drawings and 3D images critiqued by peers. Called the Screening Room—**www.animationartist.com/screeningroom/**—artists can have their work posted in a special online room where the public can analyze and critique the image. After a period of three weeks, the image is removed and the artist is encouraged to implement the suggested changes. Once the changes are implemented, both the "before" and "after" picture are put on display in the Final Cut room.

"The Screening Room is a great place for animators and students to increase their skills through valuable feedback from their peers," says Vicki Tracy, editor of *Animation Artist Magazine*. "We have created the first online environment for images to go through a thorough review process."

Rooms are split into three categories: Professional Animators, Aspiring/ Student Animators, and Young Animators (ages 7–14). The artist's name, image title, description, and questions the artist wants answered are displayed with the image. The public then views the image and fills out an easy online form to submit a critique.

Animators who use 3D programs—like Maya, SoftImage, LightWave, and 3D Studio MAX—are encouraged not to state which program was used to help create the image. Tracy says this is because she doesn't want those reviewing the images to form a bias from knowing which software assisted in the creation of the image. She wants the focus to be purely on improving the image, regardless of the software used.

George Alexa, the father of 12-year-old Christian James Alexa (currently featured in the Young Artists Screening Room) was thrilled to find this resource for his son's work to be critiqued. Christian already speaks French and Latin and plays the cello in the string ensemble for the Northern Virginia Youth Symphony. Since Christian has never taken drawing lessons, the Animation Artist Online Screening Room is turning out to be a great avenue for him to get advice from professionals on his drawings. So far he's been getting a lot of thumbs up and good advice for his original image, titled "Boy in Go-Kart."

"Christian has already started to 'upgrade' his picture, using some of the suggestions given by Screening Room visitors," says George Alexa. Once Christian's final image is received back, it will be posted to the Final Cut room for all to admire.

The Screening Room is a free service to all professional, aspiring, student, and young animators/artists.

About *Animation Artist Magazine*
Animation Artist Magazine is the nation's leading online magazine provider of animation content and interactive features. *Animation Artist Magazine* is updated 365 days a year, including holidays (even Christmas). Interactive areas on the Website include animation postcards, forums, Animation Artist Playland, and the Screening Room. The Website is located at **www.animation artist.com**. The Screening Room is located at **www.animationartist.com/ screeningroom/**.

###

Editors, please direct reader inquiries about *Animation Artist Magazine* to **www.animationartist.com** or **info@animationartist.com**. If you would like images for your story, call Joe Tracy at 805-566-2994 or email him via **jtracy@animationartist.com**.

ELEMENTS OF A PRESS RELEASE

Now that you've seen a sample press release, let's break it down to understand the various elements.

Step #1: In the top left-hand corner, place the words FOR IMMEDIATE RELEASE.

Step #2: Directly under FOR IMMEDIATE RELEASE, place the date of the release.

Step #3: Leave a blank line (double return).

Step #4: Type the word "Contact:"

Step #5: Under "Contact:" list the name, title, phone number, and email address of the person that press people should contact if they need further information regarding the release.

Step #6: Leave a blank line (double return).

Step #7: Type in the headline for your release. The more interesting you can make it, the better. In this case, my title was "New Screening Room Encourages Public Critique of Animator and Student Images." In creating this headline, I was hoping to pique an interest in what the Screening Room is, while appealing to a large audience (public, animators, students). As a general rule of thumb, don't exceed fifteen words in your headline.

Step #8: Leave a blank line (double return).

Step #9: In parentheses, place the city where your press release is originating. In this case, *Animation Artist Magazine* is located in Santa Barbara, California, so the city is named as "(Santa Barbara)."

Step #10: To the right of the location (in this example, "Santa Barbara") begin typing in the first paragraph of your press release. You want to answer the following questions (not necessarily in this order):

1. **Who?** In this case, the "who" is *Animation Artist Magazine.*
2. **What?** In this case, the "what" is the Screening Room for artists to post their work for critique.
3. **When?** In this case the "when" is immediately, since it was just "unveiled."
4. **Where?** In this case, the "where" is **www.animationartist.com/screeningroom/**.
5. **Why?** In this case, the "why" is to increase animators' skills through valuable feedback.
6. **How?** In this case, the "how" is in online rooms where the public can post critiques by going to **www.animationartist.com/screeningroom/**.

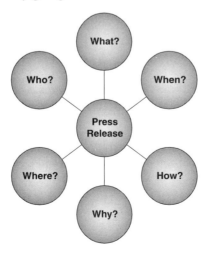

Step #11: At some point, after listing some of the facts, you will want to put a quote from a corporate executive. In this case, the executive was Vicki Tracy, the editor of *Animation Artist Magazine.*

Between each paragraph, be sure to leave an extra line space. Also, remember that quotes start separate paragraphs. When using a quote, be sure to identify the person giving the quote (for example, "says Vicki Tracy, editor of *Animation Artist Magazine*").

Step #12: Find some newsworthy and interesting elements to place throughout the body of your press release. The items we placed to help achieve newsworthiness in this press release were the following:

1. ". . . an innovative online method for animators and students to have their drawings and 3D images critiqued by peers." Notice that we placed this in the first sentence.

2. "Animators who use 3D programs—like Maya, SoftImage, Light-Wave, and 3D Studio MAX—are encouraged not to state which program was used to help create the image." Notice that we listed some popular programs by title and then added an interesting touch by saying that artists are encouraged NOT to state the name of the program.

3. "Christian already speaks French and Latin and plays the cello in the string ensemble for the Northern Virginia Youth Symphony. Since Christian has never taken drawing lessons, the Animation Artist Online Screening Room is turning out to be a great avenue for him to get advice from professionals on his drawings." I believe this is one of the most interesting aspects of the story, and it gives reporters a good angle. Here's this very talented twelve-year-old boy who has avenues for learning different languages and playing instruments professionally, but no outlet for getting advice on his drawings. Animation Artist solved that need. It adds a human interest element to the story.

If you have done any in-depth surveys or have some interesting facts to share (or quote), these are always great items to include in a press release.

Step #13: Quote a second source. You should always quote at least two sources in your press release. In this case the sources were Vicki Tracy and George Alexa. Most companies like to use company executives for both sources. I don't. My preference is to use one company executive (Vicki Tracy) and the successful story of a user (George Alexa and his son, Christian). I think the latter adds more of an interesting element to the article.

Step #14: At the end of the body of your press release, add an "About (Your Company or Website)" line, followed by a short paragraph of facts about your company or Website. What does your company or Website do? How many employees do you have? How many locations do you have? Where? Give some general, but short, information that the press should know about your company or Website.

Press Release Length
Keep your press release short. Preferably, it should be fewer than 500 words.

Step #15: Keep your press release short—no more than 500 words. The release you just read was 493 words in length from the title to the ### sign (see Step 16).

Step #16: At the end of your press release, leave a blank (double return) then three consecutive number signs—###. This signifies the end of the release.

Step #17: Leave a blank line (double return).

Step #18: Add two short sentences that tell editors where to direct people who inquire about the story and whom to contact for images. You may also want to describe the images that are available.

CRAFTING AN EFFECTIVE PRESS RELEASE

That's it! You now know the elements for writing a press release. Just knowing the elements, however, does not guarantee that the press release will be used. You must spend considerable time crafting the quality and newsworthiness of your press release.

Your first task is to ask yourself some key questions to make sure your press release has the right focus:

1. What is the purpose of your press release?
2. What do you want your press release to accomplish?
3. What group of people are you trying to reach with your press release?
4. Does the content of your press release properly target the group you are trying to reach?
5. What makes your press release newsworthy?
6. If you were an editor who received 100 press releases a day, what is it about this press release that would catch your interest?

Always read your press release out loud. How does it sound? Does it flow smoothly? Smooth out the rough parts so that it reads more naturally. Show your press release to some friends and see how long it holds their attention. Another good idea is to let the press release sit overnight. Reread it first thing in the morning with a fresh mind.

Remember that there are many different ways you can write a press release. For example, let's take the press release on the Animation Artist Screening Room that we saw earlier. This is one of the hardest types of releases to write, because many press people will see it as just being about a new area opening on a Website. That's not how I want them to see it. I want them to see it as an innovative new service for artists that is not offered elsewhere.

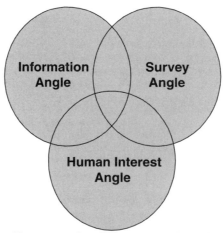

You can take different angles with your press release to increase its chances of being used.

I could have taken many different angles with the Screening Room press release. For this one, I chose the *informational angle,* in which I presented the facts while trying to add some human interest elements to enforce the information.

Likewise, I could have given the whole release a *human interest angle,* in which the entire focus was on the talented twelve-year-old boy. Here's an opening for that type of release:

> (Santa Barbara) Not many 12-year-old boys can speak three languages, play the cello for a professional youth symphony, or draw like an animator without taking any drawing courses. Christian James Alexa is all of those, but it wasn't until he found the Animation Artist Screening Room that he discovered a way to have his drawings critiqued by professional animators. . . .

Now the focus of the press release is very strong in the human interest angle, and in many ways may have a better chance of getting picked up than the information-angle release.

There's also the *survey angle,* in which the focus of the release is on a recent survey and how your product or service plays an important role somehow associated with the results of the survey. Here's an example of that angle (*Note:* I made up the survey for purposes of this demonstration):

> (Santa Barbara) A recent Wallop Poll survey found that when faced with financial difficulties, 90 percent of private schools cut special-interest courses, such as art, from the educational curriculum. The result is that students find it hard to get good training and advice, which is a primary reason why *Animation Artist Magazine* recently opened a Screening Room for people wanting an outlet to have their work evaluated. . . .

As you can see, you can take many different approaches to writing your press release. You may want to write all three for one subject and do limited releases of each to see which has the most success. Then go with that one for your massive release.

If you feel uncomfortable writing your own press release, read on . . .

HAVING SOMEONE ELSE WRITE YOUR PRESS RELEASE

You may prefer to have someone else write your press release. If this is the case, the first place you should check is some of your local public relations companies.

Step #1: Go to "Public Relations" or "Public Relations Counselors" in the Yellow Pages of your local phone book. Call the various companies to get a general idea of how much it would cost for them to write a press release and what the process involves.

Step #2: Make a list of 2 or 3 companies that impressed you the most. Have those companies send you sample press releases they have written or allow you to go to their office to look at samples.

Step #3: From the samples, you should be able to determine which local company does the best job. If the price is right, hire them to write your release. They also may be able to distribute it for you at a decent fee. If not, then look at the next section, "Press Release Distribution."

An alternative to local public relations companies is to find an online company to write your press release. Go to a search engine and search using terms such as "press release writing." I have a convenient list available for you in the *Web Marketing Applied* Online Bonus Area at **www.webmastertechniques.com/ webmarketing/**.

Once you have a release written, you need a way to distribute it to the press.

PRESS RELEASE DISTRIBUTION

So you have a killer press release . . . now what? Now you want it seen by as many people as possible within your targeted group. I've devised a free distribution method and a paid distribution method for you to consider.

Free Distribution Method. If you don't have any money to have your press release professionally distributed, there are still things you can do to get your press release into the public eye. In fact, the press release on the Screening Room in this chapter was distributed using these methods. Here's the step-by-step process:

Step #1: Go to **www.prweb.com**. This is a *free* press release distribution channel. Click on "Add a Release" and follow the directions.

Step #2: Go to a search engine and search for news sites in the category that pertains to your industry. For example, if I were the Webmaster of Dogs Daily and had a press release about my Website, I would search for "dog news." You are trying to find all the sites that publish news about your type of subject matter. If you get some matching results, go to those Websites, find a contact email, and email that person your press release.

Step #3: Go to a newsreader such as **www.deja.com**. You will need to register and become familiar with how it works. Once you're familiar, search for appropriate terms (for example,"dogs") to find newsgroups that deal with that subject. Now post your press releases in these newsgroups. Make sure that the first two words of your subject header are "Press Release:," then add a short title. Do not post your press release to newsgroups that are not relevant to your press release subject!

Step #4: Post the press release in the press area of your own Website. Be sure to use meta tags in the HTML of the page you post it on (see Chapters 2 and 3 for more information on meta tags).

Doing all of this should take two to five hours if done thoroughly. The good news is that it was two to five hours well spent. Where will most of your traffic come from out of the four steps? I've found that newsgroups is where most of my traffic comes from.

Paid Distribution Method.   If you have a budget for press release distribution, then still follow the four steps from the preceding section and then continue with Step #5:

Step #5: Study all the Websites listed here and decide which will be best for your distribution needs.

- ▶ PRW—**www.press-release-writing.com** ($220 per release as of October 1999)

- ▶ Xpress Press—**www.xpresspress.com** ($225 per release as of October 1999)

- ▶ Internet News Bureau—**www.newsbureau.com** ($225 per release as of October 1999)

- ▶ Corporate NEWS—**www.corporatenews.com** ($250 per release as of October 1999)

- ▶ Internet Wire—**www.internetwire.com** ($275 per release as of October 1999)

- ▶ Press Flash—**www.pressflash.com** ($350 per release as of October 1999)

- ▶ URL wire—**www.urlwire.com** ($295–2,000 as of October 1999)

> ▶ **Internet Media Fax—www.imediafax.com** ($.25 per faxed page as of October 1999)

> ▶ **PR Newswire—www.prnewswire.com** (varies—must join "association")

> ▶ **Business Wire—www.businesswire.com** (varies—must join "association")

When opting for one of the paid services, be sure to ask for a discount in advance (ask for a $150 or $175 "first-time rate").

It's a shame that there isn't a good service between the PR Web price range (free) and the $220 price range. Many small businesses or Websites just starting up can't afford $220 or more to reach a wide range of press. It almost makes me want to start such a service. Anyone serious about such an idea? Contact me at **joetracy@earthlink.net**.

Alternatively, you can take the time to put together your own distribution list. A solid day's work of detailed searching on the Web and in a large bookstore (magazines and newspapers) could yield a valuable list that you can use over and over. Plus, since you're searching out all the contacts, your list will be very highly targeted to your medium.

MAKING NEWS

In order for your press release to have a better chance of getting picked up, you must find something truly newsworthy to include. This sometimes means becoming more active in planning and executing events.

For example, let's assume that you run a Website that is an online business environment for your local community—a place where local shops sell stuff in one area (instead of having separate Websites). It is a strategic organizational effort. Now, let's say that this online local business community is having a Christmas sale and your job is to write a press release. Well, the chances of any media covering that are slim to none. It just isn't interesting to readers. So the question is, what can be done to *make* it interesting to readers? Here's where creative thinking comes in:

1. Try to get each company to agree to donate 5 percent of all Christmas proceeds to an important local charity. If they all agree, you have a good news angle and, more important, *you have done a great service.*

2. What if the businesses get together and throw a local Christmas party for foster children as part of the launch of the Christmas sales? There's another news angle and *strong community service.*

Try to think of different ideas that will make each event you do more news-worthy while making a greater contribution to society. It's a great way to get additional coverage.

Let's move on to another interesting area—press relations when it comes to press release distribution. Back in Chapter 3 we discussed the importance of making allies. Some of the biggest allies you can have are the press. They are also the worst enemies you can have. If you want to stay on "neutral-to-ally" ground with the press, beware of the "10 Ways to Turn Press People against You." Avoid all annoyances.

10 WAYS TO TURN PRESS PEOPLE AGAINST YOU

There are ways of getting on the bad side of the press, which is almost a guarantee that you will be ignored. Press people have spam filters too, and most know how to efficiently filter out people who annoy them, so that your email automatically goes into the recipient's trash. Here are the ten ways to turn press people (reporters, editors, and so on) against you:

1. **Misspell the contact's name.** To avoid this annoyance, always double-check to make sure the name *and title* of the press person to whom you are sending your press release is correct.

2. **Use attachments when emailing.** To avoid this annoyance, never send an attachment to a press person unless he or she requests one. Press releases should be pasted in an email message. In the email, you can direct the press person to a Website location for pictures. A major annoyance to press people is when you attach a huge demo version of a product. It's a great way to get permanently filtered.

3. **Call and ask, "Did you get my press release?"** This is one of the bigger annoyances to press people because it happens so often. If you sent it, they received it. If you don't get a call, then they're probably not interested. Calling to ask "Did you get it?" will only mark you as an annoyance.

4. **Send each press release to your contact's email, phone, fax, and snail-mail address.** A press person needs to receive only one copy of your press release, not four! Try to find out the preferred way a person likes to receive press releases, then *use only that method* when sending to that individual.

5. **Call your contact and read your press release word for word.** Talk about annoying! Some people actually call editors and, instead of giving a short rehearsed pitch for a product, actually begin reading a press release word for word. That's just as annoying as a telemarketer calling and reading from a script!

6. **Send a press release with tons of spelling errors.** With today's technological advancements and easy spell-check features, there is no reason why your press release should go out with *any* spelling errors.

7. **Send information that doesn't relate to your contact's publication.** Research a publication before you send a release to that publication. Sending your press release on high-tech mousetraps is not a story for *Airline Comfort* magazine.

8. **Don't include contact information in your press release.** If an editor likes your press release, you'd better have easy ways for him or her to contact you (email, phone, and so on) or your great press release may make it to File 13 (the garbage).

9. **Send the person a book-sized press release.** Press releases should be around 500 to 800 words, not 7,965 words! If the press release looks too long, many press people won't even look at it.

10. **Don't include a headline for your press release.** The headline is one of the most important aspects of a press release, as many press people will use it to determine whether to continue reading. Make yours catchy and newsworthy.

I'd like to comment further about which method to use when sending out a press release. If you have no way of determining the press person's preference, then use email. When working as an editor, I always preferred emailed press releases because if I decided to use information from the release, I could easily copy and paste it into a story instead of having to retype it from a faxed press release. Most press contacts I know also prefer email.

All About Press Kits (and a Tad about Media Kits)

Media kits and press kits are two different things, serving two different purposes. You create a media kit *to interest people in advertising* on your Website, while you send out a press kit *to encourage the press to cover your Website.*

Our main focus here will be the press kit, since it relates more to marketing and public relations. While I'll briefly touch on the media kit, you'll find a much more detailed explanation of it in my upcoming book, *Web Profits Applied.*

MEDIA KITS

Media kits are used to attract advertisers to your Website. A media it can be Internet-based, print-based, or both. It contains vital statistics about your Website, a breakdown of visitor demographics, your advertising prices, and so on. It is given to all potential advertisers. For our purposes, I mention the media kit only so that you know how it differentiates from the press kit, which falls directly under your public relations efforts.

PRESS KITS

Press kits are used to attract press interest to your company or Website. Here is a breakdown of what you need for your press kit:

1. **Press kit folder.** The press kit material will all fit in a standard folder that has two pockets and a slot for your business card. You can have folders professionally printed with your logo on the cover and contact information such as address, email, Website URL, and phone number on the back.

2. **Company background report.** This is a detailed summary of your Website or company, how it was founded, and where it is going. In addition, a biography of each executive and founder (including education, prior experience, and so on) should be included in the background report. Be specific with the background information you provide about your Website; it should properly summarize the history of your Website. Generally this document is two pages in length.

3. **Company fact sheet.** This is a quick list of facts dealing with your Website or company. This includes things such as when your Website

was founded, how many visitors your Website gets a month, and the URL of your home page. Any interesting facts about your Website should go here. Your fact sheet should only be one page in length.

4. **Media coverage.** If you've had any articles (online or offline) written about your Website or company, you will want to include copies in your media kit.

5. **Business card.** You'll need to include a business card, which will go in the business card slot of the press kit.

6. **Recent press releases.** Finally, your press kit needs to contain copies of any recent press releases.

Items 2, 3, and 4 will go in the left-side pocket of the folder and your recent press releases will all go in the right-side pocket. You can include photos or slides if you have such resources.

You are not restricted to these six items for your press kit. For example, you may have a great outline of upcoming features or special events for your Website that you want to include in the press kit. If you have a great print brochure about your Website, put it in! Feel free to include things you see as pressworthy, without getting carried away.

Your goal is to get your press kit into the hands of as many targeted professionals as possible. You should also script a quick letter of introduction that is personalized with the name of the editor or reporter to whom you are sending your press kit.

Visitor Relations

Throughout this book we have discussed the importance of putting your visitor first, responding immediately to emails, and so on. All of these are key aspects of public relations. Your visitors make your Website successful, and you should reward them constantly with the utmost service and respect.

Here are nine steps to improving your relationship with visitors:

Step # 1: Find out what visitors want on your Website. Consider some *private* surveys (meaning the public doesn't see the results) to determine what people want more of on your Website. Leave most of the questions open-ended, so that respondents can type in an answer instead of selecting one from a list. To get increased participation, offer a prize.

Step #2: Evaluate the results of your survey. What was the number one answer? What were number two, number three, and so on? What were some of the more unique and creative requests? Did the number one choice differ between men and women? Make a detailed list of the results.

Step #3: Implement reader requests. From the survey, you now know what visitors want; it is time to create killer new areas based on the most popular and unique answers. Remember not to spill the beans too soon about what you are doing.

Step #4: Give priority attention to visitor requests. If a visitor makes a reasonable request, follow up with the visitor and implement the request immediately. If you know that the request will take one day to implement, email the person and say that you will implement the request within the next seven days. Then email the individual immediately after fulfilling the request (within 24 hours) to let him or her know that it is complete. Be sure to include any URLs to the update. Thank the person for his or her suggestion.

Step #5: Never lie to your visitors, advertisers, or the public. If a situation arises where you were wrong, apologize. Never engage visitors in public debates (unless you are a debate Website), no matter how upset you are.

Step #6: Make someone's day. As discussed later in this chapter, practice daily the art of making another person's day brighter. Practice this in your face-to-face communications (as discussed later in this chapter under "Training for Better Relations") and in your email communications.

Step #7: Make communication easy. Make sure that your Website visitors can easily obtain your email address (or other information) in case they need to contact you.

Step #8: Reward loyal visitors. If you notice a visitor always being active and helpful on your Website (for example, participating regularly in the forums, surveys, and so on), then send that visitor a thank-you email and ask for his or her address to send a T-shirt as a thank you. When you get the address, ship the T-shirt the same day via Priority Mail.

Step #9: Protect your visitors. It seems that every Website you go to these days wants personal information, including your exact birth date and other personal information. This raises some serious concerns, such as "How is this information going to be used?" If you have any type of registration process on your Website, make sure that it never leaves your hands and that you have a privacy statement posted on your Website (see Website Marketing Idea #17 in chapter 2). This will build your credibility.

Having great visitor relations will be a tremendous advantage for your Website, but what happens when a crisis suddenly hits?

Crisis Management and Crisis Action Plans

Because public relations deals with public perceptions, the job of crisis management falls upon the public relations professional. What is crisis management? It is dealing with any major problems that are brought to the attention of the public. For example, the 1989 Exxon oil spill was a major crisis for Exxon. A plane crash is considered a major crisis for the airline. But a crisis isn't always a front-page news event. Money being misspent in a company, brought to the public's attention, is a crisis. A lawsuit against a company is considered a crisis.

Crisis management doesn't disappear on the Web. Every day Websites experience crisis situations. When a big Website such as eBay crashes, it becomes a crisis management situation for eBay, who must reassure the public that the situation is being rectified and measures being put into place so that it doesn't occur again.

Recently, a large provider of free email accounts to Webmasters (for example, yourname@yourcompany.com) had server problems for weeks that made it nearly impossible for tens of thousands of people to retrieve their email. This annoyed Webmasters who were offering the service to users. So those Webmasters started complaining to the email provider. This is a crisis situation.

The key to crisis management is to be prepared in advance for any type of crisis that may strike your Website.

The key to crisis management is to *be prepared in advance* for any type of crisis that may strike your Website. Here are a few scenarios that could happen:

1. Your server goes down and your Website is not accessible for two days or more.

2. Someone starts posting wrongful allegations about your Website in newsgroups.

3. You receive a letter from lawyers claiming that your Website URL violates the trademark of another company.

What would you do if any of these scenarios suddenly struck out of the blue? Plan your response *now* so that if any of these scenarios do strike, you are prepared for a swift reaction. Create a "crisis action plan" that outlines your response to both general and specific crisis scenarios.

For your crisis action plan, keep in mind that all reactions to crisis events could be played out in the public arena. Always be up front, keep your cool, and strive for quick resolutions.

How might a specific scenario be played out in a crisis action plan? Let's take one of the three examples and expand upon it. You can alter the plan according to how large your Website crew is and the circumstances of the situation.

"Website Not Accessible" Crisis Action Plan

▶ If any type of upcoming change (for example, a server change or maintenance) might affect the stability of the Website, post a message in advance alerting visitors to the upcoming change, when the change will happen, and the limited possibility of problems during the change.

▶ If the Website ever becomes inaccessible, immediately contact technical support, via phone or pager, to determine exactly what the problem is and what the estimated time is for the problem to be fixed.

▶ Arrange an emergency meeting with Website staff to discuss the problems and the assigned roles each will take during the duration of the crisis.

▶ If the problem is determined to be long-term, send a message to all email newsletter subscribers describing the problem. If it is determined that the problem will last more than two days, then announce that daily updates will take place via the email newsletter. *Apologize* for the problem and let readers know exactly what happened.

▶ Send an announcement to all strategic partner Websites so that they can post a notice concerning the downtime of the Website. Make sure the announcement contains newsletter subscription information and an alert that updates will take place in the newsletter until the Website is back up.

▶ Publish a news alert to all newsgroups relating to the industry your Website covers. Give subscription information for the newsletter and an announcement that updates will be posted directly to the newsletter until the Website is back up.

▶ Answer any press inquiries about the downtime immediately. Keep the press fully apprised of the situation. Set up an alert page at a different URL and post all updates. Give the URL to the press and make sure the page contains all the phone numbers of important contacts regarding the situation.

▶ When Website service is restored, post an *apology* with a commitment to fully determine and eliminate the cause of the problem. Restate and emphasize your commitment to each visitor.

The great thing about crisis action plans is that they force you to plan for various scenarios in advance, making it much easier to deal with the situation should it ever arise.

ABCNEWS.COM recently had what I consider a crisis management situation when it gave the public perception that it didn't care what its visitors thought after asking for their opinion. Read on—and be sure to avoid such mistakes.

AVOID THE ABCNEWS.COM BLUNDER

In October 1999, ABCNEWS.COM announced that it was redesigning its home page. Before putting up the new look, however, ABC posted a sneak peek area of the new look and requested the feedback of ABCNEWS.COM visitors. Soon posts started appearing; the results were an overwhelming *dislike* for the proposed new look. Many people gave constructive criticism, others flamed ABCNEWS.COM for the proposed changes, and only a handful posted any type of positive response.

I was in agreement with the majority who disliked the new look. For one, ABCNEWS.COM was changing its logo, going for a look that tied it more closely to its TV network affiliation. Not only would this disrupt ABCNEWS .COM branding of its old logo (Chapter 5), but this particular new logo did a poor job of trying to co-brand the online image with the TV image, in my opinion. Other changes forced people with smaller monitors to use the horizontal scroll bar to see text on the right-hand side of the screen, which upset a lot of people. The proposed new color changes to the Website received comments like "depressing" and "dull."

Like others, I expected ABCNEWS.COM to hear the overwhelmingly negative feedback and put a stop to the proposed changes. The majority of visitors clearly did not like the change and voiced this at the feedback section of ABCNEWS.COM, as had been requested. Since ABCNEWS.COM received a lot of great suggestions from their visitors (some of whom were professional graphic artists), it was clear to me that the route ABCNEWS.COM would take was to cancel the planned update and go back to the drawing board.

I was wrong.

Within a day or two after being slammed over the proposed changes, ABCNEWS.COM published the new look to its home page! I was astounded that they had apparently ignored all the feedback they had requested. It was a slap in the face to the overwhelming majority that had told ABCNEWS.COM that the new look was worse than the old one and shouldn't be used.

Now visitors had something new to complain about:

"Site now officially sucks. If it ain't broke, don't fix it."

"Why did you guys switch? I was sure all the smart comments posted here would make you change your mind."

"Despite the comments of so many people that the new look is bad, you still went ahead with it."

"Clearly you don't listen to what people have said, which is, incidentally, that the new design is worse than the old one."

"Can you guys at ABC read the comments people have left?"

"Can't you people leave well enough alone?"

"The general consensus is that you've fallen in love with your own image and forgotten how to serve the public."

"Well thanks ABC for messing up a great Website!"

"I can't believe you implemented this lame 'new' layout despite the overwhelming consensus from readers pointing out how much we HATED IT!!!"

ABCNEWS.COM had come across as clearly ignoring its customers and was now receiving a backlash from its decision to go ahead and publish the changes, against the advice of its visitors. Some people posted goodbye notes, telling ABCNEWS.COM that they were now headed to such ABCNEWS.COM competitors as www.cnn.com and www.usatoday.com. "I guess it's time to move on to the CNN Website for my news," said one visitor, recommending that ABCNEWS.COM get a copy of *HTML for Dummies* to learn why not to select odd colors for Website design.

This had now turned into a public relations nightmare. ABCNEWS.COM had asked the advice of the public and then had given the public the perception that it didn't care what we thought. The changes were going to occur regardless. There is no better way to irritate your users than to ask for their advice, get an overwhelming opinion, then ignore it.

Now suffering a major backlash, ABCNEWS.COM released an announcement on its front page that it had heard the requests and would be slowly implementing changes over the next several months.

The problem is that it was *too little, too late*. The damage had been done. ABCNEWS.COM should not have posted the change against the will of its visitors. It showed a lack of respect for the public's opinions—and, as one person pointed out, it showed that ABCNEWS.COM had "forgotten how to serve the public."

ABCNEWS.COM should have never asked for public opinion if there was no intent to make changes based on visitor response. If you ask for public opinion on something you've done, be prepared to make changes that are overwhelmingly requested.

All I can hope is that ABCNEWS.COM has learned from its blunder. Serving the public should be its number one priority. If it isn't, the public will go elsewhere—to www.cnn.com, www.usatoday.com, www.washingtonpost.com, or news.bbc.co.uk. The battle for news is strong on the Web and the company that can do the best job, with the best customer service, will be the one that wins out. Remember the saying, "Build it and they will come"? Here's a new one: "Ignore them and they will leave."

Prior to this event, I had been a daily visitor to ABCNEWS.COM because of its strong news coverage (particularly in the area of technology) and quickness in covering breaking news. When I was jolted awake by the 7.1 earthquake that hit Southern California on October 16, 1999, I immediately went to all the news sites for information. ABCNEWS.COM was the first with reports of the quake. But no matter how great the Website, poor customer service drives people away. Luckily, ABCNEWS.COM apparently backtracked and will now be implementing the suggested changes they received. That should minimize some of the damage, compared to if they had continued to apparently ignore user feedback. Preferably, after the blunder of publishing the changes against the will of its visitors, ABCNEWS.COM should have *apologized* for doing it and immediately implemented the old look until the requested changes were completed. This would have been the most *respectable* thing for ABCNEWS.COM to do after the fact.

If you ever ask the opinion of your visitors on your Website, be prepared for possible negative feedback. More important, listen to what your visitors tell you. If you listen, it will only strengthen their admiration of and loyalty to your Website. Good public relations means listening to your public and acting upon their requests.

Dealing with Upset People

Sometimes you will get an email or letter from someone who is really upset about something. For example, at *Animation Artist Magazine,* we once received an email from someone who was upset that we had not posted the full credit list of *The Iron Giant.* The individual felt that by publishing only a partial list of credits we were not living up to our name, Animation Artist, since all people involved in the production are of equal importance. The individual used a harsh tone to convey a point. So, how do you react to harsh emails?

Step #1: Regardless of the person's tone, analyze the situation to see whether he or she has a valid point. Upon examining the person's complaint, we determined that the problem was definitely a valid one.

Step #2: When responding to a harsh email, never attack the person back. Use the KHWK method (Kill Him/Her With Kindness). In this case we emailed the person back: "You are right and we apologize for the oversight on our part. We will have a full credit list up within four days." Also, always overestimate the time you need to correct the problem.

Step #3: Apologize when you are wrong. No one is perfect. If you make a mistake or an oversight, be willing to admit the mistake and to apologize for it. This will only increase the amount of respect people have for you.

Step #4: Immediately fix the problem. In our situation, we got our credit list and typed in each of the hundreds of names, one by one, completing the task in two days. We then immediately sent an email to the individual, letting him know the problem was corrected.

Step #5: Be amazed at the results. We have yet to be burned by responding positively to a harsh email. In the case of the credits, the person actually wrote us back apologizing for the harsh tone of his first email. We had some great communications with him after that, turning a frustrated visitor into a very satisfied "customer."

If you ever have to deal with an upset person face to face, the most important thing is to *listen.* In face-to-face conflicts, an individual is upset and has something to say. By interrupting the individual, you don't allow him or her to fully express the problem or his or her feelings on the matter. In these situations, look the person in the eye and listen very carefully to every word. *Don't interrupt.* Let the person release his or her steam, then immediately tackle the problem. Try to identify with how you would feel if you were in the customer's shoes. Put your full attention into solving this person's problem immediately. Also, apologize for the problem, even if you are not clearly at fault: "I'm very sorry that happened. I will help you immediately solve this problem."

Your biggest challenge when dealing with an angry visitor or customer is to turn him or her into a very satisfied customer! It *is* possible, depending on how you handle the situation.

Community Relations

Because the Web is its own community, few Websites give serious thought to their relations with the physical community. After all, many multimillion-dollar Web ventures started out of someone's garage or study. Take advantage of the lack of Website involvement in local community efforts. It can only work to *your* advantage, as you will make a difference in your community while promoting your Website (and getting some great tax deductions).

Join your local chamber of commerce and start getting connected with local businesses. If you have a highly successful Website, contact career counselors at your local schools and volunteer to participate in the annual Career Day event. Be involved in charity events and consider volunteering to help out with a charity Website or marketing. Participate in local fairs and festivals. Make sure to have plenty of brochures and business cards available.

For example, one event I volunteered to help out with this year is the Teen Digital Movie Making Competition—**www.teendigital.com**—a community service in Santa Barbara, California (open throughout the United States) that encourages young people to develop their filmmaking skills by entering the annual contest. I don't get paid for my marketing services, but I do get the satisfaction of making a contribution to the community. In addition, *Animation Artist Magazine* gets listed as a sponsor in all advertising material. So people are aware of Animation Artist's involvement in the community effort.

Start looking for ways that you can be actively involved in your community and get others from your Website team to join in. Help out with community events, charities, and other functions and soon you'll find yourself networked closely with the community. The result is a higher respect for you (and your Website) in the community and increased traffic to your Website as a result of your sponsorships. But best of all, you get to see the results of your efforts help make the community a better place.

Training for Better Relations

In order to be most effective at public relations, *you must practice public relations all the time,* even when "not on the job." The more you practice it, the more natural it becomes. However, you should practice public relations out of genuine desire and not out of necessity. As you apply public relations strategies to every aspect of your life, you will improve not only your world, but also the world at large.

Let's look at an example. When I lived in Oregon, I used to regularly go through the drive-through of the local Dairy Queen, usually in the evening. When the person came on to take my order, I would always start with a friendly,

"Good evening, ma'am (or sir)," place my order, and end with "please." For example, "Good evening, ma'am. I'd like a Garden Burger with no pickles and a small Oreo cookie Blizzard with vanilla ice cream, please." I tried to always be as pleasant as possible, while being as specific as possible in my order so that they didn't have to ask any added questions, such as "vanilla or chocolate ice cream?"

One day I went to the Dairy Queen as normal, except when I got to the window to collect my order, the woman said, "I knew it was you, because you are always so friendly when you order!" A few years later, when I was living in Tustin, California, I received another comment from an employee at the local Taco Bell. One day, she flat-out told me that I was her favorite customer and she always looked forward to taking my order because I was so friendly.

So what made me different from any other customer? It sure wasn't the car I drove (a 1994 Geo Metro). It wasn't the way I dressed or the music I listened to in the car (I never replaced the radio someone stole from my Geo).

The difference was *my attitude.* While I didn't realize it at the time, the attitude I exhibited toward those who took my order was actually building positive perceptions. The more I thought about it, the more sense it made. Here are hardworking people who rarely have anyone express appreciation for their service. Some fast-food employees are even verbally abused by customers on a daily basis. When someone comes along who has a genuine appreciation for the work they do, they notice it. *That is public relations.*

The attitude you exhibit toward others will determine what perceptions they have about you and your Website.

Public relations isn't about having a nine-to-five job where you write press releases and try to build positive perceptions. It is about developing a genuine appreciation for everyone and everything around you. It means greeting the local supermarket clerk as if he or she is a friend. It means saying a genuine "thank you" when someone does something for you. *What can you do to make someone's day brighter?*

When you start becoming conscious of everything going on around you and applying genuine public relations to those scenarios, you are getting better PR training than any school can teach you. Furthermore, that type of "training" will make the public relations you do for your Website 100 times more effective.

As I was writing about this scenario, I was interrupted with an incoming email message from a person in Santiago, Chile. The gentleman said his daughter was interested in animation as a career and was looking at career options. He stated that getting information on schools and universities specializing in animation was a challenge and wanted to know if I could help. I now had three options:

1. Ignore the message altogether, since it would take a long time to answer.

2. Spend 30 to 40 minutes immediately researching an answer and providing a detailed response.

3. Finish this chapter, then see whether I had time to answer the man's question.

Without hesitation, I chose option #2. Sure, I don't know the person who sent the email, but the fact is that *there is a genuine person with a problem on the other side of that email message.* He can't find the information he is looking for and has requested my assistance. If there weren't an email message (and several thousand miles) between us and he had approached me in person, would I ignore him? Of course not! But that's what I would be doing if I didn't assist him with an answer.

Picture your email messages as people approaching you in real life seeking your assistance. Realize that there is a person to whom you can be of great assistance, no matter how minute their question.

Prior to the theatrical release of the movie *ID4* (*Independence Day*), there was a really cool background score playing on the movie trailer that I absolutely loved. I downloaded the trailer online, enjoying the music as much as the preview. As soon as the *ID4* soundtrack came out, I rushed out and bought it. But guess what—the score wasn't on the CD! Now, to me this was a problem. Here was an inspirational score I really wanted, but I had no idea where it came from. Since *ID4* was put out by Twentieth Century Fox, I researched an email address for them online and sent an email inquiring about the song.

At this point, the Fox representative who received my email had two choices:

1. He or she could have thought, "I'm too busy to research the answer to what music was used in the trailer of *ID4,* especially since it doesn't effect the sales of a Fox product (since the score isn't on the CD)."

2. He or she could have taken the time to research an answer for me and email me back.

I'm very pleased to report that Fox selected number two. Within two days, I had a response from a Fox representative who had taken the time to research the answer for me. The music had come from the soundtrack for the movie *Crimson Tide.* I was ecstatic! The request may have seemed small, but I had spent hours trying to find an answer with no results. So the fact that a Fox representative took the time to research the answer for me made my week. My perceptions of Fox as a company were at an all-time high simply because someone had answered my question, no matter how minor it may have sounded. *This is good public relations,* especially since I originally thought a huge company like Fox wouldn't take the time to respond to such an inquiry. Within an hour I had the *Crimson Tide* CD in my hand and was enjoying the score (Track 5) that had played on the *ID4* trailer.

A few years after that incident, I opened up a huge fan Website dedicated to the movie *Ever After: A Cinderella Story*—**www.studiovisions.com/everafter**—and guess what? The number one question I was asked was "What was the song that played in the *Ever After* trailer? It isn't on the soundtrack!" It was a pleasure to provide the answer to every single inquiry (hundreds) because I know how frustrated I was when searching for the song on the *ID4* trailer. Responses I received from *Ever After* fans were similar to the response I sent Fox—"Thank you so much for answering my question. I've been searching everywhere for an answer and you were the first person to help me!"

Helping someone who sends an email inquiry is like helping your best friend. Think for a moment about who your best friend is. If that best friend had a problem, would you help him or her? Of course you would. Now picture everyone who sends you an inquiry as your best friend. *How will you react?*

People never forget good public relations. Likewise, they don't forget bad public relations, either. Therefore, make a conscious effort to apply public relations to every aspect of your life and it will not only brighten up the world of everyone around you—it will also brighten your own world.

QUESTIONS AND ANSWERS

QUESTION: When writing a press release, shouldn't you double-space it?

ANSWER: If you are writing a press release for mailing or faxing, then yes, it should be double-spaced on regular-sized paper (8.5″ × 11″), with one-inch margins on both sides. If the release continues past the first page, then put "-more-" at the bottom of the first page and at the top of the second page put "2-2-2-2."

So why don't you double-space in email messages? Since you are simply copying and pasting into the email message, any special formatting will be lost. You don't want to send the release as HTML code because that would be assuming that the press organizations receiving the release all have their email accounts set to properly read HTML email messages. *Never assume.*

QUESTION: Any other good or bad public relations or customer service experiences you can share?

ANSWER: Unfortunately, most of my memorable customer service and public relations experiences with larger Websites have been bad. For example, here are two recent ones:

▶ I recently had a problem when I registered a domain name through one of the newer domain name services. I emailed my problem to their contact email address and got an autoresponder message back saying that all inquiries had to go through a form on their Website. I filled out the form with a brief outline of my problem and was sent an email saying I had to call customer service. I called customer service and was given another email address where I had to forward an invoice I had received from the company for the domain name I had registered. I forwarded the invoice to the address I was told and it came back saying that all emails had to go through the form on their Website! I went back to the Website and pasted the information into the form and clicked "Submit." I received an error message that my note was too long and that I had to edit it down! I edited it down and clicked Submit again—and got the same error message. I tried calling the company again and no one would pick up the phone, even though it was still within their business hours. I went back to the Website form and had to cut and paste parts of my message into *four different forms* in order for it to go through. By the time I was done, I had spent *over three hours* just trying to get someone to pay attention to my problem. This is very bad customer service and very bad public relations. I will *never* forget this negative experience with this company and will begin looking elsewhere for future domain name service. Never force visitors to use a form on your Website for inquiries. To the contrary, you should provide five well-publicized ways of contact: email, Web form, phone, fax, and snail mail.

▶ Recently I filled out an online form requesting that a sales representative of a Website that offers chat services contact me to fulfill an immediate purchasing need. I left all required contact information, including my email address and phone number. I received no response. Twelve days later I called the company on the phone, but couldn't get beyond the secretary who said that my inquiry must be sent them via email. Instead, I sent the company a detailed letter as to why they had forever lost my business. Interestingly enough, I was contacted within three hours of them receiving that email!

If another company or Website treats you poorly or delivers terrible customer service, take your business elsewhere and never look back. Many of these places figure that you need them (versus the other way around), so they don't give a second thought to customer service. If you hang around after such shabby service, *you are only contributing to the problem.* Companies and Websites will not learn a lesson until the number of people leaving starts to affect the bottom line. I've seen some Websites so arrogant that when a person posted a complaint, the response was, "If you don't like it, then leave." I was once planning to give a considerable amount of business to one Website that offered a great service, until I saw that message ("If you don't like it, then leave") in response to another user's complaint. I immediately took my business elsewhere and have never looked back. The company was arrogant because their product was in demand. But how long will they last by telling people who have a problem to leave if they don't like it? *That depends on how long you tolerate it!*

Here are two positive customer service and public relations experiences:

▶ When I was looking for an email service with the format `yourname@animationartist.net` to offer readers, I thought I had found the dream program (it required a monthly fee, but gave you all the ad and branding space). I signed up for the service, which stated I would be contacted within 24 hours. Four days went by and I hadn't heard anything. I sent a complaint and within two hours had a response that the CEO would look into the problem for me. The next morning I received a phone call from the CEO who explained to me in detail that some new problems had arisen from the email service and that when the problems were resolved, he would give me three free months of service because they had not contacted me within 24 hours. A few days later he called me back to update me that the problem would take a while to resolve. He apologized for the problem and was very honest and up-front in answering my questions. I chose to move on and found another great service (Coconut Software) to fulfill my email needs.

Even though the first person didn't get my business, he did get my respect and I would not hesitate to do business with him again in the future, because I know he is an honest businessperson who cares about his customers.

▶ Two months after I signed up to become an Amazon.com affiliate, they sent me a T-shirt out of the blue as a "thank you" for being one of their affiliates. To date, I've worn that T-shirt at least 40 times, which is great advertising for Amazon.com. What made this a great experience is that I was not expecting a T-shirt from Amazon.com—it was a complete surprise when it arrived in the mail.

Make sure that when people remember you or your Website, is because of the *positive* experiences and not the negative ones.

QUESTION: How, exactly, do public relations and marketing go hand in hand?

ANSWER: Your Website cannot achieve ultimate success unless it has *both* strong public relations and strong marketing. This means building an integrated campaign on how you deal with publicity and customer service. I know one company that has great public relations and terrible marketing. Likewise, I know another company that has great marketing, but lousy public relations. Guess what? Both companies are failing. This is because you must integrate the strength and success of your public relations and marketing.

Let's look at some scenarios on how marketing and public relations are integrated hand in hand when it comes to your Website:

1. Let's say one of your new marketing efforts is to set up a free email service (such as the one we have at **www.animationartist.net**). If people have problems with the service, how will you address those problems to the satisfaction of your customer? That is public relations. And a good public relations plan will be prepared for scenarios before they strike. Let's say that the day you open your new email service, two people email you saying they had problems signing up for the service, three people email you to ask how you set up filters in the email program, and four people email you inquiring why an ad for your Website goes out with each message. And this is only day one! It's time for action. By the end of the day, you should not only have every question personally answered, but you should also have a FAQ posted to your Website that addresses the same questions. Now you are dealing with the problems before they arise.

2. Let's say one of your public relations efforts is to send out a press release on a new area that opened up on your Website. Because traffic to this area will increase, what will your marketing efforts be to make sure people to this new area explore other areas of your Website?

3. Let's say that one of your marketing efforts correlates with Website Marketing Idea #30 in Chapter 2, "Become a Seller on Auction Sites Such as eBay." The marketing, of course, is the launching of the program, development of your "About Me" area, and so on. The public relations part is how you deal with those who purchase an item from you. How quickly do you respond? How fast do you ship the product? How strong is your follow-up? How quickly do you post positive feedback? The two go hand in hand.

As you can see, the efforts of public relations and marketing need to be integrated together for the best results. One, without the other, will only bring limited success.

Public relations is such a vast subject that I could easily write an entire book just on the topic of public relations on the Web. Strong public relations is often overlooked by many Websites that allow email messages to go unanswered, don't put out press releases, and couldn't care less about visitor opinions. For the most part, a visitor who witnesses strong public relations is witnessing an "abnormal" experience, because it is so rare.

Now that we have traveled through the worlds of Web marketing and public relations, it is time to bring it all together. The final two chapters will assist you in creating your Strategic Website Marketing Plan, otherwise known as the blueprint to your Website's success.

9 Forming a Strategic Website Marketing Plan

This chapter and Chapter 10 are the most important chapters in this book. Why? Because they are where your entire Strategic Website Marketing Plan comes together. Everything we've discussed up to this point will do you very little good if you do not include it in a plan that moves your marketing efforts forward on a continual basis.

What exactly does a Strategic Website Marketing Plan do? Simply put, it creates a strategy for the effective implementation of your online and offline marketing ideas. It takes into account your goals, your competitors, and your relationships.

This chapter will explain all the questions listed in the worksheet pages of Chapter 10 to help you through the entire creation of your plan. Feel free to make a copy of the Chapter 10 worksheets so that you can fill out the information while following along in this chapter. Alternatively you can go to www.webmastertechniques.com/webmarketing/ and download a nice printable Word version of Chapter 10. You can also write directly in Chapter 10 if you wish.

Website Philosophy and Purpose

1. **Describe your Website's history and the products and services it offers.**

This is a simple description of your Website's history and the products and services that it offers. If someone wanted more information on your Website, but didn't know anything about it, this is the type of description you would provide. Here is an example from *Animation Artist Magazine:*

> The *Animation Artist Magazine* Website was formed in the summer of 1998 as a service to animators and animation fans who want in-depth and up-to-date information from the world of animation. The site officially opened to the public on October 8, 1998, attracting over 400 unique visitors the first day from pre-opening marketing efforts. The parent company of *Animation Artist Magazine* is Studio Visions—www.studiovisions.com—which is owned by Joe and Vicki Tracy. Joe Tracy is the publisher of *Animation Artist Magazine* and has an extensive background in print publishing. Vicki Tracy serves as the editor of *Animation Artist Magazine*. The staff is rounded out by columnists and reporters who serve on a contract basis. *Animation Artist Magazine* is headquartered in Carpinteria (Santa Barbara County), California. The Website is updated every day of the year, including Christmas Day. Services on the *Animation Artist Magazine* Website include the following:

- ▶ Daily news.
- ▶ Monthly columns.
- ▶ Monthly features.
- ▶ Inside look at upcoming animated films.
- ▶ Screening Room image review area for animators and aspiring animators.

▶ Tutorials to help aspiring animators master key skills.

▶ Monthly contests to encourage participation.

▶ Animation postcards that visitors can send to their friends.

▶ In-depth animation movie sites featuring current animated films.

▶ In-depth look at the history of animation (excellent educational resource).

▶ Affiliate links to purchase animated books, movies, music, and so on.

2. Identify the main purpose of your Website.

The first element you must identify in your Strategic Website Marketing Plan is the main purpose of your Website. Once you have a purpose in mind, you will know how to target your marketing to help achieve that purpose. Here are a few examples:

▶ The purpose of Brand X Website is to create a game zone that rewards people for playing with prizes from a variety of advertisers.

▶ The purpose of Brand X Website is to sell a self-published book on Website design. It will also serve as the base camp of a grassroots marketing effort to spread the word on the book.

▶ The purpose of Brand X Website is to provide people with detailed evaluations of theme parks across the United States, including safety numbers, prices, operating hours, and maps.

▶ The purpose of Brand X Website is to serve as a marketing and support center for customers of my offline dry cleaning store.

3. List one to three things you specifically want visitors to do when they visit your Website.

The purpose of this question is to determine exactly what you ultimately want visitors to do when they visit your Website. This usually consists of one to three key items. By determining what you want visitors to do, you can shape your marketing strategy to help accomplish that goal more quickly. Here are some examples:

▶ Visitors should voluntarily sign up to receive the Brand X Website newsletter.

▶ Visitors should register to become members of the members-only section of the Brand X Website at $12.95 a year.

▶ Visitors should purchase books through my Brand X Book Review Website.

4. Define your Website's internal goal statement.

As discussed in Chapter 1, an internal goal statement specifically identifies what you want to accomplish with your Website. Refer to Step #2 in Chapter 1 for a specific real-life example. This is a *private* document that the public does not see.

You are basically answering the following questions in the creation of your internal goal statement:

1. Why does your Website exist?
2. What do you want your visitor count to be (how many daily visitors)?
3. What do you want to accomplish with that visitor count?
4. How do you want your visitors to use your Website?

5. Define your Website's mission statement.

As discussed in Chapter 2, Web Marketing Idea #60, your mission statement is a definition of your Website's focus and commitment that is *displayed for the public*. It is a document that you should read on a daily basis to remind you of your purpose. See Chapter 2, Website Marketing Idea #60, to read the official mission statement for *Animation Artist Magazine*. As another example, here is the company mission statement for Saturn:

> *Earn the loyalty of Saturn owners and grow our family by developing and marketing U.S. manufactured vehicles that are world leaders in quality, cost and customer enthusiasm through the integration of people, technology and business systems.*

6. **Define your Website's positioning statement.**

As discussed in Chapter 5, a positioning statement defines what makes you unique and why people should visit your Website instead of the Websites of your competitors. A positioning statement is very short—usually one to three sentences. Like your internal goal statement, the positioning statement is *for your eyes only*. In many ways a positioning statement also identifies your niche. Here is *Animation Artist Magazine*'s positioning statement:

> **Animation Artist Magazine** *is the leading provider of interactive and personalized content for animators and animation fans.*

How does your internal goal statement differ from your mission statement and your positioning statement?

The internal goal statement *privately* defines why your Website exists and what you want to accomplish.

The mission statement is your *public commitment*.

The positioning statement is *how you want to be perceived* and who you want to perceive you that way (for example, "Dogs Daily is the *leading provider* of daily *dog health news and information* for *dog owners*").

Goal Setting and Objectives

7. **List three main Website marketing objectives you want to accomplish over the next month.**

This is a list of three specific objectives that you want your Website to reach within the next 30 days. Your strongest marketing focus will be on these three items, which you must update on a monthly basis. Here is an example of three objectives for *Animation Artist Magazine*:

January 2000—Objective #1: To increase mailing list memberships from 1,900 to 2,200 members.

January 2000—Objective #2: To increase traffic to the Animation Artist Playland by 25 percent over the average of the last two months.

January 2000—Objective #3: To increase the number of Animation Artist email account users from 2,600 to 3,000.

As you can see, each is a short-term objective that you strive to reach every day of the month until all three objectives are met.

8. List three main Website marketing objectives you want to accomplish over the next year.

Now we jump to the midterm objectives, which are your specific goals over a longer period of time—in this case, one year. Here is an example of three year-long marketing objectives for *Animation Artist Magazine:*

January 2000 to December 2000—Objective #1: To increase daily traffic to the home page of the Animation Artist Website from 2,000 to 10,000 unique visitors a day.

January 2000 to December 2000—Objective #2: To increase the number of Animation Radio daily listeners from 800 to 2,500.

January 2000 to December 2000—Objective #3: To hire one additional employee to deal strictly with customer service (answering phone and email inquiries).

As you can see, the midterm objectives are much more ambitious than the short-term objectives. Feel free to create some of your short-term objectives from your midterm objectives, if desired. For example, a short-term objective based on the mid-term objective in this example could be, "January 2000—Objective #1: To increase daily traffic to the home page of the Animation Artist Website from 2,000 to 2,900 unique visitors a day."

Now comes the most ambitious of all your objectives—your long-term goals.

9. List three main Website marketing objectives you want to accomplish over the next three years.

January 2000 to December 2002—Objective #1: To have a steady traffic flow of 9,000 unique visitors a day to the *Animation Artist Magazine* Website (3.2 million unique visitors a year).

January 2000 to December 2002—Objective #2: To create a strategic partnership with an animation print magazine or to branch Animation Artist into a print magazine (in addition to the Website).

January 2000 to December 2002—Objective #3: To acquire two of the top five animation Websites under Animation Artist in order to build a stronger network.

In Chapter 2, four possible categories could be developed by each idea: Initial Contact, Repeat Visits, Participation, and Loyalty & Trust. The next four questions relate directly to those categories, as you will select what you consider the top three marketing ideas for each category *that will work best for your Website.* You will then consistently focus on these ideas in your marketing efforts.

10. **List three main marketing ideas you will use to drive traffic to your Website.**

Identify, from Chapter 2, what three marketing ideas you think will work best to drive traffic to your Website. Write down the top three ideas, which will become your main marketing focus for driving traffic.

11. **List three main marketing ideas you will use to drive repeat visits to your Website.**

Identify, from Chapter 2, what three marketing ideas you think will work best to drive repeat visits to your Website. Write down the top three ideas, which will become your main marketing focus for getting people to come back to your Website on a regular basis.

12. **List three main marketing ideas you will use to drive participation on your Website.**

Identify, from Chapter 2, what three marketing ideas you think will work best to drive participation on your Website. Write down the top three ideas, which will become your main marketing focus for getting people to participate regularly on your Website.

13. List three main marketing ideas you will use to develop loyalty and trust on your Website.

Identify, from Chapter 2, what three marketing ideas you think will work best to gain loyalty and trust from your Website visitors. Write down the top three ideas, which will become your main marketing focus for gaining stronger loyalty and trust.

Your Strengths and Weaknesses

It is important to identify the strengths and weaknesses of your Website so that you can continue to build upon your strengths while taking action on your weaknesses. Try to be as open as possible with these questions. "None" is not a satisfactory answer to "What are the five biggest weaknesses of your Website?"

14. List your Website's five biggest strengths.

Here you will list the five things that you consider major strengths of your Website. Here are three examples of possible Website strengths:

▶ The Website has a strategic relationship with Brand X print magazine, resulting in higher traffic from free print ads.

▶ The forum is very active, with no fewer than 100 posts a day. At least ten new registered users are signing up daily.

▶ Website columnists are top in the industry, resulting in additional attention and respect for the site.

Analyze every bit of your Website carefully (and feedback you've received from visitors) to craft this list.

15. List your Website's five biggest weaknesses.

By honestly identifying your weaknesses, you'll be able to work on them to turn each weakness into an eventual strength. Where should you start when analyzing weaknesses? Start with your email box. What is the number one thing that people have complained about? Also, what have you personally found very difficult to execute or keep updated? Here are three examples of possible weaknesses:

- ▶ The Website has only a small staff, so we are spread so thin that it takes a while for us to answer reader inquiries.
- ▶ On three or four occasions, promised updates never occurred.
- ▶ Our busy schedule makes it hard to do multiple daily updates.

16. List a solution for each of your five biggest weaknesses.

This is where you identify the solution to each of your weaknesses so that you can turn those weaknesses into strengths. Based on the three example weaknesses I listed, here are my *solutions*:

- ▶ Set up filters to help keep email organized. Provide the sender with a response as soon as the email comes in (even if an answer is temporarily unavailable). If I allow email to pile up, it will only take longer to answer. Put emails needing further research into a "Research" folder. I will dedicate one hour every evening to answering questions in my Research folder.
- ▶ Don't promise updates. By promising and missing updates I am only contributing to a negative perception people have in my ability to update the Website. If I don't set expectations, then the problem doesn't exist if an update is delayed.
- ▶ In the next email newsletter, I will place a "Help Wanted" ad for a volunteer to take over a specific section of the Website.

Now that I've identified solutions to my weaknesses, I can work on turning them into strengths. Once that is done, I must identify more weaknesses so that I can determine solutions and execute them.

Identifying Competitor Strengths and Weaknesses

17. Identify and describe your number one competitor.

This question identifies *who* your biggest online competitor is and *why* they are your biggest competitor. Write a short description of your competitor, including the name of the Website and the URL. Here's an example using Dogs Daily:

> *The main competitor for Dogs Daily is Dogs Go Bow-Wow at* www.dogs
> gobow-wow.com. *Dogs Go Bow-Wow was formed in 1996 and was one
> of the first dog sites to hit the Web, giving it an immediate competitive
> advantage. Furthermore, Dogs Go Bow-Wow has a "Website Board of
> Directors" that consists of some of the biggest names and breeders in the
> business. This gives Dogs Go Bow-Wow instant credibility. The Dogs Go
> Bow-Wow forum gets more than 200 posts a day, and advertising
> appears to be very strong.*

18. Identify the five biggest strengths of your number one competitor.

In question #14, you identified the five biggest strengths of your Website. Now you will identify the five biggest strengths of your competitor's Website. It is better to overestimate the strength of your competitor rather than underestimate it, so be liberal in listing strengths. Here are three examples that Dogs Daily might write up on Dogs Go Bow-Wow:

▶ The Website has strong participation, with over 200 posts a day in the forum and over 500 people participating in the Dogs Go Bow-Wow Question of the Day.

▶ According to the Dogs Go Bow-Wow online media kit, they receive an impressive 4,000 unique visitors a day to their Website.

▶ Dogs Go Bow-Wow is listed as a primary sponsor at most major dog shows.

19. Identify the five biggest weaknesses of your number one competitor.

Now that you have identified the strengths of your competitor, it is time to seek out and describe five main weaknesses of your competitor's Website. Here are three examples that Dogs Daily might write up on Dogs Go Bow-Wow:

▶ Inquiries frequently go unanswered. Complaints on the forum, combined with personal tests under various aliases, have shown that Dogs Go Bow-Wow does not answer email inquiries no matter how simplistic or difficult the question being asked. The only exception was when I sent an inquiry about advertising, in which I received a response within twelve hours.

▶ Every night from ten to eleven P.M., the Website goes offline for an hour. There are no reasons posted on the Website as to why, and inquiries have gone unanswered.

▶ The interactive content on Dogs Go Bow-Wow is rarely updated. Even the Website's calendar hasn't been updated in 45 days.

20. Define actions you can take to match the strengths of your number one competitor.

This question identifies what you need to do in order to match the strengths of your number one competitor. In most cases, matching your competitor's strengths will not be an easy task, because they will have a stronghold in that area. Plus, while you're trying to match that strength, they can be getting stronger in that area. Still, you must be relentless in your pursuit of being as strong as and stronger than your competitor. Set goals that will put you on the right track.

21. Define actions you can take to capitalize on the weaknesses of your number one competitor.

By turning the weaknesses of your main competitor into your strengths, you can begin to exceed your competitor in a number of areas that visitors will pick up on. Then it is just a matter of matching your competitor's strengths and developing your niche—and suddenly you are number one! Put together some steps to help you capitalize on the weaknesses of your number one competitor.

22. Identify and describe your number two competitor.

This is the same as question #17, but it identifies *who* your second-biggest online competitor is and *why* they are your second-biggest competitor.

23. Identify the five biggest strengths of your number two competitor.

This is the same as question #18, but it identifies the five biggest strengths of your second-biggest competitor.

24. **Identify the five biggest weaknesses of your number two competitor.**

This is the same as question #19, but it identifies the five biggest weaknesses of your second-biggest competitor.

25. **Define actions you can take to match the strengths of your number two competitor.**

This is the same as question #20, but it identifies what you need to match the strengths of your second-biggest competitor.

26. **Define actions you can take to capitalize on the weaknesses of your number two competitor.**

This is the same as question #21, but it identifies what you must do to capitalize on the weaknesses of your second-biggest competitor.

Allies

27. **Identify and define three Websites that have the potential to be an ally with your Website. Also identify when you will contact these sites with a proposal.**

This question identifies the Websites within the industry your site covers with which you feel you can have a strong working relationship. This is usually a Website that covers an area of the industry you don't, while not overstepping into the coverage you provide. There is common ground where coming together can mutually benefit both parties. Here's an example, using Dogs Daily again:

> *We have identified Pretty Dog, www.prettydog.com (this URL was available as of late October 1999), as a possible ally for Dogs Daily. Pretty Dog is not a news Website, but rather a site that deals with preparing your dog for dog shows. It's not updated daily, but has already been built into an excellent resource. Since we don't cover dog shows, it would make sense to form an alliance with Pretty Dog. We will contact Pretty Dog by March 2000 with an official offer to form an alliance.*

Visitor Needs

> ### 28. Identify the main needs of your visitors and how you will address those needs.

This question requires you to find out exactly what the main needs of your visitors are and then identify how you will meet those needs. Prior to answering this question, you should do a detailed Website survey and possibly a focus group. Find out exactly what people want from a Website that covers the industry you are interested in. Identify the main need that will keep people coming back daily, then establish a plan to meet that need.

Branding

> ### 29. List your Website's slogan.

In Chapter 2 we looked at a few different slogans and the importance of a strong and catchy slogan for branding. Remember to keep your slogan short and catchy.

Cute Example: Dogs Daily—"It's a Dog's World After All"

Identifier Example: eToys.com—"The Internet's Biggest Toy Store"

Identifier Example 2: TheForce.net—"Your Daily Dose of Star Wars"

Catchy Example: California Milk Processor Board—"Got Milk?"

Be sure to run your slogan by a number of people before making it official. It will be one of the most important initial decisions you ever make. If your slogan can be cute *and* catchy *and* identify what you do all in one, then you deserve an award and should have an easier time branding your Website successfully.

> ### 30. Identify three specific ways that you will brand your logo and slogan.

Use Chapter 5 to help you identify specific ways to brand your logo and slogan. For example, one way may be to combine your logo and slogan into one (as Animation Artist has done), then place it on every single page of your Website (in the same location). Another way may be to have hundreds of T-shirts made with your logo and slogan, then give the T-shirts away.

31. **Besides a logo and slogan, identify three more specific ways you will brand your Website.**

Using Chapter 5 as a guide, come up with three other specific action items you will use to brand your Website.

Risks

32. **Identify five primary risks that your Website faces.**

This question requires careful thought and honesty as to the risks you face with your Website venture. There are definite risks in any venture, and Websites are no different. For example, do you risk losing a lot of money in hosting fees, bandwidth, and new additions to your Website if it doesn't succeed? Does the way you cover subjects (for example, tabloid journalism) open you up to possible lawsuits? What are your concerns? By identifying your risks, you can take measures to lower the chances of those risks becoming a reality.

33. **List a solution for each of your five primary risks.**

Now that you've identified your risks, you must be able to address each one to lessen the impact of each risk. For example, let's say that one risk is that you stand to lose a lot of money if your venture doesn't succeed. There are a number of solutions to this risk. The first is to not spend what you don't have. Expand as money comes in. The second is to put a stronger focus on your advertising and sales. The third is to generate a second income. Attack each risk with solutions so that the risk becomes an investment.

Public Relations

34. **Identify who will be in charge of writing your press releases.**

Press releases are an important medium for getting your message out to the public. Therefore it is critical to identify exactly who will have this duty. Is it you? Will you hire a PR firm? Will you hire a PR Website to write your releases? Will a friend with strong writing and communication skills do it?

35. Identify how your press releases will be distributed.

This question identifies whether you will distribute the press releases yourself or use a professional distribution service. If you select a professional distribution service, you must also identify which one.

36. Identify the target date for the completion and distribution of your press kit.

This question identifies your goal for completing and distributing your press kit to the press. If your Website is full of interesting adventures right now, you will want to make this date soon. If you have little to report or talk about, then make the date a year or two away. Stick with the deadline!

37. Identify your policy for responding to visitor inquiries.

When a visitor emails you a question, what is your policy for responding to that question? An example policy might be, "Answer all questions within eight hours; if an answer is not available, immediately notify the person inquiring that you are researching an answer for him or her."

38. Identify your general crisis action plan.

In Chapter 8 we discussed the importance of a crisis action plan. It is vital that you have a series of crisis action plans to deal with various potential conflicts. However, you should also have a general crisis action plan that deals with the steps you will take if an unexpected event strikes that your specific crisis action plans don't cover. The general crisis action plan should identify one spokesperson (in case the media become involved) the crisis management team, and instant response techniques to public and press inquiries.

39. Identify five community relations goals.

One of the important topics of Chapter 8 was your community relations. This question asks you to identify specific goals to improve your community relations. One of your goals may be to place free public service banners for a specific local charity on your Website. Another may be to host a chamber of commerce after-hours function. What will you do to increase your Website's involvement in the community?

Update Your Plan

The purpose of a Strategic Website Marketing Plan is not to put it away in a drawer to gather dust. You should read it *at least* once a week (to make sure you are in tune with it). Furthermore, you will need to update it monthly to reflect your new goals, accomplishments, competitors, and relationships. Every time you review it (at least once a week) you can update the plan, if needed.

Seven Important Thoughts to Remember

1. Never launch a new area of your Website without a marketing campaign to back it up.
2. Never give in to your competitor (that is, unless they want to buy you out for millions of dollars).
3. Never do marketing without public relations or public relations without marketing (see Chapter 8).
4. Schedule free time for your own sanity (and the sanity of your loved ones).
5. Enjoy what you're doing (otherwise you are wasting your time).
6. Always have at least one strong niche that your competitors don't have. Strengthen it so that it is hard to duplicate. Have another one on the back burner that you can pull up should a competitor attack your current niche.
7. Always be one step ahead of your competitor. If you can always keep your competitor on the defensive (playing catch-up, but never getting ahead), then you will be positioned as the leader while your competitor is always positioned as the follower.

QUESTIONS AND ANSWERS

QUESTION: Do I really need a Strategic Website Marketing Plan?

ANSWER: If you want your efforts to be as successful and focused as possible, then the answer is a definite *yes*. However, don't create a Strategic Website Marketing Plan if you don't plan on following it. A Strategic Website Marketing Plan will do you no good if it sits in a filing cabinet collecting dust.

Also, consider your ultimate goal with your Website. What is the best-case scenario in your mind? Is it that a bigger corporation buys out your Website for millions of dollars? Maybe it is that an investment firm channels money into your Website so that you can grow it beyond your wildest dreams. I have news for you. If your goal is to sell your Website and someone shows a serious interest, your chances of making the sale will dramatically improve if you can show the interested party both a business plan and a Strategic Website Marketing Plan. It shows that you are organized and serious. In the latter scenario, investors will insist on seeing a business plan and marketing plan before investing a single penny.

If you couldn't care less about growing your Website and you're just out to have some fun on the Web, then do what you think is best. Maybe you don't want to be bogged down with plans, objectives, and so on. If that's the case, then just apply marketing ideas from Chapter 2 at your own free will. But if you ever get serious, a Strategic Website Marketing Plan is the first thing you must create.

QUESTION: In the section on marketing objectives, you ask for three objectives for short-term, midterm, and long-term. Can I have more than three objectives in those areas?

ANSWER: By all means, yes. Just be careful not to spread your efforts too thin. You want to make sure that you can meet every single objective that you set, so be realistic with the number of objectives and with the objective itself.

QUESTION: What if I finish a marketing objective early?

ANSWER: Then set another one. In my example of long-term marketing objectives (three years), one objective I listed was to either form a strategic partnership with an animation print magazine or to turn Animation Artist into a print magazine to support the online efforts. Let's say that I formed a strategic partnership with an animation print magazine in one year. That's great! I exceeded my long-term objective by two years! I can now celebrate (always reward yourself for meeting objectives) and create a new objective to replace it.

The next chapter contains all the forms you need to craft your Strategic Website Marketing Plan. Once your plan is crafted and consistently implemented, you will be well on your way to success!

10 Strategic Planning Pages

The following several pages are worksheets for you to fill out. When you are done filling out each area, you will have your Strategic Website Marketing Plan and should begin implementing it immediately. Refer to Chapter 9, "Forming a Strategic Website Marketing Plan," for in-depth details on how to fill out each area in this chapter.

Strategic Website Marketing Plan

1. Describe your Website's history and the products and services it offers:

_____

_____

_____

_____

_____

_____

_____

_____

_____

_____

_____

_____

_____

_____

_____

_____

_____

_____

_____

_____

_____

_____

_____

2. Identify the main purpose of your Website:

_____

_____

_____

_____

_____

_____

_____

_____

_____

_____

_____

_____

_____

_____

3. List one to three things you specifically want visitors to do when they visit your Website:

1. _____

_____

2. _____

_____

3. _____

_____

4. Define your Website's internal goal statement:

_____

_____

_____

---

5. Define your Website's mission statement:

---

6. Define your Website's positioning statement:

_____

_____

_____

_____

_____

7. List three main Website marketing objectives you want
   to accomplish over the next month:

   1. _____

   _____

   2. _____

   _____

   3. _____

   _____

8. List three main Website marketing objectives you want
   to accomplish over the next year:

   1. _____

   _____

   2. _____

   _____

   3. _____

   _____

9. List three main Website marketing objectives you want
   to accomplish over the next three years:

   1. _____

   _____

   2. _____

   _____

3. _____
_____

10. List three main marketing ideas you will use to drive traffic
to your Website:

1. _____
_____

2. _____
_____

3. _____
_____

11. List three main marketing ideas you will use to drive repeat visits
to your Website:

1. _____
_____

2. _____
_____

3. _____
_____

12. List three main marketing ideas you will use to drive participation
on your Website:

1. _____
_____

2. _____
_____

3. _____
_____

13. List three main marketing ideas you will use to develop loyalty and trust on your Website:

1. _____

_____

2. _____

_____

3. _____

_____

14. List your Website's five biggest strengths:

1. _____

_____

2. _____

_____

3. _____

_____

4. _____

_____

5. _____

_____

15. List your Website's five biggest weaknesses:

1. _____

_____

2. _____

_____

3. _____

_____

4. _____

_____

5. _____

_____

16. List a solution for each of your five biggest weaknesses:

1. _____

_____

2. _____

_____

3. _____

_____

4. _____

_____

5. _____

_____

17. Identify and describe your number one competitor:

_____

_____

_____

_____

_____

_____

_____

_____

_____

_____

_____

18. Identify the five biggest strengths of your number one competitor.

    1. _____

    _____

    2. _____

    _____

    3. _____

    _____

    4. _____

    _____

    5. _____

    _____

19. Identify the five biggest weaknesses of your number one competitor:

    1. _____

    _____

    2. _____

    _____

    3. _____

    _____

    4. _____

    _____

    5. _____

    _____

20. Define actions you can take to match the strengths of your number one competitor:

_____

_____

_____

_____
_____
_____
_____
_____
_____
_____
_____

21. Define actions you can take to capitalize on the weaknesses
    of your number one competitor:

_____
_____
_____
_____
_____
_____
_____
_____
_____
_____
_____

22. Identify and describe your number two competitor:

_____
_____
_____
_____
_____

_____

_____

_____

23. Identify the five biggest strengths of your number two competitor:

1. _____

_____

2. _____

_____

3. _____

_____

4. _____

_____

5. _____

_____

24. Identify the five biggest weaknesses of your number two competitor:

1. _____

_____

2. _____

_____

3. _____

_____

4. _____

_____

5. _____

_____

25. Define actions you can take to match the strengths of your number two competitor:

_____

_____

_____

_____

_____

_____

_____

_____

_____

_____

_____

_____

26. Define actions you can take to capitalize on the weaknesses of your number two competitor:

_____

_____

_____

_____

_____

_____

_____

_____

_____

_____

_____

_____

27. Identify and define three Websites that have the potential to be an ally with your Website. Also identify when you will contact these sites with a proposal:

1. _____

_____

Contact by: _____

2. _____

_____

Contact by: _____

3. _____

_____

Contact by: _____

28. Identify the main needs of your visitors and how you will address those needs:

_____

_____

_____

_____

_____

_____

_____

_____

_____

_____

_____

29. List your Website's slogan:

_____

_____

30. Identify three specific ways that you will brand your logo and slogan:

    1. _____
    _____

    2. _____
    _____

    3. _____
    _____

31. Besides a logo and slogan, identify three more specific ways you will brand your Website:

    1. _____
    _____

    2. _____
    _____

    3. _____
    _____

32. Identify five primary risks that your Website faces:

    1. _____
    _____

    2. _____
    _____

    3. _____
    _____

    4. _____
    _____

    5. _____
    _____

33. List a solution for each of your five primary risks:

1. _____
   _____

2. _____
   _____

3. _____
   _____

4. _____
   _____

5. _____
   _____

34. Identify who will be in charge of writing your press releases:

_____

35. Identify how your press releases will be distributed:

____ I will use a professional distribution service. Which one?

_____

____ I will build my own database and distribute the press releases myself.

36. Identify the target date for the completion and distribution of your press kit:

_____

37. Identify your policy for responding to visitor inquiries:

_____
_____
_____
_____

_____
_____
_____
_____
_____

38. Identify your general crisis action plan:

_____
_____
_____
_____
_____
_____
_____
_____
_____

39. Identify five community relations goals:

1. _____
   _____

2. _____
   _____

3. _____
   _____

4. _____
   _____

5. _____
   _____

Closing Statement

I thank you for your purchase of *Web Marketing Applied* and hope that you have found this book at least 100 times more valuable than the price you paid for it. Throughout this book, I have been committed to helping you achieve strong success through the marketing of your Website. I would like nothing more than to see your dedication to these ideas result in one of the most valuable resources on the Web—*your Website*. I hope that you will personally keep me posted on that success.

If you have any questions, comments, or suggestions, please feel free to email me at my direct email address—joetracy@earthlink.net. I will try my best to respond in a timely fashion. If there is something you would like to see expanded upon in any future updates to this book, please let me know. I greatly value your feedback and am honored that you have selected this book to assist you in your marketing efforts.

Wishing you much success always,

Joe Tracy, author
Web Marketing Applied
joetracy@earthlink.net

Index